V.KAIROS

ELEMENTIA
A SPARKS OF A GENESIS

V.KAIROS

ELEMENTIA A SPARKS OF A GENESIS

CONTENT

ABOUT THE AUTHOR

CHAPTER 1   A NEW CYCLE

CHAPTER 2   UNSEEN PROPHECY

CHAPTER 3 TIME TO REMEMBER

CHAPTER 4 IMPENDING DANGER

CHAPTER 5 FIVE A NEW HOME

CHAPTER 6 LESSONS BEGIN!

CHAPTER 7 STRICTLY TRAINING SESSION

CHAPTER 8 BURDENED AND BOUND

CHAPTER 9 UNEXPECTED CHALLENGE

CHAPTER 10 OLD LEGACY REAWAKENED

CHAPTER 11 ELEVEN STRANGE NIGHT

CHAPTER 12 THE CHASE

CHAPTER 13   ENDANGERED TEMPLECHAPTER 14 TEMPLE BRAWL

CHAPTER 15 TERRAKA SCROLL RETRIEVED

CHAPTER 16 START OF AN RIVALRY

CHAPTER 17 KHAOS KOLLECTIVIT

V.KAIROS

Copyright © 2024 by V.KAIROS

All rights reserved. No part of this book may be used or reproduced in any form whatsoever without written permission except in the case of brief quotations in critical articles or reviews.

Printed in the United States of America and Canada

For more information, or to book an event, contact :
Publish By COJ BOOKZ PUBLISHING
Email; INFO@COJBOOKZ.COM

Cover design by V.KAIROS

ISBN - Paperback: 978-1-998120-60-4

About The Author

I chose the pen name V. Kairos for a few personal reasons, the first being privacy. My real name can be a bit difficult for most people to pronounce, and I thought a pen name would just be more practical. The "V" comes from the first letter of my real name, and "Kairos" is inspired by an anime character I admired, not the Greek god. It felt right. Growing up, writing and reading were always more than just hobbies for me—they were passions that shaped who I am today. I was that kid who always had their nose in a book, and whenever I wasn't reading, I was dreaming up stories. The idea of becoming an author one day, of sharing my creativity with others, felt like a natural goal. It wasn't something I talked about much when I was younger, though. I was always a bit too shy to openly say that I wanted to write books. Back then, I feared no one would support me or that my dreams were unrealistic. But as I got older, that self-doubt began to fade. It was around sixth grade when I first entertained the idea of being an author, though I kept it to myself. I didn't feel motivated enough to chase it back then. I was always a little afraid that no one would take me seriously. But by seventh grade, things started to change. I had more friends, and I began to feel more confident in sharing my stories. My writing journey started with something simple: My Hero Academia fanfiction. I created my own characters and wove them into the universe of the show. I shared my stories with my friends on Google Docs, and to my surprise, they really enjoyed them. That first taste of positive feedback gave me the push I needed to keep going. By the end of seventh grade, I had written a full series of fanfiction, two parts deep. It was exciting—finally seeing my stories take shape, seeing my characters come alive on the page. But by eighth grade, things took a turn. Some of my friends drifted away, and I found myself isolated. I didn't talk much to anyone unless they spoke to me first. I felt like an outsider, rejected by people who didn't understand me or my past actions. I didn't know how to rebuild those connections, and I began to struggle with trust issues. My mind would often tell me, "Why bother? They're just going to leave you too." That isolation was one of the biggest challenges I faced during those years. Despite feeling alone, I didn't give up on my dream. I began to realize that being an author didn't depend on my social life. In April of that year, I stopped worrying about being alone and started focusing on what truly mattered to me. I found inspiration in something I had loved since childhood—Lego Ninjago. The idea of elemental ninjas captivated me, and I thought, "Why not make a story like that? But different. Something unique." And so, I began building my own world. I spent hours planning out characters, their backstories, and their arcs. It wasn't easy, but the process of creating something from scratch kept me motivated. For the first time, I felt like I was living out my dream, even if the rest of the world didn't understand.

Eighth grade was probably the hardest year of my life—not just because I lost friends, but because of the mental state I was in. I often felt like I didn't matter, like I was invisible. There were days when I'd think, "What's the point? Why even bother?" It felt like everyone hated me, and I started to believe that there was no reason to try to connect with anyone. I'd make excuses to stay home from school, convincing myself that it was better than facing the uncertainty of social interactions. The idea of walking into school, facing the people I once called friends, filled me with anxiety. Every day felt like a battle. I was constantly walking the hallways with this deep sense of fear and self-doubt. I didn't know if I was going to get jumped or hurt by my old friends, and that fear weighed on me more than I realized. The pressure of it all was overwhelming. I started avoiding places where I might run into people, retreating to the bathroom whenever things got too rough or when I couldn't bear the anxiety any longer. It was just the feeling that I wasn't safe in a place that was supposed to be my school, my refuge. The isolation was suffocating, and I often questioned why I was even trying to exist in that space at all. It got so bad that later in mid-April I had to be in RVH in Barrie for three days to get the help I needed and support and stay away from school for a couple of days to get a lot more help and support from my mom so I'm grateful for her and I managed to move past this and continue to stay alive to actually like completely my goal. I write because I want to share my ideas and my stories with others, but more importantly, I want to reach those who feel like they're alone. I want to inspire kids who, like me, have struggled with depression, anxiety, or the feeling that they don't matter—that no one would miss them if they were gone. It's heartbreaking to think that anyone feels that way because it's simply not true. I want to remind them, through my writing, that they do matter. Their existence has meaning, even when it feels like the world doesn't notice. I don't say this to be harsh or dismissive, but because I truly believe no one should feel like they're invisible or unimportant. To wrap it all up, I envision my book series spanning 4 to 7 books, which is probably how long it'll take to bring the story to its final chapter. But that's just the start—I want to explore other genres too, like romance, horror, sci-fi, and more. I hope that, through everything I create, people can find something that speaks to them. So that's all, and peace out... Keep going, even when it feels like no one's watching. Your story matters, and it's only just beginning.

ELEMENTIA A SPARKS OF A GENESIS

CHAPTER 1

A NEW CYCLE

In a bygone era, humanity witnessed the emergence of elemental powers within its populace. Legend has it that these abilities originated from the air, sparked by a mysterious meteorite that struck the earth.

As a result, life became increasingly turbulent... until three visionary individuals, driven by a desire for peace, intervened to restore balance to the world. Empowered by their own elemental abilities, they were hailed as saviors of the earth. They established dojos and temples, where future generations could harness their elemental powers and reach their full potential. However, one member of this trio began to doubt the wisdom of saving individuals who could potentially perpetuate chaos.

This led them down a dark path, culminating in a brutal war that claimed millions of lives and pitted elements against each other. Ultimately, the remaining two members, who had maintained their faith, emerged victorious. Tragically, they were executed for their association with the instigator of the war.

Yet, they died with smiles on their faces, knowing that they would one day be reincarnated, and perhaps, learn from their past mistakes."

As the three friends sat on the mountain top, enjoying the peaceful sunny day, birds flying in the sky, cars passing by, and trees swaying in the breeze, they talked and laughed together. The girl, with her Straight-messy-ish, amber brown hair blowing in the wind, and her blue eyes shining with excitement, spoke up first. "Is it just me or am I the only one who's happy to be on summer break right now?" she asked with a happy smile, turning to the boy with two-toned dreadlocks. Her strains of hair mostly covered her face.

"Ehh, I mean yeah, we should have fun this time instead of just being locked up in the house like last summer," the two-toned-haired boy declared, laughter filling his voice. "But of course, Neveah is going to be a scaredy cat and not wanna explore abandoned places with me and Michael," he added, causing Neveah to roll her blue eyes.

"Shut up," Neveah said, clearly disapproving of the boy's mischievous suggestion.

"Or we could go to a birthday party and pop balloons there!" Michael, the boy with medium-length pink hair that was parted by a black headband, spoke up with a wink, making Neveah and Jasiah give him a side eye.

"Hell no, Michael," Jasiah said, clearly disapproving of his friend's idea.

Michael snorted and rolled his eyes, scoffing, "Whatever,

Jah." Neveah spoke up, agreeing with Jasiah, Neveah spoke up, her voice laced with conviction, "I wholeheartedly agree with Jasiah, Mike. That would utterly ruin that kid's birthday." Michael responded with a nonchalant chuckle, his eyes glinting with mischief. "Boo hoo, I don't care!" he exclaimed, causing both Neveah and Jasiah to simultaneously face-palm in frustration.

Michael's grin only seemed to widen, his amusement palpable as he continued, "Or are you guys going to confess your undying love to each other?" Jasiah shot him a withering look, his eyebrows raised in incredulity, while Neveah glared at him with an intensity that could melt steel.

The tension was palpable, the air thick with unspoken emotions as they all sat there in silence, waiting for the inevitable response. Michael's attempt at humor had fallen flat, and the weight of his failed joke hung in the air like a challenge. Suddenly, Jasiah burst into laughter, his body shaking with mirth as he slapped his knee and rolled his eyes at Michael's attempt at humor. "As if we'd ever do something like that," he said, shaking his head in disbelief.

Neveah chimed in, her voice dripping with venom. "Michael, you know better than to make jokes like that. It's just not funny." Michael scoffed, his eyes rolling heavenward in exasperation. "Whatever!!!" he exclaimed, not feeling the slightest bit guilty for his unfunny joke. Neveah's response was immediate, her words laced with venom. "Stupid idiot," she said openly, her anger simmering just below the surface. Michael shrugged, his hands ruffling through his pink hair as he retorted, "You're just mad because you're not as cool as me." Neveah jabbed back, her words razor-sharp. "If I were you, I'd want to be anyone else..."

Michael scoffed, his hand still tangled in his hair as he replied, "Of course you'd say that." He removed his hand, his gaze flicking between Neveah and Jasiah, who remained quiet, his expression a mask of neutrality. He sighed, the sound a gentle whisper in the tension-filled air.

The silence that followed was oppressive, Michael's gaze lingered on Neveah, his expression a mixture of defiance and indifference. Jasiah, still quiet, his eyes fixed on the grass.

Neveah's anger seemed to simmer down, her eyes narrowing as she studied Michael's face. "You know, Mike," she said, her voice laced with a hint of curiosity, "sometimes I wonder what goes on in that head of yours." Michael smirked, his pink hair tousled from his earlier hand-ruffling. "Oh, you know, just the usual. World domination,, and embracing my inner awesomeness." Jasiah's eyes flicked up, his gaze meeting Neveah's, a silent understanding passing between them. Michael, oblivious to the unspoken communication, continued, "Besides, someone's got to keep things interesting around here." Neveah's expression turned skeptical. "Interesting? You call making bad jokes and irritating people interesting?" Michael shrugged, his grin still plastered on his face. "Hey, someone's got to keep the mood light. You're always so serious, Neveah. Lighten up." The tension in the air seemed to thicken, Neveah's anger simmering just below the surface once more. Jasiah intervened, his voice a gentle calming presence. "Hey, guys, let's not fight, okay? We're all friends here." Michael rolled his eyes, his apathy kicking in.

"Oh? I'll stop fighting when Neveah here can take a joke." Neveah scoffed, her lips curling in derision. Jasiah sighed, his gaze fixed on the grass, as he predicted, "And this is where you all are going to start arguing, isn't it...?" Neveah's response was swift, her tone laced with annoyance.

"And I won't fight with Mike when he stops being an ass..." Jasiah's sigh was a gentle whisper, his eyes clouding with concern. "Can't we all just get along?" he pleaded, his voice tinged with exasperation.

The silence that followed was heavy, the air thick with unspoken emotions. Michael's grin had faltered, his expression a mask of indifference. Neveah's anger still simmered, her eyes flashing with irritation. Jasiah's attempt at mediation seemed to have fallen flat, the fragile peace hanging by a thread. As they sat there, the tension between them palpable, it seemed as though the storm was far from over. The question on everyone's mind was: what would it take to calm the tempest brewing between them? Michael's eyes remained fixed on Neveah, his gaze challenging.

Neveah's anger simmered, her eyes flashing with irritation. Jasiah's attempt at mediation seemed to have fallen flat, the fragile peace hanging by a thread.

Michael's voice was laced with sarcasm as he spoke, "Oh, I'm an ass, huh? That's rich coming from Miss Perfect over here." Neveah's response was swift, her tone laced with venom. "At least I don't make a fool of myself in front of everyone, Michael." The argument was escalating, the tension between them palpable.

Jasiah's eyes darted between the two, his expression a mixture of concern and frustration. "Guys, stop," he pleaded, his voice rising above the din. "This is getting out of hand." But Michael and Neveah were beyond reason, their anger and frustration boiling over. "You're just mad because you can't take a joke, Neveah," Michael sneered, his pink hair quivering with rage. "You're always so uptight, so serious. Can't you just relax for once?" Neveah's response was a cold, calculated fury. "I'm not uptight, Michael. I'm just not willing to stop at your level. You're a joke, and you know it." The words hung in the air, the silence that followed deafening. Jasiah's sign was a gentle whisper, his eyes clouding with despair. "This is exactly what I was afraid of," he muttered, shaking his head. The storm had finally broken, the tempest brewing between Michael and Neveah threatening to consume them all. The grassy field slope, once a serene backdrop for their gathering and talking, was now a battlefield.

Michael and Neveah stood facing each other, their voices raised in anger The air was thick with tension, the only sound the rustling of leaves and the distant chirping of birds. "Oh, I'm a joke?" Michael said, his voice dripping with confidence. "I was the top of my class back when we were still in school, and I'm going to do the same thing when we're in high school when summer ends." He sneered, his eyes quivering with rage.Neveah's response was blunt, her tone laced with skepticism. " Jasiah is able to keep up with you... And I bet he will surpass you in math." Her words hung in the air, a challenge to Michael's boasts. Michael's smile was condescending, his tone dripping with arrogance. "Oh? Nah, I think not. He had three scores lower than me in the final math test, so... and he never got a higher score, so..." He trailed off, his words hanging in the air like a gauntlet thrown. Neveah's eyes flashed with anger, her face reddening with indignation.

"That's not the point, Michael," she spat, her voice venomous. "The point is that you're always so full of yourself, always thinking you're better than everyone else just because you're good at math." Michael's sneer deepened, his eyes glinting with malice. "And what's wrong with being confident, huh? You're just jealous because you're not as smart as me." The words were a low blow, aimed directly at Neveah's insecurities. Jasiah's eyes darted back and forth between the two, his expression a mixture of concern and frustration. "Guys, stop," he pleaded, his voice rising above the din. "This is getting out of hand."

Michael and Neveah were beyond reason, their anger and frustration boiling over like a pot about to overflow.

The argument continued to escalate, with Michael and Neveah trading barbs and insults. Jasiah's attempts to intervene were met with indifference, and he finally threw up his hands in defeat. "Forget it," he muttered, pulling out his phone and scrolling through TikTok. Michael and Neveah didn't even notice, too caught up in their own bitter argument. "You're just mad because you're not as popular as me," Michael sneered, his pink hair quivering with rage. "Oh, please," Neveah shot back, her voice venomous. "I'd rather be unpopular and have actual friends than be a fake like you, with your shallow relationships and pretentious attitude. " The insults flew back and forth, each one landing with a precision that left the other reeling. Jasiah winced at the cruelty of their words, but he didn't bother intervening. He'd tried, and it was clear that Michael and Neveah were beyond reason. As the argument continued to rage on, Jasiah's phone became a welcome distraction. He scrolled through his feeds, watching videos of dancing dogs and lip-syncing teens. Anything to take his mind off the toxic fight unfolding before him.

Meanwhile, Michael and Neveah continued to tear each other apart, their anger and frustration boiling over like a pot about to overflow. The air was thick with tension, the only sound the rustling of leaves and the distant chirping of birds.

 It was a scene that would leave scars, and Jasiah knew it. But for now, he was just going to sit back, scroll through TikTok, and let the drama unfold. The argument continued to simmer, with Michael and Neveah trading barbs and

insults. But Jasiah had had enough. "Guys, wanna go explore an abandoned house?" he said, interrupting the argument.

To his surprise, Neveah and Michael said "Sure!" at the same time, their eyes locking in a fierce glare. Jasiah sighed and started walking down the grassy mountain, Neveah quickly following behind him. She glanced back at Michael, sticking her tongue out at him, and Michael groaned,quickly running after them. As they walked, the tension between them was still palpable, but they seemed to be enjoying the distraction from their argument. "When I get older, I'm definitely gonna be the very best lawyer," Michael said, looking at Jasiah with a competitive glint in his eye. "And let me guess, you wanna be a stupid officer?" Michael said, his voice dripping with sarcasm. Jasiah bristled, his face reddening in defense. "Hey, police officers help people, you know?" he said, his tone firm. Michael rolled his eyes, his expression dismissive.

"And what about you, Neveah?" he asked, his voice bitter and condescending.

Neveah shrugged, her expression open-minded. "Hmm, I think I wanna stay forever young and be pretty," she said, her voice cheerful. Michael snorted, his hands behind his head as he walked in front of Neveah, alongside Jasiah. "Lame," he said, his tone dripping with disdain their argument seemed to fade into the background, replaced by the thrill of discovery and adventure.

But as they made their way back down the mountain, the tension between them began to simmer once more.

Finally, they reached the bottom of the mountain, where Neveah and Michael had left their bikes. They climbed onto their respective vehicles, Neveah adjusting her helmet while Michael pedaled lazily in place.

Jasiah, meanwhile, pulled out his skateboard, the wheels creaking as he stepped onto it. "Alright, let's go," Michael said, his eyes glinting with competition. "Losers buy ice cream and then we'll explore the abandoned place" Neveah grinned, her ponytail bouncing as she nodded. "Game on." Jasiah just rolled his eyes, his skateboard hovering inches above the ground. "You guys are going to regret this," he said, his tone dry. Neveah and Michael were already off, their bikes accelerating rapidly as they sped down the sidewalk.

Jasiah waited for a moment, watching as they gained distance, before pushing off with his back foot and launching himself forward. The wind whipped through his hair as he picked up speed, his senses alive with the rush of adrenaline. He could see Neveah and Michael up ahead, their bikes weaving in and out of pedestrians as they competed for the lead.

Jasiah grinned, his heart pounding with excitement. This was what he loved about skateboarding - the freedom, the thrill, the sense of living on the edge.

As he drew closer to Neveah and Michael, he could see the determination etched on their faces. They were giving it their all, their bikes eating up the distance as they hurtled towards the finish line. Jasiah dug deep, his legs pumping furiously as he surged forward.

He could feel the wind rushing past him, his skateboard vibrating beneath his feet as he hurtled towards the finish.

It was going to be close, he could sense it. But Jasiah was determined to come out on top, to prove that his skateboard was more than a match for Neveah and Michael's bikes. The finish line loomed ahead, a blur of colors and sounds as Jasiah, Neveah, and Michael crossed it in a flurry of motion. Who would emerge victorious? Only time would tell.

As they crossed the finish line, the three friends skidded to a stop, their chests heaving with exhaustion. For a moment, they just looked at each other, grinning from ear to ear. Then, in perfect sync, they let out a whoop of excitement, pumping their fists in the air. "Yes!" Neveah screamed, her ponytail bouncing with the motion. "I did it!" Michael high-fived her, his eyes shining with competitive spirit. "You won, Neveah! I was right behind you!" Jasiah chuckled, his skateboard still vibrating beneath his feet. "You guys are crazy," he said, shaking his head in admiration. "I didn't think I was going to catch up to you." Neveah turned to him, her face flushed with excitement.

"You were so close, Jasiah! I thought you were going to pass me at the end." Jasiah shrugged, his grin still plastered on his face. "I gave it my all, but you guys were just too fast." The three friends stood there for a moment, basking in the glow of their competitive spirit. Then, as one, they turned and pushed off towards the ice cream truck parked nearby. "Ice cream is on me," Jasiah said, digging into his pocket for some cash. Neveah squealed with delight, her eyes shining with excitement.

"Yes! I'm getting a triple scoop cone!" Jasiah just rolled his eyes, laughing. "You guys are something else." As they walked towards the ice cream truck, the tension between them was all but forgotten, replaced by the joy of friendly competition and the thrill of adventure. They knew that no matter what, they would always have each other's backs, whether they were racing down the sidewalk or exploring the unknown. And as they Bits into their ice cream cones, the sweet taste of victory was all theirs. As they savored their ice cream cones, the sweet flavors and cold temperatures were a perfect complement to the warm summer day. Neveah was in heaven, her triple scoop cone a towering masterpiece of chocolate, vanilla, and strawberry.

Jasiah and Michael, meanwhile, opted for more modest single-scoop cones, but were no less enthusiastic about their treats. After they finished their ice cream, Michael spoke up, his eyes sparkling with mischief.

"Now we can go to the abandoned house now that we ate!" he said, and started biking off in the direction of the mountain. "He never changes.." Jasiah said, shaking his head in amusement as he got on his skateboard.

Neveah followed close behind on her bike, her ponytail bouncing with each pedal stroke. As they made their way back up the mountain, the abandoned house loomed before them, its boarded-up windows and crumbling facade a testament to its neglect. But to Jasiah, Neveah, and Michael, it was a symbol of adventure, a challenge to be explored and conquered.

 They parked their vehicles at the entrance, the rusty gate creaking in the wind as they stepped through.

The air inside was musty and stale, the only sound the creaking of the old wooden floorboards beneath their feet. "Alright, let's split up and see what we can find," Michael said, his voice low and conspiratorial. "Meet back here in 20 minutes and compare notes." Neveah nodded, her eyes shining with excitement. "I'll take the upstairs bedrooms." Jasiah shrugged, his skateboard tucked under his arm. "I'll check out the kitchen and living room." And with that, they set off in different directions, their footsteps echoing through the empty halls as they began their exploration of the abandoned house As Jasiah made his way to the kitchen, his eyes scanned the room for any signs of interest. The

countertops were old and worn, the sink stained with rust and grime. He opened the cabinets, finding nothing but empty shelves and a few stray utensils. Moving on to the living room, Jasiah's gaze fell upon the old couch, its upholstery torn and faded. He lifted up the cushions, searching for any hidden treasures or clues,
but found nothing.

 The bookshelf was bare, the books long gone or destroyed. Meanwhile, Neveah was exploring the upstairs bedrooms, her heart racing with anticipation.
She searched through the dusty closets, finding old clothes and forgotten trinkets. But nothing seemed out of the ordinary, no hidden messages or secrets waiting to be uncovered. As the 20 minutes drew to a close, Jasiah and Neveah met back in the entrance hall, their faces reflecting their disappointment. Michael, however, was nowhere to be found. "Michael, where are you?" Neveah called out, her voice echoing through the empty halls. There was no response.
Jasiah frowned, a hint of concern creeping into his voice. "Jah, I think we should find Michael."
Neveah nodded, her eyes scanning the area. "Let's split up and search for him." Jasiah nodded, and they set off in different directions, their footsteps echoing through the empty halls once more. But as they searched, they couldn't shake off the feeling that they were missing something, that there was more to the abandoned house than met the eye. Despite their initial disappointment, neither Jasiah nor Neveah was ready to give up. They were determined to uncover the secrets of the abandoned house, to find out what

lay hidden beneath its crumbling facade. As Jasiah and Neveah searched the lower floors, they couldn't help but feel a sense of unease. It was as if they were being watched, their every move being monitored by some unseen presence.

But they shook off the feeling, focusing instead on their mission to uncover the secrets of the abandoned house. Meanwhile, Michael had wandered off on his own, his curiosity getting the better of him.

He had discovered a narrow staircase leading up to the attic, and his instincts told him that this was where he would find something interesting. As he pushed open the creaky door, a musty smell wafted out, and Michael's eyes adjusted to the dim light.

The attic was cluttered with old trunks, dusty boxes, and forgotten memorabilia. But Michael's gaze was drawn to a small, intricately carved treasure box in the corner. He approached it slowly, his heart pounding with excitement.

This was it, he was sure of it. This was where he would find the treasure. With a confident grin, Michael opened the box, and his eyes widened in amazement. Inside, nestled in a bed of velvet, was an orange crystal-looking thing that seemed to pulse with an inner fire. "Whoa, that's so cool!" Michael exclaimed, reaching out to grab it. As soon as his fingers made contact with the crystal, a fiery barrier erupted around it, and Michael yelped in pain as his finger was burned. "Gah! What the...?" he muttered, clenching his finger in agony.

The sudden noise echoed through the attic, and Jasiah and Neveah, who were still searching the lower floors, froze. They exchanged a worried glance, their hearts racing with concern.

"What was that?" Neveah whispered, her eyes wide with fear. Jasiah shook his head, his face grim. "I don't know, but we need to go check it out."

Without hesitation, they rushed towards the attic, their senses on high alert. What had Michael found, and what was the significance of the strange crystal? And what lay behind the eerie, pulsing fire that seemed to emanate from it?

As Jasiah and Neveah rushed into the attic, they were met with a scene of chaos. Michael was clutching his burned finger, his face contorted in pain and annoyance. "Mike, you okay?" Jasiah asked, dropping to his level and placing a hand on his shoulder.

Michael shook his head, his eyes flashing with irritation. "No, that crystal in the box burned me!" he said, his voice laced with frustration. Jasiah's gaze followed Michael's, and he spotted the treasure box in the corner.

His curiosity piqued, he walked over to the box and peered inside.

The orange crystal glowed with an otherworldly light, its flames pulsing with an eerie energy. As Jasiah reached out to grab the crystal, Neveah's voice rang out, sharp with warning. "Don't!" she said, her eyes wide with concern. "If Michael got burned, why are you doing it?" But Jasiah was undeterred. He managed to grab the crystal, and to everyone's surprise, he didn't flinch. "Hey, it doesn't hurt guys!" he said, his face breaking into a happy smile. Michael's jaw dropped, his eyes wide with astonishment. "How the fuck-" he started to say, but Neveah cut him off with a stern rebuke. "Language, Michael!" Jasiah, meanwhile, was entranced by the crystal. He gazed down at it, the flames' reflection dancing in his green eyes. The crystal seemed to be pulsing with an energy that was both mesmerizing and unsettling.

As the group stood there, frozen in awe, the attic seemed to grow quieter.

The creaks and groans of the old house receded into the background, leaving only the soft hum of the crystal's power. It was as if the very fabric of reality was shifting, drawn into the vortex of the mysterious crystal's energy. What secrets lay hidden within the crystal's depths? And what would be the cost of unlocking its power? As the group stood there, transfixed by the crystal's power, a sudden and inexplicable phenomenon occurred. The crystal, still pulsing with energy, began to float in mid-air. It hovered above Jasiah's outstretched hand, its flames dancing with an otherworldly intensity. "Uh... am I being schizophrenic or is that crystal floating?" Neveah asked, her voice laced with confusion and wonder. "It's not just you!" Michael spoke up, his eyes wide with amazement. "I don't know what's happening, but I'm oddly calm about this," Jasiah said, his voice eerily serene. The crystal, as if responding to Jasiah's words, began to move of its own accord. It floated around Jasiah, its flames leaving trails of glittering sparks in its wake.

The group watched in stunned silence, unsure of what to make of this bizarre spectacle. As the crystal continued to orbit Jasiah, its power seemed to grow stronger.

The air around them began to vibrate with an electric tension, as if the very fabric of reality was being reshaped by the crystal's energy.

Suddenly, the crystal came to a stop, hovering inches from Jasiah's chest.

For a moment, it seemed to pause, as if gathering its strength. Then, in a flash of light, it plunged into Jasiah's chest, disappearing from view. The group stood there, frozen in shock, unsure of what had just happened. "Okay..." Michael said, his voice barely above a whisper. The silence that followed was oppressive, heavy with the weight of uncertainty.

What had just occurred? What secrets lay hidden within the crystal's depths, and what would be the cost of unlocking its power? As they stood there, unsure of what to do next, the attic seemed to grow darker, the shadows deepening into twisted, eerie shapes. It was as if the crystal's power had awakened something ancient and malevolent, something that lurked just beyond the edge of perception. What lay ahead for the group, now that the crystal had taken its mysterious journey into Jasiah's chest? Would they be able to unlock its secrets, or would they succumb to the darkness that lurked within?

As the group stood there, frozen in shock, Jasiah's gaze wandered around the attic. His eyes landed on a corner of the room, and his face lit up with excitement. "Guys, there's two more!" he exclaimed, his voice echoing through the attic.

Michael and Neveah turned to follow Jasiah's gaze, and their eyes widened in amazement. Two more crystals sat on a dusty old shelf, each one radiating an otherworldly energy. One of the crystals was a deep green and brown, with vines and stone etched into its surface. It seemed to pulse with a gentle, earthy power. The other crystal was a brilliant blue, with water swirling inside its depths.

It glittered like a sapphire, and its power seemed to reverberate through the air. Jasiah, still grinning from ear to ear, took a step forward. He reached out a hand to touch the blue crystal, but before he could make contact, a sudden barrier of water erupted around it. The barrier pushed Jasiah back, sending him stumbling across the attic floor. "what the hell!" Jasiah exclaimed, his blue Nike jacket now soaked through.

Michael burst out laughing, while Neveah's face seemed to pale with worry. "Dude, are you okay?" Michael asked, still chuckling. Jasiah nodded, his grin still plastered on his face. "Yeah, I'm fine. But what's up with these crystals? They're like, defending themselves or something." Neveah's brow furrowed, her eyes fixed on the crystals. "I think we should be careful," she said, her voice laced with caution. "We don't know what kind of power they possess." But Jasiah was undeterred. He took another step forward, his eyes fixed on the blue crystal. "I think I can handle it," he said, his confidence radiating through the air. As he reached out to touch the crystal again, the water barrier reformed, pushing him back once more. Jasiah stumbled, his eyes wide with surprise. What secrets lay hidden within the crystals' depths, and what would be the cost of unlocking their power?

The group stood there, frozen in uncertainty, as the attic seemed to grow darker and more ominous.

It was as if the crystals' power was growing, drawing them into a vortex of uncertainty. What lay ahead for the group,

now that they had stumbled upon these ancient, mysterious relics? As the group stood there, frozen in uncertainty,
Michael suddenly sprang into action. He strode forward, his eyes fixed on the blue crystal, and reached out to grab it. The water barrier dissipated, and the crystal seemed to pulse with energy as Michael's hand closed around it. At first, nothing seemed to happen.
But then, in a burst of light, the blue crystal began to orbit around Michael's body, its power coursing through the air.
Michael's eyes widened in amazement, and he stumbled backward, his arm outstretched as if trying to keep the crystal at bay. "Hey, wait... It's actually working?" Michael said, his voice laced with incredulity. Neveah s eyes seemed to pop out of her head, her face pale with surprise. Jasiah's jaw dropped, his eyes fixed on Michael in awe. The blue crystal continued to orbit around Michael, its energy pulsing with an otherworldly power. It was as if the crystal had recognized Michael as its master, and was now submitting to his will. The air seemed to vibrate with an electric tension, as if the very fabric of reality was being reshaped by the crystal's power. "Dude, what's going on?" Jasiah asked, his voice barely above a whisper.

Neveah shook her head, her eyes wide with confusion. "I don't know, but it looks like Michael's connected to the crystal or something." Michael's face seemed to glow with an inner light, his eyes fixed on some distant horizon. It was as if he was seeing something that the others couldn't,
some hidden truth that only the crystal could reveal. The attic seemed to grow quieter, the shadows deepening into

dark, mysterious pools. The group stood there, transfixed by the spectacle, unsure of what to make of this bizarre and wondrous phenomenon.

As the blue crystal continued to orbit around Michael, it suddenly lunged forward, plunging into his chest with a burst of light. The crystal disappeared from view, leaving Michael standing there, his eyes still fixed on some distant horizon.

Neveah rolled her eyes, her envy and frustration palpable. "Great, so now both you and Jasiah have grabbed a crystal and none of us knows what happens next! Great!" she scoffed, her voice laced with sarcasm. "What's next? We're going to drop through the floor like this is some kind of superhero movie?" Neveah said, raising a brow.

Jasiah chuckled awkwardly, his eyes darting around the attic. "Maybeee?" Jasiah said, his voice hesitant. Michael, still basking in the afterglow of the crystal's power, turned to Neveah with a condescending smirk. "Stop complaining, Neveah. You could try grabbing the green one," Michael said, his tone dripping with arrogance. Neveah scoffed, her eyes flashing with anger. "Hell no. You can forget it," Neveah said, her voice firm. "I'm not going to risk getting possessed by some ancient relic just because you two are too curious for your own good." The attic seemed to grow darker, the shadows deepening into dark, mysterious pools.

The group stood there, frozen in uncertainty, unsure of what lay ahead. "What's going to happen to us?" Neveah asked, her voice barely above a whisper. Jasiah shrugged, his eyes fixed on Michael. "I don't know, but I think we're in for a wild ride," Jasiah said, his voice laced with excitement. Michael, still basking in the crystal's power, smiled enigmatically, his eyes fixed on some distant horizon. Neveah scoffed, her eyes flashing with anger, but then suddenly, she reached out and grabbed the green and brown crystal. The crystal seemed to pulse with energy as Neveah's hand closed around it, and for a moment, the group stood there,

frozen in shock. But then, Michael's eyes widened as a realization dawned on him.

"Wait, guys? What if the reason why I couldn't touch the orange crystal but Jasiah could was because the crystal chose him for some reason?" Michael said, his voice filled with excitement. "And then the blue crystal chose me, but wouldn't choose Jasiah," Michael continued, his eyes darting between Jasiah and Neveah. "And then the green and brown crystal chose Neveah." Neveah's eyes narrowed, her face still etched with anger, but Jasiah's face lit up with sudden understanding. "For once, you say something likable," Jasiah said, his voice filled with amusement.

 The group stood there, frozen in silence, as the implications of Michael's words sank in.

It was as if the crystals had somehow chosen them, each one selecting a specific individual for some unknown purpose.

The attic seemed to grow darker, the shadows deepening into dark, mysterious pools. The group stood there, transfixed by the spectacle, unsure of what lay ahead. "What does it mean?" Neveah asked, her voice barely above a whisper. Jasiah shrugged, his eyes fixed on Michael.

ELEMENTIA A SPARKS OF A GENESIS

CHAPTER 2

UNSEEN PROPHECY

Suddenly, a strange gas seemed to permeate the air, filling the attic with a noxious mist. It was as if the very atmosphere itself was conspiring against them, making the trio feel lethargic and disoriented. "Guys...? What's going on...?" Michael exclaimed, his voice slurred and uncertain. Jasiah's eyes darted around the room, trying to identify the source of the gas. "I don't know! Everybody hold your breath!" Jasiah shouted, his voice panicked. But it was too late. Neveah, who had been standing quietly to the side, suddenly slumped to the floor, her eyes glazed over in a deep sleep.

Jasiah's eyes widened in horror as he realized Neveah had been overcome by the gas. He tried to shake off the feeling of drowsiness that was creeping over him, but it was no use.

The gas was too potent, and soon he found himself stumbling towards the floor, his vision blurring.

Michael, still trying to fight off the effects of the gas, stumbled backwards, his eyes fixed on Jasiah and Neveah.

He knew he had to get out of there, but his legs felt like lead, and his senses were rapidly deteriorating. As the gas continued to spread, the attic grew darker and more ominous, the shadows deepening into dark, mysterious pools. The group lay there, overcome by the mysterious gas, unsure of what lay ahead. Would they awaken to find themselves trapped in some kind of ancient curse, or would they be able to escape the attic and uncover the secrets that lay beyond? Only time would tell.

Jasiah's eyes fluttered open, but he was not in the attic anymore. He found himself in a dreamlike world, surrounded by an ethereal mist that swirled and eddied around him. The air was thick with an otherworldly energy, and Jasiah could feel his heart pounding in his chest. Before him, a figure emerged from the mist. It was a being of pure flame, its body a blazing inferno that seemed to pulse with an ancient power.

Jasiah tried to speak, but for some reason, he couldn't. His mouth was covered in flames, and his voice was silenced by the intense heat. The flame figure loomed over him, its eyes blazing with an intense ferocity. Jasiah tried to step back, but his legs were rooted to the spot. He was trapped, unable to move or speak, as the flame figure began to speak to him in a voice that was both ancient and eternal. "You have been chosen," the flame figure intoned, its voice like thunder in Jasiah's mind. "You have been selected to fulfill an ancient prophecy, one that will determine the fate of the world."

Jasiah's mind reeled as the flame figure's words echoed through his consciousness.

What prophecy was this? And why had he been chosen to fulfill it? The questions swirled in his mind, but he was unable to ask them aloud. The flame figure raised a hand, and Jasiah felt a surge of energy course through his body. He was being imbued with a power that was both ancient and mysterious, a power t hat would change him forever. As the energy coursed through him, Jasiah felt his senses expanding, his mind opening up to new possibilities and new realities. He was becoming something more, something greater, and he knew that he would never be the same again.

The flame figure continued to speak, its voice echoing through Jasiah's mind. "So welcome back, Aria. It's been a couple of years." The words were like a puzzle, each one fitting together in a way that Jasiah couldn't quite understand. He knew his name wasn't Aria, and he had no idea who this flame figure was or why it was calling him by that name. But Jasiah's confusion was compounded by the fact that he still couldn't speak. His mouth was still covered in flames, and his voice was silenced by the intense heat.

The flame figure seemed to sense Jasiah's confusion, and it continued to speak, its words only adding to the mystery.

"You've been gone for so long, Aria. I thought I'd lost you forever. But now you're back, and everything can begin again. "Jasiah's mind was reeling. What was this flame figure talking about? And who was Aria? He didn't know anyone by that name, and he certainly didn't know any flame figures.

But the flame figure continued to speak, its words weaving a web of confusion and mystery around Jasiah. "The prophecy is clear, Aria. You are the chosen one, the one who will bring balance to the world. And I am the one who will guide you on your journey." Jasiah's eyes were wide with confusion. What prophecy was this?

And what journey was the flame figure talking about? He

didn't know anything about any of this, and he was starting to feel like he was trapped in some kind of nightmare. The flame figure continued to speak, its words only adding to the mystery.

"You've been given a great gift, Aria. The power of the elements is within you, and with it, you will be able to wield the very fabric of reality. But be warned, Aria, there are those who will seek to take this power from you. You must be careful, for the fate of the world hangs in the balance."

Jasiah's mind was reeling. What power was this? And what elements was the flame figure talking about? He didn't know anything about any of this, and he was starting to feel like he was losing his grip on reality.

The flame figure continued to speak, its words only adding to the confusion. "You will meet others on your journey, Aria. Ones who will aid you and ones who will hinder you. You must be cautious, for the line between friend and foe is thin indeed." Jasiah's eyes were wide with confusion.

What journey was this? And who were these others that the flame figure was talking about?

He didn't know anything about any of this, and he was starting to feel like he was trapped in some kind of never-ending dream. The flame figure continued to speak, its words only adding to the mystery. "And then there is the one who will be your greatest ally and your greatest enemy. The one who will stand by your side and the one who will seek to destroy you. You must be prepared, Aria, for the fate of the world hangs in the balance." The flame figure continued to speak, its words weaving a web of confusion around Jasiah.

"The threads of fate are complex, Aria. You are entwined with destiny, and your path is fraught with peril. You must be cautious, for the forces of darkness seek to claim you." Jasiah's eyes were wide with frustration. He didn't know what this flame figure was talking about, and he was getting tired of being called Aria.

"Hey, my name isn't Aria!" Jasiah finally managed to speak, his voice shaking with anger.

"My name is Jasiah!" The flame figure paused, its flames dancing in surprise. "Ah, Jasiah, then," it said, its voice dripping with an otherworldly tone.

"You are still unaware of your true nature, but that will soon change. The threads of fate are converging, and your destiny awaits." Jasiah's face twisted in frustration. "And I don't know what you mean by enemy," he continued. "I'm just a normal kid! Leave me out of your supernatural Aria thing you have going on!" The flame figure chuckled, its flames crackling with amusement. "Ah, Jasiah, you are so much more than that.

You are a key player in the grand tapestry of fate. And as for your enemy, you will soon discover that it is one who walks in the shadows, waiting for the perfect moment to strike." Jasiah's eyes narrowed in confusion. "What shadows? What are you talking about?" The flame figure leaned forward, its flames dancing with an intense energy. "The shadows of the past, Jasiah. The shadows of your own heart. You must confront them if you hope to survive the trials that lie ahead." Jasiah's face twisted in disgust. "Trials? What trials? I just want to go home and forget this whole thing ever happened!"

The flame figure's words hung in the air like a challenge, its flames dancing with an intense energy.

Jasiah's face twisted in disgust, his mind reeling with the implications of what the flame figure was saying. "After you grabbed the orange crystal, there was no going back," the flame figure said,

"It's been destined for us to meet again after centuries!" Jasiah's eyes widened in shock, his face pale with fear. "I never knew you!" he yelled out, his voice echoing through the attic. "And for centuries?

There's no way I'm only fourteen! In eighth grade! And going to ninth grade in September!" The flame figure chuckled, its flames crackling with amusement. "Ah, Jasiah, you are so caught up in the mundane concerns of your mortal life. You have no idea what lies beyond the veil of reality.

But soon, you will remember. Soon, you will recall the life you lived before, the life that bound us together across the centuries." Jasiah's face twisted in confusion, his mind reeling with the implications of what the flame figure was saying. "What life? What are you talking about?" he demanded, his voice shaking with anger. The flame figure leaned forward, its flames dancing with an intense energy.

"The life of Aria, Jasiah. The life you lived as Aria, a powerful Hero who wielded the elements with ease. You were my enemy, my greatest foe, and yet, my dearest friend. And now, you have been reborn, returned to this world to fulfill the prophecy that binds us together." Jasiah's eyes widened in shock, his mind reeling with the implications of what the flame figure was saying.

He didn't know what to believe, didn't know if he was caught up in some kind of crazy dream or if this was all real.
But one thing was certain - he didn't want any part of it. "I don't want to be Aria," Jasiah said, his voice firm with determination. "I don't want to be some kind of Hero or fulfill some prophecy. I just want to go home and forget this whole thing ever happened." "And do you want other people to be Aria?" the flame creature asked, its flames dancing with an intense energy. "What? No!" Jasiah said, his voice firm with determination.

"Then you must break the cycle," the flame creature spoke, its voice dripping with an otherworldly tone. "Here, in this era, is where the story of Aria and Mael ends." Jasiah's eyes narrowed in confusion. "Who the hell is Mael!?" he spoke, his voice laced with frustration. The flame creature chuckled, its flames crackling with amusement. "A very evil man... Who was worse than me," it said, its voice dripping with an air of mystery. "But I can't say exactly who." Jasiah's face twisted in anger. "Why not?!" he asked, his voice demanding an answer.

The flame creature leaned forward, its flames dancing with an intense energy. "Because the truth is hidden, Jasiah," it said, its voice dripping with an air of secrecy. "And only you can uncover it.
You must break the cycle, Jasiah. You must fulfill the prophecy and put an end to the story of Aria and Mael." Jasiah's eyes widened in shock, his mind reeling with the implications of what the flame creature was saying.

He didn't know what to believe, didn't know if he was caught up in some kind of crazy dream or if this was all real. But one thing was certain - he didn't want any part of it. "I don't want to break any cycle," Jasiah said, his voice firm with determination. "I don't want to fulfill any prophecy.

I just want to go home and forget this whole thing ever happened." The flame creature chuckled again, its flames crackling with amusement. "Ah, Jasiah, it's too late for that," it said, its voice dripping with an air of inevitability. "You have already been chosen, already been bound to the prophecy. You will fulfill your destiny, no matter the cost."

Jasiah's face twisted in anger, his eyes flashing with determination. "I won't do it," he said, his voice firm with defiance. "I won't fulfill any prophecy or break any cycle.

I'll just go home and forget this whole thing ever happened." the flame creature reached out and placed a hand on his forehead. Suddenly, visions flooded Jasiah's mind, images of people dying and begging for help from elemental powers years ago. Jasiah's eyes widened in horror as he saw the destruction and chaos that had been unleashed upon the world. "What the..... hell...?" Jasiah muttered out, his voice barely audible. He felt sick seeing that. Up until now, he didn't even know elemental powers actually existed.

The flame creature removed its hand, its flames dancing with an intense energy. "So, are you sure you don't want to break the cycle?" it asked, its voice dripping with an air of persuasion. Jasiah's eyes narrowed, his face twisted in anger. "If I don't, that will happen again?" he asked, his voice laced with frustration.

The flame creature nodded, its flames crackling with affirmation. "Yes, Jasiah. If you don't break the cycle, the same destruction and chaos will be unleashed upon the world once more." Jasiah's face twisted in determination, his eyes flashing with justice. "Fine, I'll do it," he said, his voice firm with resolve. "But I'm not Aria. I don't know who she is or why you called me that or what kind of weird thing this is.
But I will walk my own damn path."
The flame creature chuckled, its flames crackling with amusement. "I like your spirit, Jasiah," it said, its voice dripping with an air of approval. "But first, you must learn to harness your powers. Jasiah looked confused, his eyes squinting in skepticism. "Huh, like what powers?" he asked, making the flame creature's face palm. "Well, I don't know, take a lucky damn guess?" the flame creature said, its flames dancing with amusement. Jasiah's face scrunched up in thought. "Uh, am I gonna be able to use bankai?" he asked, making the flame creature sigh. "No, Jasiah, you have the power of Courage," the flame creature said, its voice dripping with an air of importance. "Which means you have the power of flames... and another power you were indeed born with, but I can't state what exactly." Jasiah's eyes widened in confusion. "What do you mean? What's this other power?" he asked, his voice laced with curiosity. The flame creature's flames danced with an intense energy.
"Ah, Jasiah, that's for you to discover," it said, its voice dripping with an air of mystery. "But first, you must learn to harness your power of Courage. You must learn to control the flames within you." Jasiah's face twisted in determination.

"Okay, fine," he said, his voice firm with resolve. "I'll learn to control my powers. But I'm still not Aria, and I still don't know what the hell is going on." The flame creature chuckled, its flames crackling with amusement. "Ah, Jasiah, you will learn," it said, its voice dripping with an air of confidence. "And when you do, you will fulfill your destiny, and put an end to the story of Aria and Mael."

Jasiah's eyes narrowed, his face twisted in determination. "I'll do it," he said, his voice firm with resolve. "But I'm doing it my way, not because of some prophecy or destiny. I'm doing it because I want to make a difference." Jasiah's eyes sparkled with curiosity, his face etched with a mixture of excitement and skepticism. "So, once I wake up from my dream, I'll be able to shoot out flames?" he asked, making the flame creature shake its head. "No, Jasiah, it's not that simple," the flame creature said, its voice laced with a hint of sternness. "You'll have to prove to the flames, which is me, that you are worthy, like actually worthy, to wield the flames. Then, and only then, will you be able to use them."

Jasiah's face scrunched up in confusion. "Prove myself worthy? What do you mean?" The flame creature's flames danced with an intense energy, illuminating the dark surroundings. "I mean, Jasiah, that you'll have to demonstrate your courage, your determination, and your will to master the flames. It's not just about shooting out flames like a firework, it's about harnessing the elemental power within you." Jasiah's eyes widened, his face twisted in understanding. "I see," he said, his voice laced with a hint of determination. "And what about this other element you mentioned earlier?

The one I was born with?" The flame creature's flames crackled with amusement. "Ah, yes, that element.
I can't identify it yet, but I sense that it's powerful, very powerful.
It could amplify the flames, making them stronger than they should be, but it may take years for you to master or even awaken it." Jasiah's eyes bulged, his face twisted in shock. "YEARS?" he exclaimed, his voice laced with incredulity. "You mean I have to wait years to master my powers?" The flame creature nodded, its flames dancing with an intense energy.
"Yes, Jasiah, it's a long and arduous journey ahead of you.
But I'll be here to guide you, to mentor you, and to help you unlock your true potential." Jasiah's face twisted in determination, his eyes flashing with resolve. "I'll do it," he said, his voice firm with conviction. "I'll master my powers, no matter how long it takes. I'll prove myself worthy, and I'll fulfill my destiny."

Jasiah's eyes finally snapped completely open, his green eyes confused as he fixed his two-toned dreads. He sat up, rubbing his temples, trying to process the wild dream he just had. As he looked around, he saw Michael and Neveah already awake, sitting on the floor, their hair disheveled. "Oh, you're up," Michael said, his pink curly hair slightly messy, a lazy grin on his face. Neveah was brushing her brown hair, which was now in messy brown curls, as she tied it up into a ponytail, stray strands of her hair framing her face. "Did you also have a weird dream after the gas put us to sleep?" she asked, her eyes curious. "I saw a stone-earthy-like creature in mine, and it told me about some... type of balance and harmony, and stuff. Like, I have earth powers now or something.. and that I also have Miracle or something." Michael nodded, an arrogant smile on his face. "Same here, but mine was like a sea monster, and it said I have Pride and water powers... or something." Jasiah's eyes widened as he listened to their accounts, his mind racing with the implications.

"You guys too?" he asked, his voice laced with excitement. "Mine called me Aria, and said that I have to end the story between Aria and Mael or something, and said I have Courage and fire..." Neveah's eyes rolled, a hint of annoyance in her voice. "Mines called me... Caelum... Like, I am NOT a boy." She shook her head, her ponytail bouncing. Michael's eyes lit up, calculating glint in his eye. "Wait, Jasiah, you said it called you Aria? Mine called me Mael..." The trio's eyes widened, a collective gasp escaping their lips. Neveah's voice was laced with concern. "Wouldn't that mean you two have to fight one day?" The room fell silent, the only sound the soft creaking of the old attic.

Jasiah's eyes locked onto Michael's, a spark of rivalry igniting between them. Neveah's eyes darted back and forth, her brow furrowed in worry. The tension hung in the air, the trio realized that their lives had just taken a dramatic turn. They were no longer just ordinary teenagers; they were now players in a grand, mysterious game, with their destinies entwined in ways they couldn't yet comprehend.

And as they sat there, the darkness of the attic looming over them, they knew that their journey was only just beginning, a journey that would test their courage, their resolve, and their very souls...

Jasiah's face broke into a wide grin, his eyes sparkling with excitement. "Once we both master our elemental powers, me and you, Mike, will have a fight!" he exclaimed, his voice laced with anticipation. Michael's confident smile grew even wider, his eyes flashing with arrogance. "You're on, just remember, water beats fire, idiot," he said, his voice dripping with condescension. Neveah's eyes widened, her brow furrowed in concern. "Guys, I don't think that's a good idea," she said, her voice laced with caution. "We don't even know what we're capable of yet, or what the consequences of our actions might be." Jasiah and Michael ignored her warnings, their competitive spirits fueled by their encounter with the mysterious creatures. They began to banter back and forth, their words laced with bravado and confidence. "Oh, I'll take you down with my flames," Jasiah said, his eyes flashing with determination. "Yeah, right, like your little sparks can take on my tidal wave," Michael retorted, his voice dripping with sarcasm. Neveah's eyes rolled, her ponytail bouncing as she shook her head. "You guys are impossible," she muttered, her voice laced with exasperation. As the trio continued to argue, the tension in the attic grew thicker, the air electrified by their competitive energies.

It was clear that their encounter with the mysterious creatures had awakened something within them, something that would drive them to push their limits and test their resolve. And as they sat there, the darkness of the attic looming over them, they knew that their journey was only just beginning, a journey that would take them to the very limits of their strength, their courage, and their souls...

Little did they know, their destinies were intertwined, their fates bound together by the mysterious forces that had awakened their elemental powers. And as they sat there, poised on the threshold of their journey, they had no idea what lay ahead, no idea what challenges they would face, or what sacrifices they would be forced to make.

The next day, they gathered in Jasiah's mansion backyard, eager to test their elemental powers. "Alright, let's see if we can use our elemental power!" Jasiah exclaimed, apples perched precariously on his head as the target. Michael stretched, a cocky grin spreading across his face. "Easy peasy," he spoke arrogantly, confident in his ability to wield water. Neveah rolled her eyes, a skeptical expression on her face as she scoffed. "Yeah, right," she muttered under her breath. Michael put his hand forward, expecting water to gush out and soak the apples.

Nothing happened. Not a single drop of water emerged. "Uh, lemme try again!" Michael said, his confidence faltering for a moment. He tried again, but still, nothing happened. "Come on, water!" he shouted, his voice laced with frustration. But it seemed that Michael's elemental power was not as easy to harness as he thought. He tried again and again, but each time, his attempts ended in failure.

The apples remained dry, mocking him with their intactness. Neveah shook her head, her ponytail bouncing as she chuckled. "Maybe you should try a different approach, Mike," she suggested, her voice laced with amusement. Jasiah, however, was undeterred. He focused his energy, his eyes flashing with determination as he summoned his inner flames. A small spark erupted from his finger, singeing the nearest apple. "Yes!" Jasiah exclaimed, pumping his fist in triumph. But Michael's eyes narrowed, his competitive spirit ignited. "That's nothing," he muttered, his jaw clenched in determination. "I'll show you my true power." And with that, Michael launched himself into a series of elaborate gestures, shouting "Water, come forth!" at the top of his lungs. But no matter how hard he tried, no matter how loud he shouted, not a single drop of water emerged.

As the sun began to set, the trio reluctantly admitted defeat. It seemed that mastering their elemental powers would not be as easy as they thought. But they were determined to persevere, to practice and train until they could wield their powers with precision and skill. Michael tried moving the water with his powers, his eyes fixed intently on the liquid, his brow furrowed in concentration. But nothing was happening. The water remained still, as if mocking his attempts. "I don't think that's gonna work," Neveah spoke, blowing a bubble gum that popped with a loud smack. "Shhh... I'm trying to concentrate," Michael said, feigning annoyance, his eyes still fixed on the water. But then, suddenly, the water began to move. It rippled and churned, as if an invisible force was stirring it. "GUYS, I DID IT!" Michael exclaimed, his voice loud and triumphant, making Neveah choke on her gum. "Wait, really?" Neveah said, her eyes wide with surprise, as she coughed out the gum. "Yeah, I just moved it!" Michael exclaimed, his excitement palpable, his face beaming with pride. But his excitement was short-lived, as Jasiah emerged from the water, a mischievous grin spreading across his face. "Nah, pranked ya! You thought!" Jasiah said, teasing and laughing, pointing at Michael's triumphant expression.

Neveah burst out laughing, her laughter echoing through the backyard, as Michael's face fell, his annoyance and embarrassment evident. "Hey, that's not fair!" Michael said, his voice laced with indignation, his glare fixed on Jasiah. Jasiah just chuckled, his eyes sparkling with amusement. "Gotcha, Mike," he said, still laughing.

Neveah finally managed to compose herself, wiping tears from her eyes. "Sorry, Mike, but that was just too funny," she said, still chuckling. Michael scowled, his annoyance evident, but deep down, he couldn't help but laugh at the absurdity of it all.

After all, it was just a prank, and Jasiah had gotten hi good. But as they all laughed and joked, they knew that their journey was far from over.

They still had to master their elemental powers, and they couldn't afford to let their guard down. The stakes were too high, and the challenges ahead would require all their strength, courage, and determination.. Neveah, determined to prove herself, strode over to a massive boulder in Jasiah's backyard, her eyes fixed intently on the rock. Michael, always up for a challenge, hopped onto the boulder, a teasing grin spreading across his face. "Come on, use your girly preppy power," Michael said, his voice laced with sarcasm, his eyes sparkling with amusement. Neveah's face flushed with annoyance, but she refused to be deterred. She took a deep breath, her eyes fixed on the boulder, her hands spread wide as she summoned her elemental power. A gentle breeze rustled through the air, whispers of wind that seemed to caress the boulder. But Neveah's power was growing, her energy building as she focused her mind. "I will knock you off there, shut up," Neveah said, her voice low and even, her eyes flashing with determination. Michael chuckled, his grin growing wider as he settled in, ready to ride out Neveah's attempt. But Neveah was not to be underestimated. With a swift motion, she raised her hands, and a blast of air shot out, lifting the boulder off the ground. Michael's eyes widened in surprise as he felt himself rising into the air, the boulder hovering beneath him.

Neveah's power was growing stronger, her control more precise as she manipulated the air. But just as it seemed like Neveah had finally mastered her power, the boulder began to wobble, Michael's weight shifting precariously. Neveah's eyes narrowed, her focus wavering for a moment, and the boulder crashed back down to the ground, Michael tumbling off with a laugh.

Neveah's face fell, her disappointment evident, but Michael was quick to offer her a thumbs-up. "Nice try, Neveah! You're getting there!" he said, his grin infectious. Neveah couldn't help but laugh, her annoyance forgotten in the face of their friendly banter. Jasiah, who had been watching from the sidelines, nodded in agreement. "Yeah, Neveah, you're close. Just need to work on your control a bit more." And with that, the trio continued their training, determined to master their elemental powers and face whatever challenges lay ahead. The stakes were high, but they were ready to take on the world, one prank at a time...

As they continued their training, Jasiah tried to summon a flame in his palm, his eyes fixed intently on his hand. "Come on, flames, come out!" he muttered, his brow furrowed in concentration. But nothing happened. Not a single spark emerged from his palm, leaving Jasiah frustrated and disappointed. He shook his head, trying to clear his mind, and attempted again, but the result was the same - nothing. Meanwhile, Michael was still trying to move the water in the pool, his eyes fixed on the liquid as he waved his hand in a circular motion. But no matter how hard he tried, the water remained still, refusing to budge even an inch. Michael scowled, his annoyance evident, as he tried again and again, but to no avail. Neveah, determined to master her power, was trying to lift up the boulder, her arms aching from the effort. She grunted, her face contorted in concentration, as she strained to lift the massive rock. But despite her best efforts, the boulder refused to budge, weighing her down with its immense weight. As they struggled to master their powers, the air was filled with the sounds of frustration and disappointment. Jasiah muttered curses under his breath as he failed to summon a flame, while Michael growled in annoyance as the water refused to move. Neveah, on the other hand, let out a series of loud grunts as she struggled to lift the boulder, her face reddening with exertion.

But despite their struggles, they refused to give up. They knew that mastering their elemental powers was key to their survival, and they were determined to succeed no matter what. So they kept trying, kept pushing themselves to the limit, as they struggled to tap into the deep reservoir of power that lay within them. As the sun began to set, casting a golden glow over the backyard, the trio finally took a break, exhausted and frustrated but not defeated.

They slumped to the ground, panting and sweating, their faces etched with determination.

As the sun dipped below the horizon, casting a warm orange glow over the backyard, the trio finally took a break, exhausted and frustrated but not defeated. They slumped to the ground, panting and sweating, their faces etched with determination. As the stars began to twinkle in the night sky, Jasiah walked back into his house, emerging a moment later with an ice pack in hand.

"Here, you must need it!" he said, handing it to Neveah with a concerned expression. Neveah took the ice pack gratefully, placing it on her shoulders with a sigh of relief. "Thanks, Jah!" she said, her voice laced with appreciation. Jasiah smiled, settling into one of his chairs and leaning back with a contented sigh. "No problem, Neveah. You guys looked like you could use a break.

" Michael, still scowling in frustration, scoffed at the sight of Neveah with the ice pack. "Geez, how hard is it to manipulate water?" he asked, groaning in annoyance.

Neveah shot him a withering look, her eyes flashing with exasperation. "I don't know, Michael," she spoke, her voice strained. "Earth is way more difficult. It's way too hard to move a whole boulder." Michael raised an eyebrow, his skepticism evident. "Really? I thought it was just a matter of focusing your energy or something." Neveah shook her head, her ponytail bouncing with the motion. "It's not that simple, Michael. Moving a boulder requires a huge amount of energy and control. It's not just about focusing your mind, it's about tapping into the fundamental forces of nature." Jasiah nodded in agreement, his eyes thoughtful.

"Yeah, I've been trying to get a flame to appear in my palm, but it's not easy. It's like trying to harness a tiny piece of the sun's energy." Michael looked at them both, his expression thoughtful. "I never realized how hard it was to master our powers. I just thought it would come naturally or something." Neveah smiled wryly. "Trust me, Michael, if it were that easy, we'd all be masters by now. But it takes practice, patience, and perseverance. And even then, it's no guarantee." As they sat there, surrounded by the quiet of the night, they knew that they still had a long way to go.

They were determined to succeed, no matter what it took...

CHAPTER 3

TIME TO REMEMBER

As they sat there, surrounded by the quiet of the night, they knew that they still had a long way to go. But they were determined to succeed, no matter what it took. Just then, Jasiah's mom walked out into the backyard, a gentle smile on her face. "Alright, kids, it's getting late. Time to settle in for the night," she said in a polite tone. Michael groaned, his face falling in disappointment. "Aw, man, wait, Ms.Adolescence, did you ask my parents if I can sleepover?" he asked, his eyes pleading.

Jasiah's mom nodded, a smile spreading across his face. "Yeah, I did, and they said you can. They'll drop off your clothes and stuff later," she said, relieved. Jasiah's mom turned to Neveah, her eyes warm with kindness. "And yes, Neveah, you can stay over too, sweetie!" she said, her voice gentle. Neveah's face lit up with gratitude. "Thanks, Ms. Adolescene!" she exclaimed, her eyes shining with excitement. With that, the trio walked towards Jasiah's room, a cozy space that reflected his personality. The walls were painted a soothing blue, and the desk was cluttered with photos, a computer, and an Xbox Series X.

A bookshelf stood tall in one corner, filled with Jasiah's favorite novels and comics. His drawings and artwork adorned the walls, showcasing his creative talent. Air mattresses were set up for Michael and Neveah, and Jasiah slumped onto his bed, exhausted but content.

"Make yourselves at home, guys," he said, his voice tired but warm. Michael flopped onto his air mattress, letting out a relieved sigh. "Thanks, man. I'm beat," he said, his eyes already closing.

Neveah settled in beside him, her eyes scanning the room with interest. "This is so cool, Jasiah," she said, her voice soft. "I love your room." Jasiah smiled, feeling a sense of pride and belonging. "Thanks, Neveah. I'm glad you like it," he said, his eyes drifting shut as he let out a contented sigh.

The room was quiet for a moment, the only sound being the gentle hum of the Xbox Series X and the soft rustling of the air mattresses. Michael and Neveah were already dozing off, their eyelids heavy with exhaustion. Jasiah, too, was feeling the weight of his fatigue, his eyes drifting shut as he let out a contented sigh. But suddenly, Michael spoke up, his voice piercing the silence.

"I'm bored, y'all wanna play like a game on the Xbox?" he said, looking at Jasiah's Xbox Series X with a mischievous glint in his eye. Jasiah's eyes snapped open, his gaze fixed on Michael with a warning. "No, my mom's strict when it's time for bed," he said, his voice firm but gentle. "We can play tomorrow, maybe." Michael pouted, his face falling in disappointment.

"Aww, come on, Jasiah. Just one game? It'll be quick, I

promise," he said, his eyes pleading. Neveah, who had been watching the exchange with interest, spoke up. "Yeah, Jasiah, it's not like we're going to stay up all night or anything," she said, her voice soft and persuasive. But Jasiah was unmoved. "No, guys, I'm serious. My mom will kill me if she finds out we're gaming at this hour," he said, his voice firm. "Besides, we need to get some rest. We've got a big day ahead of us tomorrow." Michael sighed, his body language defeated. "Fine, fine. I'll go to sleep," he said, his voice sulky. Neveah smiled, her eyes twinkling with amusement.

"Good choice, Michael. We can play tomorrow, like Jasiah said," she said, her voice soothing. For about thirty minutes, the room was quiet, the only sound being the soft rustling of their breathing as they drifted off to sleep. But then, Jasiah spoke up, his voice barely above a whisper. "Guys... I can't sleep," he said, his voice laced with frustration. Michael, who had been pretending to sleep, suddenly sat up, a mischievous grin spreading across his face. "Would a kiss goodnight make it better?" he said, winking at Jasiah. Jasiah's face was a picture of horror, his eyes wide with disbelief. "No, you're weird as hell, bro," he said, giving Michael a blank look that made him snicker.

Neveah, who had been quietly observing the exchange, finally spoke up, her voice firm but playful.

"Can you both shut up? A girl needs her beauty sleep," she said, her eyes flashing with amusement.

Michael and Jasiah looked at each other, both of them

grinning like fools. "Sorry, Neveah," they chimed in unison, their voices teasing. Neveah rolled her eyes, a soft sigh escaping her lips. "You guys are impossible," she said, shaking her head in exasperation.

Despite their apologies, Neveah couldn't shake off the feeling of restlessness. She tossed and turned on her air mattress, her mind racing with thoughts of the day's events. Michael and Jasiah, too, seemed to be struggling to fall asleep, their bodies fidgety and restless. The room was quiet, but not peaceful.

The air was thick with tension, the silence punctuated by occasional rustlings and sighs. Neveah threw off her blanket, getting out of bed to grab a glass of water from the nightstand. As she walked back to her air mattress, she noticed Michael and Jasiah watching her, their eyes gleaming with mischief.

"What's going on, guys?" Neveah asked, her voice soft and curious. Michael shrugged, his shoulders barely rising off the mattress.

"I don't know, I just can't sleep," he said, his voice laced with frustration. Jasiah nodded in agreement, his eyes dark with fatigue. "Yeah, me neither. My mind's racing," he said, his voice barely above a whisper. Neveah sat down on her air mattress, her eyes scanning the room with a sense of desperation. "This is ridiculous," she said, her voice firm. "We need to do something to relax." Michael and Jasiah looked at each other, their faces lighting up with a sudden idea. "Let's have a midnight snack!" Michael exclaimed, his voice loud and enthusiastic.

Neveah raised an eyebrow, her skepticism evident. "Are you

guys serious?" she asked, her voice incredulous. But Michael and Jasiah were already getting out of bed, their faces set with determination. "Yeah, we're serious," Jasiah said, his voice firm. "We need something to take our minds off things." Neveah sighed, her shoulders sagging in defeat. "Fine, but if we get caught, I'm blaming you guys," she said, her voice resigned.

With that, the trio slipped out of the room, their hearts pounding with excitement and their stomachs growling with hunger. The night was young, and they were ready to take on whatever adventures came their way...

As they crept out of the room, the darkness of the hallway enveloped them like a shroud. The only sound was the soft creaking of the floorboards beneath their feet, and the distant hum of the refrigerator in the kitchen. Neveah led the way, her eyes fixed on the door at the end of the hall, her heart racing with anticipation. Michael and Jasiah followed close behind, their eyes darting back and forth, as if searching for any signs of danger. They were all thinking the same thing: what if they got caught?

What if Jasiah's mom woke up and found them rummaging through the kitchen? The thought sent a shiver down their spines, but they pressed on, driven by their hunger and curiosity. They reached the kitchen, Neveah pushed open the door, her eyes scanning the room like a hawk. The kitchen was dark and silent, the only light coming from the faint glow of the microwave clock.

Michael and Jasiah slipped in behind her, their eyes fixed on the pantry, where they knew the snacks were kept. Neveah moved quickly, her hands darting in and out of the pantry like a magician's. She emerged with a bag of chips, a box of cookies, and a jar of peanut butter. Michael and Jasiah cheered, their eyes lighting up with excitement. But just as they were about to dig in, they heard a faint creaking sound coming from the hallway.

It was soft at first, but it grew louder, until it sounded like someone was walking towards the kitchen. Neveah's eyes went wide, her face pale. "What was that?" she whispered, her voice trembling. Michael and Jasiah exchanged a nervous glance. They didn't know what to do, but they knew they had to act fast. Without a word, they scrambled to hide, Neveah diving behind the kitchen island, Michael slipping into the pantry, and Jasiah hiding behind the door.

The creaking grew louder, until it sounded like someone was right outside the kitchen door. Neveah held her breath, her heart pounding in her chest. Suddenly, the door swung open, and a figure loomed in the doorway...

The figure stood tall, its silhouette illuminated by the faint light from the hallway. Neveah's heart was racing, her mind racing with worst-case scenarios. Was it Jasiah's mom? Had she caught them red-handed? But as the figure took a step forward, Neveah realized it wasn't Jasiah's mom. It was... the family cat, Mr. Whiskers. He was an old, scrappy tabby with a wonky eye and a perpetual scowl. Neveah let out a sigh of relief, her heart still pounding in her chest.

Michael and Jasiah emerged from their hiding spots, their faces sheepish. "Dude, that was close," Michael said, his voice still shaking with laughter. Jasiah chuckled, his eyes crinkling at the corners. "Yeah, I thought we were busted for sure." Neveah rolled her eyes, her face still pale. "You guys are idiots," she said, her voice stern but playful. Mr. Whiskers, sensing the commotion, padded over to the trio, his tail twitching with curiosity.

Neveah reached out to pet him, her fingers stroking his soft fur. The tension broken, the trio settled in to enjoy their midnight snack. Michael opened the bag of chips, Jasiah unscrewed the peanut butter jar, and Neveah poured herself a glass of milk. They munched in silence, the only sound being the crunch of chips and the occasional sniffle from Mr. Whiskers. But as they ate, Neveah couldn't shake off the feeling of unease. It wasn't just the close call with Mr. Whiskers; it was something else. Something that had been nagging at her all night. "Guys," she said, her voice low and serious. "I think we should talk about what happened earlier." Michael and Jasiah looked at her, their faces quizzical.

"What do you mean?" Michael asked, his voice casual. Neveah hesitated, her eyes darting back and forth between her friends. "I mean, the midnight snack. The sneaking around. It feels like we're getting away with something." Michael's brow furrowed, his eyes narrowing as he considered Neveah's words.

"What if we can't sleep is because of the fact we haven't been able to activate our elemental powers yet?" Michael asked, his voice laced with uncertainty. Jasiah nodded, his eyes serious. "Probably," he said, his voice barely above a whisper. Jasiah shrugged, his shoulders barely rising off the countertop.

"Eh, it's probably not," he said, his voice skeptical. "Until we can use our elemental abilities for the first time, let's just live life as normal teenagers, k?" Neveah exhaled, her shoulders sagging in defeat. "Yeah, maybe you're right," she said, her voice resigned. The trio lapsed into silence, the only sound being the distant hum of the refrigerator and the occasional creak of the house. They knew that their lives were about to change forever, but they didn't know how or when.

As they stood there, lost in thought, the weight of their uncertainty hung in the air like a thick fog. They knew that their lives were about to change forever, but they didn't know how or when. The silence was oppressive, heavy with unspoken thoughts and doubts. Finally, Jasiah broke the silence, his voice low and casual. "Hey, let's just forget about it for now, okay? We can deal with it in the morning." Neveah nodded, her eyes still fixed on the floor. "Yeah, okay." Michael shrugged, his shoulders barely rising off his chest.

"I'm good with that." Without another word, the trio turned and headed back to Jasiah's room, the snacks still clutched in their hands. They settled in, munching on chips and cookies, the only sound being the crunch of snacks and the occasional rustle of wrappers. As they ate, the tension began to dissipate, replaced by a sense of nostalgia and longing. They started to talk about the last day of 8th grade, reminiscing about the good times and the bad. "Hey, remember when Mrs. Johnson yelled at us for pulling off that epic prank in class?" Michael said, a grin spreading across his face.

Neveah chuckled, her eyes sparkling with amusement. "Oh man, that was classic. I thought we were going to get in so much trouble." Jasiah snorted, his laughter low and husky.

"Yeah, and then we had to clean up the entire classroom as punishment. That was a blast." The trio laughed, their eyes shining with mirth and nostalgia.

They talked about their favorite teachers, their worst subjects, and their most embarrassing moments. As they chatted, the darkness of the night receded, replaced by the warm glow of friendship and camaraderie.

They forgot about the uncertainty of their futures, forgot about the elemental powers that seemed to hang over them like a sword of Damocles.

As they delved deeper into their conversations, the room seemed to shrink, the walls closing in on them as they basked in the warmth of their shared memories. The darkness of the night receded, replaced by the warm glow of friendship and camaraderie.

They reminisce about the time they accidentally set off the fire alarm during a science experiment, and how they had to evacuate the entire school. They laughed about the embarrassing moment when Neveah tripped on her own feet during a school assembly, and how Jasiah had tried to help her up, only to trip himself. As they chatted, their voices grew softer, their laughter more subdued. The room began to feel cozy, the air thick with the scent of snacks and friendship.

The uncertainty of their futures, the elemental powers that had been hanging over them like a sword of Damocles, seemed to fade into the background. The conversation turned to their summer plans, with Michael regaling them with stories of his upcoming family vacation to the beach.

Neveah talked about her plans to attend a summer camp for aspiring artists, and Jasiah shared his hopes of getting a part-time job at the local arcade one day.

As the night wore on, their voices grew sleepy, their words slurring together in a gentle rhythm. The room seemed to grow darker, the shadows deepening as the moon rose high in the sky. One by one, they began to nod off, their heads drooping as they fought to stay awake. Michael's eyes fluttered closed first, his chest rising and falling in a slow, steady rhythm. Neveah followed soon after, her eyelids drooping as she let out a soft sigh. Jasiah was the last to fall asleep, his eyes fixed on the ceiling as he listened to the sound of his friends' gentle snores. He smiled to himself, feeling a sense of contentment wash over him.

As he drifted off to sleep, the room fell silent, the only sound being the distant hum of the refrigerator and the occasional creak of the Mansion. The trio slept peacefully

The trio slept peacefully, their dreams filled with visions of summer fun and adventure. The room was quiet, the only sound being the distant hum of the refrigerator and the occasional creak of the old house. The moon had reached its peak, casting a silver glow over the room.

As the first light of morning crept into the room, Michael woke up with a start, his eyes flying open as he sat up in bed.

He rubbed the sleep from his eyes, his gaze falling on Jasiah and Neveah, who were still fast asleep. "Good morning, guys," Michael said, his voice low and husky, noticing that his friends were still sleeping. He stretched, his arms extending above his head as he let out a loud yawn. The sound seemed to echo through the room, but Jasiah and Neveah didn't stir. Michael chuckled to himself, shaking his head in amusement.

He swung his legs over the side of the bed, his feet dangling in the air as he looked around the room. The remnants of their midnight snack lay scattered on the floor, crumbs and wrappers strewn about. Michael sighed, knowing they'd have to clean up the mess later. He got up, his movements silent as he padded over to the window.

He pulled back the curtains, letting in a flood of morning light. The sky was a brilliant blue, with just a hint of pink on the horizon. As the light streamed in, Jasiah and Neveah began to stir, their eyes fluttering open as they sat up in bed.

They rubbed their eyes, their faces still sleepy, but their eyes shining with a sense of excitement and anticipation. "Morning," Jasiah mumbled, his voice still husky with sleep. Neveah yawned, her eyes still half-closed. "What time is it?" Michael glanced at his phone, his eyes widening as he saw the time. "It's already 9:30. We slept in late."

The trio looked at each other, their faces still sleepy, but their eyes shining with a sense of excitement and anticipation. They knew that today was a new day, a day filled with possibilities and promise. As they sat there, still waking up, they heard the sound of footsteps outside the room. Jasiah's mom, Mrs. Adolescence, walked in with a bright smile on her face. "Good morning, kids! Breakfast is ready! Come on down!" The trio's eyes lit up at the mention of food, and they quickly scrambled out of bed. Michael, still half-asleep, stumbled towards the door, his eyes fixed on the floor.

Just as they were about to head downstairs, Mrs. Adolescence called out, "Last one there has a crush on me!" Michael, always up for a challenge, grinned mischievously and took off, racing down the stairs of the mansion. Jasiah, caught off guard, shouted "Hey, wait what- he took off after Michael, Neveah hot on his heels. The three of them thundered down the stairs, their footsteps echoing off the walls. Neveah tried to get in front of Jasiah, dodging and weaving around him as they raced down the stairs. Jasiah, determined to win, pushed himself to go faster, his heart pounding in his chest.

The three of them burst into the kitchen, out of breath and laughing. Mrs. Adolescence looked up from the stove, a warm smile on her face. "Ah, looks like you all are hungry! Good thing I made plenty of pancakes." The trio collapsed into their seats, grinning at each other as they dug into their breakfast. The pancakes were fluffy and golden, the syrup sweet and sticky.

They chatted and laughed, savoring their food and each other's company. As they ate, they couldn't help but tease each other about their performance in the race. Michael gloated about his victory, while Jasiah and Neveah good-naturedly ribbed him about his slow start.

The three of them finished their breakfast, their plates clean and their bellies full. Jasiah pushed his chair back and stood up, a look of excitement on his face. "Hey, Mom, can we go outside?" he asked, his eyes shining with anticipation.

Mrs. Adolescence smiled and nodded. "Of course, just be back by 2 P.M. and don't trust strangers!" she cautioned, her voice warm and caring. Jasiah nodded enthusiastically. "Don't worry, we won't!" he promised, already heading out of the kitchen. Neveah and Michael followed him, the three of them making their way to Jasiah's room. Jasiah stopped in front of the mirror, gazing at his reflection as he examined his two-toned dreads.

The right side was black, and the left side was white, a striking contrast that made his eyes sparkle. "Eh, maybe next month I'll make the white side a yellow color or purple, I don't know," Jasiah mused to himself, his brow furrowed in thought. Meanwhile, in the bathroom, Michael was changing into his white soccer shirt and black shorts, his pink curly hair parting as he tied his black headband around his forehead. Neveah, on the other hand, was putting on her orange blouse and blue ripped jeans, her straight brown hair tucked into a neat bun.

  Once they were all dressed,they headed to the front door, their energy and excitement palpable. The sun was shining brightly outside, casting a warm glow over the entire scene. As they stepped out into the bright morning light, the trio couldn't help but feel a sense of freedom and adventure. They had the whole day ahead of them, and they were ready to make the most of it.

As they stepped out into the bright morning light, the trio couldn't help but feel a sense of freedom and adventure.

They had the whole day ahead of them, and they were ready to make the most of it. Without a second thought, they decided to head to the park, eager to indulge in some good old-fashioned fun. As they walked to the park, they couldn't help but act like kids again. They skipped and jumped, their laughter echoing through the streets.

They played "I Spy" with the buildings and trees, making silly bets on who could spot the most ridiculous thing.

When they finally arrived at the park, they ran straight for the swings, their eyes shining with excitement. Michael pumped his legs furiously, trying to reach new heights, while Neveah giggled uncontrollably as she spun around in circles. Jasiah, meanwhile, tried to do backflips on the trampoline, his two-toned dreads bouncing with each attempt. As they played, they attracted a few strange looks from grown adults. One woman, sipping a latte on a bench, raised an eyebrow at their antics. A businessman, typing away on his phone, shook his head in disbelief. But the trio didn't care - they were too busy having the time of their lives. After a while, they decided to take a break and have a snack.

Neveah pulled out a bag of goldfish crackers, and they sat down on a blanket, munching away as they watched the world go by. Michael started making up silly songs, his pink curly hair bobbing up and down as he sang. Jasiah and Neveah joined in, their harmonies blending together in a hilarious mix of off-key warbling and crazy dance moves. As they sat there, they noticed a group of kids staring at them in awe. One little boy pointed at Michael's hair, his eyes wide with wonder. "Mommy, Mommy, look at that boy's hair!" he exclaimed. Michael grinned, striking a pose as the kid's mom tried to usher him away.

The trio laughed and waved at the kids, feeling like rockstars for the moment. They knew they were being silly, but they didn't care - they were too busy having fun. As they finished their snack, they decided to move on to the next adventure.

They spotted a group of ducks waddling around the pond and decided to follow them, making quacking noises and flapping their arms like wings. The ducks, seemingly entertained by the trio's antics, swam closer, quacking and splashing in response. The scene was pure chaos, with the trio laughing and chasing after the ducks, their silly noises echoing across the park. It was a moment of pure joy, As they chased after the ducks, they stumbled upon a group of picnickers, who were startled by the trio's sudden invasion of their tranquil afternoon. Michael, still flapping his arms like wings, accidentally knocked over a blanket, sending sandwiches and fruit flying in all directions.

Neveah, trying to help, ended up stepping on a squishy sandwich, causing her to slip and slide across the grass.

Jasiah, laughing too hard to stand up straight, stumbled after his, his two-toned dreads bouncing wildly as he tried to catch his balance. The picnickers, initially shocked, couldn't help but laugh at the absurdity of it all. One of them, a little girl with pigtails, started giggling uncontrollably, her eyes shining with mirth. The trio, still chasing after the ducks, didn't even notice the commotion they were causing. They were too busy having the time of their lives.

  They ran around the pond, making silly faces and noises, and generally causing chaos wherever they went. As they played, they lost track of time. It wasn't until Neveah glanced at her watch that they realized it was now 1:20 PM. They only had forty minutes left before they had to head back home.

"Whoa, time flies when you're having fun!" Michael exclaimed, still out of breath from all the excitement. "Yeah, we have to make the most of it!" Jasiah agreed, his eyes sparkling with mischief. The trio looked at each other, grinning from ear to ear. They knew they had to make the most of their remaining time, and they were determined to do just that.

"Let's go find some more trouble to get into!" Neveah exclaimed, her curly brown hair bouncing with excitement. And with that, the three of them took off, racing around the park, causing chaos and mayhem wherever they went. They were like a trio of mischievous pixies, spreading joy and laughter wherever they wenT. As they ran around the park, they stumbled upon a group of benches and decided to have an impromptu dance party. Michael started spinning around in circles, his pink curly hair flying in every direction.

Jasiah jumped up on a bench, his two-toned dreads bouncing with each move. Neveah twirled around, her orange blouse fluttering like a butterfly's wings. Their laughter and music attracted a crowd, with some people stopping to watch in amusement.

However, a few adults looked on with concern, whispering to each other and glancing at the trio with suspicion. One woman, sipping a latte, raised an eyebrow, muttering to herself, "Are they high or something?" The trio didn't care - they were too busy having the time of their lives. They took a break from dancing to take some group photos, striking silly poses and making funny faces. They took a photo with Jasiah sitting on Michael's shoulders, Neveah perched on top, all three of them grinning from ear to ear. Next, they took a photo with Michael doing a backbend, Jasiah and Neveah standing on either side, their arms outstretched like wings.

A photo was taken with Neveah sitting on a bench, Jasiah and Michael on either side, all three of them making silly monkey faces. As they snapped away, they attracted even more attention, with people stopping to watch and take their own photos. The trio lapped up the attention, hamming it up for the cameras and making silly jokes.

One group of teenagers, inspired by the trio's antics, started taking photos with them, asking them to pose with silly props and making funny faces. The trio obliged, laughing and joking with the teens, who were thrilled to be a part of the fun.

The minutes ticked away, the trio knew they had to make the most of their remaining time. They took a few more photos, including one with Jasiah riding on Michael's back, Neveah holding onto Jasiah's shoulders, all three of them making funny animal noises. Walking away from the park, the trio couldn't stop talking about their adventure. "Man, that was fun!" Jasiah said with a grin, still recovering from the laughter. "Right!" Michael said, throwing his shoulder over Jasiah's shoulder. "That's one count for the summer!" Michaels exclaimed, and Jasiah smirked, playfully rolling his eyes.

Neveah, however, rolled her eyes for a different reason.

"You two are so weird," she said, shaking her head. Michael teased her, "Hey, weren't you the one who was crushing on that one guy two years ago in grade six?" Neveah's face reddened, and she spoke sharply, "Shut the hell up, please." She scoffed, shooting Michael a warning glare. The trio continued to banter back and forth, their laughter and jokes filling the air as they walked towards Jasiah's mansion. They were about 20 minutes away from the house, and they knew they had to hurry if they wanted to make it back in time. As they strolled down the sidewalk, they couldn't help but relive the highlights of their adventure. "Oh man, remember when we chased those ducks?" Michael asked, chuckling. "And then we took those silly photos?" Jasiah added, grinning.

Neveah playfully rolled her eyes again, but couldn't help but smile. The sun was still shining brightly overhead, casting a warm glow over the scene. The air was filled with the sweet scent of blooming flowers, and the sound of birds chirping in the distance. It was a perfect summer day, and the trio was determined to make the most of it.

They were nearly there, they saw and heard screaming and police cars coming from the other street. "What the hell?" Jasiah said, running to the side of his house to check it out. "Jah, where the hell are you going?!" Neveah said, running after him. "Oh my gosh..." Michael said, running after them. When they got to the scene, they saw a grown man with gray disheveled hair and muscular build, wearing a sleeveless white shirt and blue jeans. He had striking features, but it was his actions that caught their attention. He was using... Shadow elemental power? And he was beating up the police - one of them was dead - and trying to rob an old woman.

"We don't even have our elemental powers yet, plus it's just an old woman, she's gonna die one day anyway, so let's get out of here, Jasiah!" Michael said in an urgent tone. Neveah didn't agree with Michael's rude statement, but she did agree with running away. However, Jasiah didn't go anywhere. He walked closer to the scene, his eyes fixed on the man. "Jah, what the hell?!" Michael said, turning around, but Jasiah didn't respond. He just kept walking, his heart pounding in his chest. He knew he didn't know how to use his fire power yet, but he had to do something.

He couldn't just stand by and watch as this man terrorized innocent people. The man, sensing Jasiah's approach, turned around. His eyes narrowed, and he sneered at Jasiah. "And what do we have here? A little hero, trying to save the day?" He took a step closer to Jasiah, his shadowy aura flaring up. "You think you can stop me? I'll crush you like the insignificant insect you are!" Jasiah didn't back down, despite the fear that was creeping up his spine. He took another step forward, his fists clenched. "Leave her alone," he said, his voice firm. "Leave them all alone.

CHAPTER 4

IMPENDING DANGER

The man chuckled, his crooked teeth glinting in the sunlight. Jasiah, sensing an opportunity, took a chance without thinking. He threw his phone at the man's face, hoping to distract him. The phone hit the man squarely on the nose, and for a moment, the two stood in awkward silence. The man's expression turned from amusement to anger, and he raised his hand. A dark, shadowy blast erupted from his palm, hitting Jasiah with incredible force. Jasiah was sent flying backward, crashing into a nearby car with a loud thud. The impact was immense, and Jasiah's body crumpled to the ground, dazed and disoriented. Michael's eyes widened in alarm as he rushed to Jasiah's side.

"Jasiah! Oh man, are you okay?" he exclaimed, helping Jasiah to his feet. Neveah's concern was etched on her face as she watched Jasiah stumble, still trying to regain his bearings. The man, unfazed by Jasiah's bravery, took another step closer. "You think a little phone trick is going to stop me? I'll show you what real power looks like." He raised his hand again, and the air seemed to darken around him.

The old woman, who had been cowering in fear, let out a terrified scream as the man's shadowy aura enveloped her.

Michael and Neveah exchanged a worried glance. They knew

they had to do something, but what? They didn't have their elemental powers yet, and they were no match for this man's abilities.

They couldn't just stand by and watch as he terrorized innocent people. Jasiah, still reeling from the shadow blast, gritted his teeth. He knew he had to try again, no matter how scared he was.

Jasiah continued to fight with his bare hands, determined to protect the old woman and take down the man. But it was a losing battle. The man's shadow powers seemed to be getting stronger by the minute, and Jasiah's punches and kicks were having little effect. The man laughed, a cold, mirthless sound, as he summoned another shadowy blast. Jasiah tried to dodge, but the blast caught him square on the chest, sending him flying backward. He crashed to the ground, the wind knocked out of him.

Michael and Neveah rushed to his side, helping him to his feet. "Jasiah, we have to get out of here!" Michael exclaimed. "We can't take on this guy without our powers!" But Jasiah was resolute. "I won't leave her," he said, nodding towards the old woman, who was still cowering in fear. "I have to protect her." Neveah's eyes were filled with concern. "Jasiah, you're not thinking clearly. You're going to get yourself killed." But Jasiah was beyond reason. He charged forward, fists clenched, determined to take down the man once and for all. The man, however, was ready for him. He summoned a wave of shadowy tendrils, which snaked around Jasiah's arms and legs, immobilizing him.

Jasiah struggled and kicked, but it was no use. He was

trapped. The man sneered, his eyes glinting with triumph. "You're no match for me, little hero," he said, his voice dripping with contempt. "You're just a foolish mortal, playing at being a hero." Jasiah's face twisted with rage and frustration. He knew he was losing, but he refused to give up. He continued to struggle, trying to break free from the shadowy bonds that held him captive. But it was no use. The man's powers were too strong, and Jasiah was no match for him. He was trapped, and he knew it. The only question was, how long would it take for the man to deliver the final blow?

Neveah, witnessing Jasiah's struggles, let out a desperate cry. "Don't!! He's just a kid!" she pleaded to the man, her voice trembling with fear and urgency. "Leave him alone!" The man, however, was unmoved by Neveah's words. He laughed, a cold, mirthless sound, his eyes glinting with amusement.

"A kid, you say?" he repeated, his voice dripping with sarcasm. "He's been playing hero, and now he's paying the price." Neveah took a step forward, her eyes flashing with anger. "You're a monster," she spat, her voice venomous. "You're terrorizing innocent people, and now you're going to hurt a child?" The man chuckled, his eyes never leaving Jasiah's struggling form.

"Innocent people?" he repeated, his voice heavy with irony. "You humans are so naive. You think you're innocent, just because you haven't done anything wrong? Ha! You're all guilty, in one way or another. And as for this little hero..." he nodded towards Jasiah, "he's just a foolish mortal, playing at being something he's not." Michael, who had been watching the scene unfold, took a step forward, his eyes blazing with anger. "That's enough," he growled, his voice low and menacing. "You're going to leave him alone, right now." The man turned to Michael, a sneer still plastered on his face. "Or what?" he taunted, his voice dripping with contempt. "You'll try to stop me? Ha! You're just a couple of kids, playing at being heroes. You're no match for me." Neveah's eyes were filled with tears, as she watched Jasiah struggle against the shadowy bonds that held him captive.

She knew they were running out of time, and she didn't know what to do. The man's powers were too strong, and they were no match for him. All they could do was watch, as Jasiah's fate was decided. Jasiah, with a surge of determination, took a deep breath and tried to break free from the shadowy bonds that held him captive. He strained against the bonds, his muscles flexing with effort, but they refused to budge. The man, anticipating Jasiah's attempt, sneered with satisfaction. "You think you can break free?" he taunted, his voice dripping with contempt. "You're just a weak little kid, playing at being a hero." With a sudden motion, the man slammed Jasiah into the ground, the impact sending shockwaves through Jasiah's body. Jasiah's eyes widened in pain as the man started punching him, his fists flying in rapid succession.

"See what happens when you wanna be a hero, kid?" the man snarled, his face twisted with cruelty. "You get beat to the ground like THIS!" He punctuated his words with a particularly vicious punch to Jasiah's face, the blow sending Jasiah's head reeling. Jasiah's eyes began to glaze over, his vision blurring from the repeated blows. He tried to defend himself, but the man's shadowy fists were too fast, too powerful. "And then you die," the man spat, his voice dripping with malevolence. "You'll be just another casualty, another foolish mortal who thought they could take on the likes of me." With a final, vicious punch, the man sent Jasiah crashing to the ground,

the young hero's body limp and still. The man stood over him, his chest heaving with exertion, his eyes blazing with triumph. Neveah and Michael watched in horror, their eyes fixed on Jasiah's motionless form. They knew they had to do something, but they were powerless against the man's shadowy powers. The man turned to them, a sneer still plastered on his face. "And as for you two," he said, his voice dripping with menace, "you're next."

Neveah and Michael exchanged a terrified glance, their hearts racing with fear. They knew they were no match for the man's powers, and they were powerless to stop him. But just as the man was about to strike, a weak voice echoed

through the air. "Don't... hurt them," Jasiah said, his voice barely above a whisper. Neveah and Michael turned to see Jasiah crawling towards them, his green eyes unfocused and blood dripping from his head. He looked like he was on the verge of collapse, but he refused to give up. "Oh my gosh...

Young boy, just stop," the old lady exclaimed, her voice trembling with concern. "You're hurt, Jasiah. You need to rest." But Jasiah refused to listen. He dragged himself closer to Neveah and Michael, his eyes fixed on the man.

"Don't... hurt them," he repeated, his voice growing stronger with determination. The man sneered at Jasiah, his eyes blazing with contempt. "You're still trying to play hero, even when you're on the brink of death?" he taunted. "You're pathetic, kid." Neveah and Michael watched in awe as Jasiah continued to crawl towards them, his body broken and battered, but his spirit unbroken.

They knew they had to do something, but they were still powerless against the man's shadowy powers.

Despite his broken and battered body, Jasiah managed to summon a surge of adrenaline, allowing him to stand up on unsteady legs. His green eyes were still unfocused, but there was a hint of something in them, a spark of determination that seemed to fuel his actions.

"Lay a finger on them and I'll kill you," Jasiah said, his voice low and menacing, his fist clenched at his side. The man let out a laugh, a cold, mirthless sound. "Oh? That's funny coming from you! I can just-" he said, before Jasiah gave a sudden burst of speed, running towards him with a fierce cry. As Jasiah approached, a spark of flames erupted on his hand, and he punched the man with all his might. The man stumbled back, his eyes wide with shock, as Jasiah's fist connected with his chest. The flames from Jasiah's hand seemed to ignite the man's clothing, and he let out a scream of pain as his skin began to burn. Neveah and Michael watched in awe, their eyes fixed on Jasiah as he stood tall, his chest heaving with exertion. They had never seen him like this before, so fierce and determined. The man stumbled back, clutching at his burning chest, his eyes blazing with anger. "You little brat," he snarled, his voice dripping with venom. "You think you can take me down? I'll show you my true power!" As the man spoke, his body began to change, his shadowy aura growing stronger and more menacing.

His eyes turned a deep, burning hatred and his skin seemed to ripple and writhe like a living thing. Jasiah stood tall, his eyes fixed on the man, his fist still clenched and burning with flames. He knew he had to end this, once and for all. He took a step forward, his eyes blazing with determination. "Bring it on," Jasiah said, his voice low and deadly. "I'm not afraid of you."

With a sudden flick of his wrist, the man sent a wave of shadowy energy hurtling towards Jasiah. Jasiah raised his hand, and a small spark of flame erupted from his fingertips, but it was no match for the man's powerful attack. The shadowy energy engulfed Jasiah, sending him stumbling back. The man advanced, his eyes burning with hatred. He raised his hand, and a torrent of shadowy tendrils burst forth, wrapping around Jasiah like a living noose. Jasiah struggled to break free, but the man's grip was too strong.

With a desperate cry, Jasiah summoned all his strength and managed to conjure a small flame on his hand. He thrust his hand forward, sending the flame shooting towards the man, but it was easily deflected by the man's shadowy aura. The man retaliated with a blast of dark energy, sending Jasiah flying across the room. Jasiah crashed to the ground, his body bruised and battered. He struggled to get up, but the man was too quick, pinning him to the ground with a shadowy tendril. "You're no match for me, little brat," the man sneered, his eyes blazing with triumph. "I'm the master of shadows, and you're just a foolish mortal playing with fire." Jasiah's eyes flashed with determination, and he summoned all his remaining strength to conjure a small spark of flame on his hand. He thrust his hand forward, sending the spark shooting towards the man, but it was easily extinguished by the man's shadowy aura. The man laughed, his eyes gleaming with sadistic pleasure. "You're so pitiful," he sneered. "You can't even conjure a decent flame." Jasiah's eyes fell, his body weakening from the relentless assault. He knew he was no match for the man's shadowy abilities, and he was running out of time.

Jasiah's eyes fell, his body weakening from the relentless assault. He knew he was no match for the man's shadowy abilities, and he was running out of time. Despite his exhaustion, Jasiah summoned all his remaining strength to try and conjure a flame once more. He focused all his energy, his hand shaking with effort, but instead of a flame, only a few sparks erupted from his fingertips. The sparks died out quickly, and Jasiah's eyes fell in defeat. He knew he was beaten, and the man's shadowy aura seemed to be closing in around him like a suffocating shroud. Neveah and Michael watched in horror, their eyes fixed on Jasiah's struggling form.

"Crap, what do we do, Mike?!" Neveah exclaimed, her voice trembling with fear. "There's no way Jasiah is going to win!" Michael's eyes were wide with worry, his face pale with fear.

"We have to do something," he muttered, his voice barely above a whisper "We can't just stand here and watch him get killed." But despite their desperation, they were powerless to stop the man's relentless assault. The man's shadowy powers seemed to be growing stronger by the minute, and Jasiah's flames were no match for them. The man raised his hand, and a wave of shadowy energy washed over Jasiah, sending him stumbling back. Jasiah's eyes were glassy, his body swaying unsteadily, and the man's eyes gleamed with triumph. "It's over," the man sneered, his voice dripping with contempt. "You're finished, little brat.

Now, it's time for you to pay the price for your foolishness."

As the man's shadowy energy washed over him, Jasiah's body began to heat up, his skin glistening with sweat. His eyes were glassy, his body swaying unsteadily, and the man's eyes gleamed with triumph. But before the man could deliver the final blow, Michael intervened, his voice laced with arrogance. "Tch, hey ugly!" Michael said, referring to the man. "Why attack him when you have someone your size?" Michael spoke with a confidence that belied his concern for Jasiah's well-being. He rolled his eyes, a gesture that seemed to infuriate the man. The man's eyes narrowed, his face twisted in anger. He turned to Michael, his shadowy aura swirling around him. With a sudden flick of his wrist, the man sent a shadowy ball hurtling towards Michael.

Michael slightly stepped back, avoiding the attack by a hair's breadth. But the man was relentless, summoning a shadowy clone that seemed to materialize out of thin air. The clone grabbed Michael, its shadowy arms wrapping around him like a vice. Michael struggled to break free, but the clone's grip was too strong. It kneeled down, holding Michael in place, and the man's eyes gleamed with sadistic pleasure. "You think you can talk back to me, boy?" the man sneered, his voice dripping with contempt. "You think you're worthy of taking on someone like me?" Michael's eyes flashed with defiance, but he knew he was no match for the man's shadowy powers. He was trapped, and the man's clone was holding him in place, ready to deliver the final blow.

Neveah watched in horror, her eyes fixed on Michael's struggling form. She knew she had to do something, but what? The man's shadowy powers seemed invincible, and Jasiah was still recovering from his earlier attack. As the man's clone held Michael in place, the man raised his hand, preparing to deliver the final blow.

Neveah knew she had to act fast, or risk losing her friends to the man's shadowy powers.

As the man raised his hand, preparing to deliver the final blow, Neveah knew she had to act fast, or risk losing her friends to the man's shadowy powers. But before she could react, a sudden and unexpected development occurred.

On Jasiah's arm, a whole orange flame erupted, its bright, fiery light illuminating the dark, shadowy atmosphere. The flame was so intense that it melted the shadowy tendrils that had been binding Jasiah, sending them dissipating into nothingness. The man didn't even flinch, so caught up was he in his own triumph. But Jasiah, suddenly empowered by the flame, took advantage of the distraction. His eyes blazing with determination, he punched the man with his burning hot hand, sending him stumbling back a few feet. The man's eyes widened in shock, his face contorting in pain as he clutched at his chest. Smoke began to waft from the sides of his mouth, a testament to the intense heat of Jasiah's flame.

Jasiah took a step forward, his flame still burning brightly on his arm. He seemed to be gaining strength from it, his body language exuding a newfound confidence. The man, still reeling from the unexpected attack, took a step back, his eyes darting between Jasiah and Michael, who was still being held by the shadowy clone. Neveah watched in awe, her eyes fixed on Jasiah's flaming arm.

She had never seen anything like it before. The flame seemed to be fueling Jasiah's determination, giving him the strength he needed to take on the man's shadowy powers. As the man regained his composure, his eyes locked onto Jasiah with a fierce intensity. "You think a little flame like that can stop me?" he sneered, his voice dripping with contempt. "I'll show you what real power looks like." With a sudden flick of his wrist, the man summoned a massive wave of shadowy energy, its dark, swirling tendrils hurtling towards Jasiah like a living thing.

As the man summoned the massive wave of shadowy energy, Jasiah knew he had to act fast. With a swift motion, he backflipped, his movements slightly sloppy as he slid under the tendrils. The shadows grazed his skin, but he managed to avoid the full force of the attack. As he landed on his feet, Jasiah swiftly raised his hand, the one still ablaze with flames. With a fierce cry, he uppercutted the man, the flames on his hand illuminating the dark atmosphere. The man's eyes widened in shock as Jasiah's flames connected with his jaw, sending him stumbling back.

The flames danced across his face, leaving behind a trail of scorched skin. As quickly as they had appeared, the flames on

Jasiah's hand disappeared, leaving behind a wispy trail of smoke. Jasiah's hand was left slightly charred, the skin reddened from the intense heat. The man stumbled back, clutching at his face, his eyes watering from the pain. Neveah watched in awe, her eyes fixed on Jasiah's hand, still smoking from the flames. Michael, still held by the shadowy clone, took advantage of the distraction. With a sudden burst of strength, he broke free from the clone's grasp, sending it dissipating into nothingness.

The man, still reeling from Jasiah's attack, took a step back, his eyes darting between the two friends. His face was twisted in anger, his skin still smoldering from the flames.

As the man went to finish off Jasiah, suddenly a small stream of water came from Michael's fingertip, hitting the man squarely in the eyeball. Michael grinned mischievously, his eyes sparkling with amusement. "Didn't like that?" he said with a teasing look. Neveah, watching from the sidelines, was thinking how she could use her earth elemental power to help her friends. She knew she had to act fast, or risk losing the battle against the man's shadowy powers. The man, wiping his eyes with a snarl, took a step back. "Annoying ass brats, just drop dead!" he snarled, his face twisted in anger.

Michael just chuckled, a reckless glint in his eye. "Jah now!" he said, and Jasiah nodded, taking advantage of the distraction. With a swift motion, Jasiah conjured a small fire blast, directing it at the man's shoulder. The flames erupted with a soft whoosh, and the man growled in anger, his eyes blazing with fury. "DIE!" the man bellowed, his fist flying towards Jasiah's face. But Jasiah was quick, catching the man's fist with a firm grip. "Really? Telling kids to die is a little... immature, you know?" Jasiah spoke with annoyance, his eyes flashing with irritation. But before he could react further, the man summoned a sword made of shadows, its dark blade glinting with malevolent energy. Jasiah's eyes widened in alarm, and he swiftly let go of the man's hand, stumbling back to avoid the blade. The man swung the sword with a swift, deadly motion, and Jasiah barely avoided the blow.

But in his haste, he forgot to dodge the follow-up attack, and the sword sliced across his cheek, leaving a shallow gash. Blood dripped from the wound, and Jasiah stumbled back, his eyes watering from the pain. "Gah!" Jasiah exclaimed, clutching at his cheek. The man sneered, his eyes gleaming with triumph. "You're no match for me," he sneered. The man's eyes blazed with fury as he jumped onto the hood of a nearby car, his shadowy aura swirling around him like a dark vortex. "This is it, I've had enough of you brats," he snarled, his voice dripping with malice. With a swift motion, he charged up a shadowy blast, a huge ball of dark energy forming in his hand. Jasiah's eyes widened in alarm as he backed up, his heart racing with fear. Michael, still struggling to break free from the clone's grasp, tried to call out to Jasiah, but his voice was muffled

by the clone's dark tendrils. Neveah, realizing she had to act fast, turned to run, hoping her elemental power would kick in and allow her to escape. But as she turned, her eyes locked onto a figure emerging from the shadows. It was a young man, his slicked-back black hair reaching ear-length, and his height eerily similar to that of a high schooler.

His eyes gleamed with an otherworldly intensity, and his hand grasped a sword that seemed to pulse with a poison-like aura. The sword's blade seemed to absorb the light around it, leaving a dark void in its wake. The young man's gaze locked onto the man on the car, his eyes flashing with a fierce determination. "You're not taking them down today," the young man said, his voice low and deadly. The man on the car sneered, his shadowy blast still charging up. "And who's going to stop me?" he snarled. The young man didn't respond, instead charging forward with a swift, deadly motion.

The sword sliced through the air, leaving a trail of darkness in its wake. And then, everything froze. The blast of shadowy energy, the young man's sword, the clone's grasp on Michael - everything seemed to hang in suspended animation. The only sound was the heavy breathing of the combatants, and the distant hum of the city's traffic.

The air was thick with tension, and the outcome of the battle hung precariously in the balance.

CHAPTER 5

FIVE A NEW HOME

Everything went black. Back to a few minutes earlier... The boy with slickly black hair and brown eyes, a nice prominent jawline, stood on the rooftop of a building, conversing with an older man. The cityscape stretched out before them, a vast expanse of concrete and steel. "So, you're saying we're going to just take those three kids?" the boy asked, his voice filled with annoyance. "Are we even sure they have elemental powers? I mean, the two-toned boy is getting his ass kicked." The older man smiled, his eyes crinkling at the corners. "I am certain those three kids have the elemental power," he said, his voice dripping with confidence. The boy raised an eyebrow, his expression skeptical. "Tch.

 Don't think I'm going to be all buddy-buddy with them," he said, his voice firm. "But that two-toned boy sure has guts... I don't know if he's just being stupid or brave, but I don't care much." The boy's tone was dismissive, but there was a hint of curiosity in his voice.
He seemed intrigued by Jasiah's boldness, even if he wouldn't admit it. The older man ruffled his own brown hair, a thoughtful expression on his face. "We'll see about that soon enough," he said. "Our scouts have been tracking them for weeks. We have reason to believe they're connected to an ancient prophecy... One that could change the course of our world forever." The boy's eyes narrowed, his interest piqued.

"An ancient prophecy, you say? What kind of prophecy?" The

older man's smile grew wider, his eyes glinting with excitement. "Ah, that's for later. First, we need to secure those three kids. And then... well, we'll see what kind of power they truly possess." The boy scoffed, his expression dismissive. "Whatever... But what if they refuse?" he said in a judgemental tone, his brown eyes flashing with skepticism. "They're probably in middle school at best," he continued, his voice dripping with disdain. The older man's smile remained unwavering, his eyes glinting with amusement. "Well, then, if they refuse, they refuse. We can't force them to do it," he said, his voice calm and collected. The boy's gaze narrowed, his eyes piercing as he shot the man a warning glare. "I will use poison on you, shut up," he said, his voice low and deadly.

The man chuckled, his crimson red eyes lightening with amusement "Whoa, you're forgetting who taught you all this stuff," he said, his voice tinged with a hint of nostalgia. The boy just scoffed, his expression unimpressed. "You think you're so great just because you taught me how to wield a sword?" he said, his voice dripping with sarcasm. The older man's smile grew wider, his eyes twinkling with amusement. "Hanuel, you're so predictable," he said, his voice warm with faffection. "You're so quick to anger, so quick to lash out. But that's what makes you so strong, so capable." The boy's face reddened, his eyes flashing with anger. "Shut up," he said, his voice barely above a whisper.

The older man chuckled, his eyes sparkling with mirth. "I'm just telling the truth, Hanuel," he said.

"You're a talented young man, with a bright future ahead of you. And with the power of the vortex corps behind you, there's no limit to what you can achieve."

Kamar chuckled, his eyes sparkling with mirth as he gazed at his young protégé. His weathered face, etched with lines of experience and wisdom, seemed to glow with a warm, paternal affection. His brown hair, trimmed short and neat, framed his face like a halo, giving him an aura of authority and wisdom. "I'm just telling the truth, Hanuel," Kamar said, his voice warm and gentle, like a summer breeze on a hot day. "You're a talented young man, with a bright future ahead of you. And with the power of the vortex corps behind you, there's no limit to what you can achieve."

Hanuel's glare faltered, his anger dissipating like mist in the morning sun. He looked away, his eyes drifting towards the cityscape below, the towering skyscrapers and bustling streets a blur as his mind whirled with thoughts and emotions. Kamar's words were like a balm to his soul, soothing his anger and calming his fears.

He knew that Kamar was right - he was talented, and with the vortex corps behind him, he could achieve great things. But it was hard to shake off the feeling of inadequacy, of being a pawn in a game much larger than himself. "Sensei," Hanuel said, his voice barely above a whisper, his lips trembling with emotion. "Why do I have to be the one to get them? Why can't someone else do it?" Kamar's expression remained calm and collected, his eyes shining with a knowing glint. "Because, Hanuel," he said, his voice measured and deliberate, "you're the only one who wasn't busy at the base." Hanuel's eyes twitched, his face reddening with indignation. "Well, Aiyden was literally playing video games!" he complained, his voice rising in pitch. "And Camila was making a TikTok! You could've asked them!" Kamar's smile grew wider, his eyes sparkling with amusement. "Eh, you also looked bored," he said, his voice dripping with humor. Hanuel's face darkened, his eyes flashing with anger. "I was not bored!" he protested, his voice loud and defensive.

Kamar chuckled, his shoulders shaking with mirth. "Oh, Hanuel, you're so easy to read," he said, his voice warm and teasing. "Your eyes glaze over whenever you're not in the thick of things. And besides, I needed someone with your... unique skills." Hanuel's expression softened, his anger dissipating like mist in the morning sun. He knew that Kamar was right - he did get bored easily, and his skills were well-suited for this kind of mission. "Fine," Hanuel said, his voice resigned. "I'll get them. But don't expect me to be all smiles and rainbows about it." Kamar's smile grew wider, his eyes shining with approval. "I wouldn't have it any other way, Hanuel," he said, his voice warm and affectionate."Now, go".

" Hanuel nodded, his determination crystallizing like ice in the cold. He turned to leave, his footsteps echoing through the rooftop as he jumped towards his destiny.

The scene shifted back to the present time, where Hanuel stood on the car his poison-tipped sword at the ready. With a swift motion, he slashed the man across the back, both horizontally and vertically, making the man's shadow ball slowly shrink and then disappear completely.

"I feel dizz-" The man said, collapsing forward and falling off the car, his face planting on the pavement with a sickening thud. Hanuel twirled his sword and put it on his back, his eyes scanning the ground from on top of the car as he gazed at Jasiah, Michael, and Neveah. Before they could say anything, he knocked all three of them out, his movements swift and precise.

Kamar jumped down from the rooftop, his eyes narrowing as he gazed at Hanuel. "You didn't need to knock them out, y'know?" he said, his voice tinged with amusement. Hanuel shrugged, his expression impassive. "I don't wanna deal with this, so let's just get back to base before they wake up," he spoke, lifting up Neveah as Kamar took Michael and Jasiah. As they stood there, Kamar noticed Jasiah's phone on the ground, slightly shattered. The old lady was scared, her eyes wide with fear.

Kamar simply picked up the phone and started walking away from the scene, his movements calm and collected. Hanuel and Kamar quickly body-flickered to a nearby forest, their movements swift and precise. As they materialized amidst the trees, Kamar spoke, his voice low and analytical. "It seems like this boy got the most damage," he said, placing down Jasiah on the forest floor.

Hanuel sighed, his expression concerned. "Yea... seems like it," he said, glancing at Michael, who was still unconscious. "And the pink-haired boy doesn't seem as bad," Hanuel added, his gaze flicking towards Michael's pale face.

Hanuel's eyes roamed over the trio, his expression a mixture of concern and annoyance. "I swear to God, if they're loud, I swear I might just quit right then and there," Hanuel muttered out, his voice low and exasperated.

Kamar chuckled, his eyes crinkling at the corners. "Oh, Hanuel, you're such a drama queen," he said, his voice teasing. Hanuel shot him a withering look, but Kamar just smiled, his expression unrepentant. "You know it's only a matter of time before they start making a ruckus," Hanuel said, his voice resigned. Kamar nodded, his expression serious.

"Yes, we should prepare ourselves for the worst," he said, his voice dry.

They just stayed in the forest and eventually brought them to the base. Michael was the first to wake up, and as he opened his eyes, he found himself tied to a chair in a bedroom. The walls looked like stone, and there was a master bed with a nightstand beside it. An office desk sat in one corner, with a unique aqua-like crest on the wall above it. A pair of clothes lay on the desk, and there was even a TV, but no windows. The room was lit up with torches, and the door was made of wooden planks. Michael's eyes scanned the room, but he didn't see Jasiah or Neveah. "Hello?!" he called out, his voice echoing off the stone walls.

Just then, Kamar walked in, a smile on his face. "Ah, so you're awake!" he said, his eyes sparkling with amusement. Michael analyzed the figure in front of him, his expression confused. "Who the hell are you? Are you associated with the guy who used shadows?" Michael asked, his voice laced with suspicion. Kamar chuckled. "No, no! He's someone me and my students have been trying to catch. And I see you might be a straightforward person. However, you remember grabbing a crystal a few days back, when you explored an abandoned house, right?" Kamar asked, his eyes piercing.

Michael's eyes widened in shock. "How do you know that?!" he exclaimed. Kamar shrugged. "Hm, because when I went there, they weren't in the chest nor on the shelf, and I saw you shooting water from your fingertip... when you fought that man," Kamar explained, his voice matter-of-fact. Michael nodded, his expression thoughtful. "Ah, I see..." "But then, why am I here?" Michael asked, his voice laced with curiosity. Kamar smiled. "It's a life-changing offer... really," he said, his voice tantalizing. Michael's eyes narrowed. "Well, what kind of offer is it?" he asked, his voice impatient.

Kamar leaned forward, his eyes serious. "Well, I'm assuming you already met the crystal's protectors when you first grabbed the crystals, so it's the same... your first option... either go back to your normal life, and let me extract the power from your soul with no memory of the elemental power, or join us and stay here, but you'll no longer be able to have education like a normal kid. You'll potentially miss out on all years of high school... And you won't be able to visit your parents, but we'll help you master your water element, since you can only use water streams from your fingertip," Kamar explained, his voice measured. Michael's eyes widened as he considered the options. "I already asked your two friends, and Jasiah said to stay here with no hesitation, while Neveah had a disagreement but she ended up also joining," Kamar continued.

Michael sighed, his expression resigned. "Fine, I'll stay, but only because they're my friends... Not because I want to save people," Michael spoke bluntly, his voice laced with a hint of annoyance. Kamar nodded, a smile on his face. "I expected as much," he said, his voice dry.

As the ropes fell away, Michael rubbed his wrists, his eyes narrowing at Kamar. "Thanks for the hospitality," he said, his voice laced with sarcasm. Kamar chuckled. "Anytime, Michael. Now, let's get you settled in.

You've got a lot to learn," he said, his eyes sparkling with amusement. Michael followed Kamar out of the dormitory, his eyes scanning the unfamiliar surroundings.

They walked down a long corridor, the walls lined with stone and the air thick with the scent of old books. As they turned a corner, Michael saw Jasiah and Neveah waiting for him in the training room. Jasiah was leaning against a wooden beam, his

arms crossed and a look of displeasure on his face.
Neveah was standing beside him, her eyes fixed on Michael. "Oh, you chose to stay too?" Jasiah said, his voice not really happy about the idea of having to leave his mom without her knowing and ruin his education.
Michael scoffed. "Yup," he said bluntly. "Only because you guys chose to," he added, his eyes flicking towards Jasiah and Neveah. Jasiah's expression darkened, his eyes flashing with anger. "You're only staying because of us?" he asked, his voice low and dangerous. Michael shrugged. "What else am I supposed to do? You guys are my friends, and I'm not going to leave you to deal with this mess on your own,"
he said, his voice firm. Neveah stepped forward, her eyes shining with understanding. "Thanks, Michael," she said, her voice soft. "We appreciate it." Jasiah's expression softened, his eyes flicking towards Neveah before turning back to Michael. "Yeah, thanks, man. I guess we're in this together now," he said, his voice gruff.
 The trio waited until Kamar walked into the training room, carrying a few mysterious objects in his hands. "First, you guys need to complete this obstacle course," he said, pointing to the walls as platforms appeared, and lasers flashed to life. Michael's eyes widened in excitement. "I'll go first!" he said confidently. Kamar nodded, a small smile on his face. "Alright," he said, walking over to Michael and placing a blindfold over his eyes. Michael's expression changed from confidence to confusion. "Huh, what the... I can't see!" he exclaimed, his hands flailing in front of him. Kamar's voice was wise and calm. "That's the point. Focus your mind to moving water itself. Focus until you can see the water crystal. Focus on that until you can feel the water in your blood.

Focus your pride," he said, his words dripping with encouragement.

Jasiah and Neveah watched in rapt attention as Michael took a deep breath, his face scrunched up in concentration. The air around him seemed to ripple, as if the water molecules were responding to his inner turmoil. Suddenly, Michael's expression cleared, and he took a step forward, his hands outstretched. The blindfold stayed in place, but his movements were deliberate, as if he was being guided by an unseen force. The platforms on the wall began to glow with a soft blue light, and the lasers hummed to life, creating a complex pattern of beams that crisscrossed the room. Michael's hands moved in time with the beams, as if he was conducting an invisible orchestra. The room was silent, the only sound the soft hiss of the lasers and Michael's steady breathing. Jasiah and Neveah watched in awe as Michael navigated the obstacle course, his movements becoming more fluid and confident with each step.

As Michael continued to navigate the obstacle course, his movements became more fluid and confident with each step. His hands waved and gestured, as if he was conducting an invisible orchestra, and the lasers responded in kind, weaving a complex pattern of light and sound around him. Jasiah and Neveah watched in awe, their eyes fixed on Michael as he danced across the room. They could feel the air charged with energy as if the very molecules themselves were responding to Michael's inner power. But as Michael approached the final platform, his movements began to falter. His hands trembled, and his steps became hesitant.

The lasers, sensing his uncertainty, began to waver, their beams flickering and dimming. Kamar's voice was calm and encouraging. "Focus, Michael. You're almost there. Feel the water within you, guiding you towards the Money."

Michael took a deep breath, his eyes fixed on the platform ahead. He could see the Money, its facets glinting in the dim light of the room.

He reached out a hand, his fingers closing around the Money as if it were a tangible thing. But just as he thought he had succeeded,

his grip faltered. The Money slipped from his grasp, and Michael's eyes snapped open, his face twisted in a mixture of frustration and disappointment. The room fell silent, the only sound the soft hiss of the lasers as they died away. Jasiah and Neveah exchanged a worried glance, their faces etched with concern.

Michael's face twisted in a scowl. "I was so close," he muttered, his fists clenched in frustration. Kamar placed a hand on his shoulder. "You were. And you will be again. Let's try it again, and this time, focus on the sensation of the water within you. Feel its power coursing through your veins, guiding you towards the prize " Michael nodded, his eyes flashing with determination.

He took a deep breath, and the room fell silent once more, as if the very air itself was holding its breath in anticipation. With a sudden burst of energy, Michael launched himself forward, his hands waving and gesturing as he navigated the obstacle course once more. The lasers hummed to life, their beams weaving a complex pattern of light and sound around him. This time, as he approached the final platform, Michael's movements were fluid and confident.

As Michael approached the final platform, his movements were fluid and confident. He jumped onto the platform with a triumphant cry, but his victory was short-lived. His foot slipped on the slick surface, and he managed to stumble off, landing on the mat with a thud.

Neveah couldn't help but burst out laughing at Michael's misfortune. "I'd do better!" she said, a smirk on her face. Michael scoffed, his pride wounded. "Then you try, idiot!" he said, his voice loud and defensive. Jasiah's face palmed, and he shook his head, muttering under his breath. "Great, now they're going to start arguing again..." Neveah didn't seem to mind, though. She walked confidently in front of the obstacle course, a determined look on her face. "I'll show you how it's done," she said, and started the course. At first, she did well, navigating the platforms with ease. But as she reached the fifth platform, her legs started to wobble, and she tumbled off, landing on the mat with a giggle.

Meanwhile, Kamar walked over to Jasiah, a mischievous glint in his eye. "While you wait, Jasiah, you can lift this," he said, handing Jasiah a massive 200-pound weight. Jasiah's jaw dropped in shock. "Wait, what?!" he exclaimed, his eyes fixed on the weight. Kamar nodded casually. "Yup. Or you can give me 500 pushups," he said with a grin, clearly enjoying Jasiah's distress. Jasiah hesitated for a moment, then nodded reluctantly.

"Yeah, uhm, I'll just lift the weight," he muttered, his face scrunched up in effort. In the background, Michael and Neveah were still trying to master the obstacle course, but they were failing miserably. Michael stumbled off the platform for the fifth time, while Neveah got stuck on the third platform, her legs tangled in the laser beams. Jasiah, meanwhile, was struggling to lift the weight, his face red with effort. He grunted and groaned, his arms shaking with the strain, but he refused to give up.

As the minutes ticked by, none of them were making any progress. Michael was still stuck on the obstacle course, unable to navigate the complex pattern of laser beams. Neveah was getting frustrated, her attempts to lift herself up onto the platform resulting in spectacular failures. Jasiah, meanwhile, was still struggling to lift the massive weight, his face red with effort and his arms shaking with the strain. Kamar walked around the room, offering words of encouragement and advice, but it seemed like no matter what they did, they just couldn't get it right. Michael's movements were stiff and awkward, Neveah's legs were trembling with exhaustion, and Jasiah's arms were on the verge of giving up.

The room was filled with the sound of their struggles, the air thick with the smell of sweat and frustration. Michael's face was twisted in a scowl, Neveah's eyes were flashing with anger, and Jasiah's expression was a mix of determination and desperation.

As the minutes turned into hours, it seemed like they were getting nowhere. Michael's attempts to navigate the obstacle course were getting slower and more labored, Neveah's jumps were becoming weaker and more hesitant, and Jasiah's lifts were getting more and more feeble. Kamar's expression was calm and encouraging, but even he seemed to be getting worried. He walked over to each of them, offering words of advice and encouragement,

but it seemed like no matter what he said, they just couldn't get it right.

As the hours dragged on, the trio's attempts only grew weaker and weaker. Michael's legs trembled with exhaustion as he tried to navigate the obstacle course, his movements slow and clumsy.

Neveah's jumps were barely clearing the platform, her legs wobbling with fatigue. And Jasiah's lifts were getting more and more miserable, his arms shaking with the strain.

Kamar's words of encouragement were starting to sound hollow, even to himself. He walked around the room, trying to offer advice and motivation, but it seemed like no matter what he said, they just couldn't muster up the strength to succeed.

Michael stumbled off the platform for the tenth time, his face twisted in frustration. Neveah's legs gave out on her, and she collapsed to the mat, her chest heaving with exhaustion. Jasiah's lift barely cleared the ground, his arms collapsing under the weight. The room was silent, the only sound the heavy breathing and grunting of the trio as they struggled to overcome their limitations.

It was a scene of pure despair, a testament to the futility of their efforts.

"It's okay, guys. You've done enough for today. Let's take a break and come back to it tomorrow." But even as he spoke, he knew that it was a hollow promise. They were never going to master their elemental powers, not at this rate.

And as the three of them stumbled out of the room, exhausted and defeated, The trio couldn't help but wonder if they had made a grave mistake.

Kamar led them to the dining table, where a feast of delicious foods awaited them. Bowls of steaming hot spaghetti, mashed potatoes, and chicken sat alongside plates of crispy fries, corn, and luscious watermelon. The aroma of sizzling steak wafted through the air, making Michael's and Jasiah's mouths drool in anticipation.

As they took their seats, they noticed a few other kids already seated at the table. One of the girls had straight, dark brown hair that fell down her back like a rich, chocolate waterfall, with a few stray strands framing her heart-shaped face. Her warm brown eyes were glued to the screen of her phone, and she hadn't noticed the trio yet. Beside her was Hanuel, his eyes fixed intently on Jasiah, Michael, and Neveah. Michael, never one to mince words, spoke up as he took his seat. "So, you gonna talk or you just gonna sit there like a retard?" he said to Hanuel, making the other boy's glare harden. "You just got here and this is our first time interacting, and I already don't like you," Hanuel said, his voice dripping with disdain. The argument between Michael and Hanuel made the girl with straight brown hair look up, but she quickly noticed Neveah and her face lit up. "Oh my god, finally another girl here!! Hiii!!" she exclaimed, bouncing up from her seat. Neveah waved, a little shyly.

"Hey!" she said, while Jasiah was too busy helping himself to the food and sharing his plate with Michael to pay attention to the drama.

The girl introduced herself as Camila and she looked like she was around sixteen. She was bubbly and enthusiastic, chatting with Neveah like they were old friends. Meanwhile, the argument between Michael and Hanuel continued, with Kamar trying to intervene and calm things down.

As the argument between Michael and Hanuel escalated, Camilla's eyes darted back and forth between the two boys, her expression a mix of concern and amusement. Neveah, seemingly oblivious to the tension, chatted excitedly with Camilla, asking her about her interests and hobbies. "I'm so into photography," Camilla said, her eyes lighting up. "I love capturing moments and beauty through my lens. What about you, Neveah? What do you like to do in your free time?" Neveah's face lit up. "I'm super into music. I play the guitar and piano, and I love writing my own songs. I'm actually thinking of starting a YouTube channel to share my music with others." Camilla's eyes widened. "That's amazing! I've always wanted to learn how to play the guitar. You'll have to teach me sometime." Meanwhile, Michael and Hanuel's argument was getting more heated by the minute. "You're just a clueless newbie who thinks he can come in here and disrespect me?" Hanuel sneered.

"I'm not disrespecting you, I'm just calling you out on your attitude," Michael shot back. "You're acting like you're better than everyone else just because you've been here longer." Kamar intervened, his voice calm but firm. "Okay, guys, let's not forget that we're all here to learn and grow together. Let's focus on building each other up, not tearing each other down." But Michael and Hanuel were too far gone to listen. They continued to bicker and argue,

their voices rising until they were almost shouting. Jasiah, meanwhile, was too busy munching on his food to care about the drama unfolding around him. He shared his plate with Michael, who was too caught up in the argument to notice. As the meal went on, the tension in the air was palpable. Camilla and Neveah's conversation was the only bright spot in an otherwise stormy atmosphere. They chatted and laughed, exchanging stories and getting to know each other.

As the meal finally came to a close, Kamar stood up, his eyes scanning the table. "Alright, everyone. Let's take a break and get some fresh air. We can continue our discussion later." The table erupted into a cacophony of sounds as everyone pushed back their chairs and stood up.

Michael and Hanuel were still arguing, their voices fading into the background as the group made their way out of the dining room.

Neveah and Camilla walked side by side, chatting and laughing like old friends. Jasiah trailed behind, his eyes fixed on the remnants of the meal, his stomach still growling with hunger. As they stepped out into the evening air, the tension seemed to dissipate, replaced by a sense of unease. It was clear that this was only the beginning of a long and complicated journey, one that would test their limits and push them to their breaking points.

As they stepped out into the evening air, the cool breeze seemed to do little to calm the lingering tension. Michael and Hanuel continued to argue, their voices growing louder as they walked further away from the dining room. "You think you're so much better than me, don't you?" Hanuel sneered, his eyes flashing with anger. "You think you can just waltz in here and take over?" "I'm not trying to take over anything," Michael shot back, his face reddening with frustration. "I'm just trying to point out that your attitude is ridiculous. You're acting like you're the king of the castle just because you've been here a little longer." "Oh, so now you're an expert on me?" Hanuel's voice dripped with sarcasm.

 "You've known me for all of five minutes and you think you can psychoanalyze me?" "I don't need to psychoanalyze you to see that you're being a jerk," Michael retorted. "You're acting like a spoiled brat who can't handle the fact that someone new is getting attention." Hanuel's face darkened, his eyes narrowing into slits. "You have no idea what you're talking about," he growled. "You have no idea what it's like to be here, to be a part of this group. You're just a newbie who thinks he can come in and change everything." The argument continued to escalate, with neither boy willing to back down. Neveah and Camilla watched in discomfort, their earlier laughter and chatter replaced by worried glances. Jasiah, still trailing behind, shook his head. "Guys, come on," he muttered. "Can't we just get along?" But Michael and Hanuel were too far gone to listen. They continued to shout and argue, their voices echoing through the empty corridors of the mansion. As they walked, the group's pace slowed, the tension between Michael and Hanuel growing thicker with every step. It was clear that this was only the beginning of a long and complicated journey, one that would test their limits and push them to their breaking points.

Hanuel's smug grin spread across his face as he sneered at Michael. "Well, at least unlike you, I can actually use my elemental power," he said, his voice dripping with condescension. Michael's eyes flashed with anger, his fists clenched at his sides. "Elemental power or not, I'd still kick your ass," he growled, his words barely contained. Hanuel's grin grew even wider as he raised his hand, a dark, poison aura swirling around it. "Oh, really?" he said, his eyes glinting with malice as he took a step closer to Michael.

Before Hanuel could strike, Camilla sprang into action. Her eyes flashed with determination as she raised her own hand, summoning vines from the nearby plants to restrain Hanuel. "Hey! No attacking the weak!" she exclaimed, her voice firm as she glared at Hanuel. Hanuel's eyes narrowed, his poison aura faltering as he gazed at Camilla's vines. He sighed, his expression annoyed, before deactivating his poison hand. "Good," Camilla said, retrieving her vines with a satisfied nod. Neveah's eyes widened in amazement as she watched the scene unfold. "Whoa, that was kinda cool!" she exclaimed, her eyes fixed on Camilla.

"So, you have a plant power?" Camilla's smile was radiant as she nodded. "Yeah, and what about you?" she asked, her curiosity piqued. Neveah chuckled, her eyes sparkling with amusement. "Eh, I'm supposed to have earth," she said, her voice tinged with uncertainty. Camilla's laughter was infectious, and Neveah couldn't help but join in. "That partially makes us distant relatives, I suppose," Camilla said, her eyes twinkling with mirth. As the two girls laughed, the tension between Michael and Hanuel began to dissipate, replaced by a sense of wonder and curiosity. Jasiah, who had been watching the scene unfold, nodded in agreement. "Yeah, it's pretty cool to see people using their elemental powers," he said, his voice filled with excitement.

Michael, still visibly shaken by Hanuel's poison aura, nodded reluctantly. "Yeah, I guess it's not all bad," he said, his eyes flicking towards Hanuel.

As the group dispersed, each member retreating to their respective dorms, Jasiah couldn't shake off the feeling of unease that had settled in the pit of his stomach. He trudged along the dimly lit corridor, his footsteps echoing off the stone walls as he made his way to his dorm. Finally, he arrived at the entrance of his dorm, the fire crest emblazoned on the wall a warm, golden glow that seemed to mock him. Jasiah's eyes fell upon the crest, and he felt a pang of inadequacy wash over him. He slumped down onto the bed, his body language defeated, as he questioned how he could

possibly learn to harness his elemental power.
"I'm supposed to be a fire wielder," he muttered to himself, his voice laced with frustration. "But how do I even begin to control it?" Jasiah's mind raced with thoughts of his failed attempts to conjure even a spark of flame. He thought back to the argument between Michael and Haneul, and how Camilla had effortlessly summoned her plant elemental power to restrain Haneul.

 Why was it so easy for them, and yet so impossible for him? As he lay there, Jasiah's gaze wandered around the room, taking in the Spartan decorations and the neatly made bed. It was a far cry from his cluttered, chaotic bedroom back home, but it was a reminder that he was here to learn, to grow, and to master his elemental power.

With a newfound determination, Jasiah pushed himself off the bed and began to pace around the room. He couldn't give up With a newfound determination, Jasiah pushed himself off the bed and began to pace around the room. He couldn't give up now, not when he had finally discovered his true potential. As he walked, his mind
raced with thoughts of how he could possibly master his elemental power. In a moment of impulsive decision, Jasiah snuck out of his dorm, unsure if there were rules against it, but he didn't care. This was his first day here, and he was determined to make the most of it.

He made his way to the training room, his heart pounding with excitement and anticipation. As he entered the room, he was surprised to see Michael already there, back to doing his parcour training.

Jasiah's eyes widened as he watched Michael's fluid movements, his body bending and twisting with ease. "Oh,

Michael, you're here too?" Jasiah asked, trying to sound nonchalant, despite his eagerness to join in. Michael turned, a fierce glint in his eye. "Yeah, I'm gonna train and beat up that bastard named Hanuel. With my water, his poison won't be able to do anything to me." Jasiah nodded, his mind racing with ideas. "Hm... what if we had a hand-to-hand combat? Maybe then our elemental powers will work?" Michael's eyes narrowed, his interest piqued. "What do you mean?" Jasiah's eyes sparkled with remembrance. "Remember a few hours ago, when we were fighting the man with the shadow powers? I was able to make a whole arm of flames.
" He spoke with conviction, his voice filled with determination. "So maybe I can do that again." Michael's face broke out into a wide grin. "Sure," he said, his voice filled with excitement. "Let's do it." Without another word, the two boys faced off, their bodies tense and ready. Jasiah's hands clenched into fists, his heart pounding with anticipation. He was going to master his elemental power, no matter what it took.

The two boys faced off, their bodies tense and ready, their eyes locked in a fierce stare. The air was electric with tension as they circled each other, their movements fluid and calculated. Jasiah's hands clenched into fists, his heart pounding with anticipation. He was going to master his elemental power, no matter what it took. Michael, sensing Jasiah's determination, grinned with excitement. He had been itching for a fight, and now he had one. With a swift kick, he launched himself at Jasiah, his body a blur of movement. Jasiah dodged the kick with ease, his reflexes honed from years of martial arts training.

He countered with a swift punch, his fist flying towards

Michael's face. Michael blocked the punch with his arm, his eyes flashing with anger. The two boys exchanged blows, their movements lightning-fast, their bodies clashing in a flurry of motion. Jasiah's eyes blazed with determination, his heart pounding with excitement. He was finally getting the chance to test his elemental power, to see if he could harness it in the heat of battle.

As they fought, Jasiah's mind raced with thoughts of his elemental power. He could feel it simmering beneath the surface, waiting to be unleashed. He focused all his energy on summoning the flames, his body tensing with anticipation. The air was electric with tension as they circled each other, their eyes locked in a fierce stare. It was going to be a battle of wills, a test of strength and determination. But Jasiah was ready.

The two boys charged at each other, their bodies clashing in a flurry of punches and kicks. Jasiah's fists flew towards Michael's face, but Michael dodged with ease, countering with a swift kick to Jasiah's stomach. Jasiah doubled over, gasping for breath, but he refused to give up. He launched himself at Michael, their bodies crashing together in a flurry of movement. Michael's arms wrapped around Jasiah's waist, pulling him into a tight headlock.

    Jasiah's eyes bulged as he tried to break free, but Michael's grip was like iron. With a burst of strength, Jasiah managed to wriggle free, sending Michael stumbling back. Michael's eyes flashed with anger, and he charged at Jasiah with a fierce cry. The two boys exchanged blow after blow, their bodies clashing in a flurry of motion. Sweat dripped from their brows, their chests heaving with exhaustion. But neither of them would give up, their determination to win driving them forward. As they fought, Jasiah's mind raced with thoughts of his elemental power. He focused all his energy on summoning the flames, but nothing happened. Michael, too, seemed to be struggling to harness his water power.

The two boys were evenly matched, their physical strength and determination the only things driving them forward. The battle raged on for what felt like hours, the two boys giving it their all. But in the end, it was clear that neither of them had managed to harness their elemental power. Michael stumbled back, panting heavily, his eyes wide with exhaustion. Jasiah stood tall, his chest heaving with exertion, his eyes blazing with determination. "Well, that didn't work..." Michael panted, his voice laced with disappointment. "No shit," Jasiah said, panting too, his face twisted with frustration. Jasiah's eyes scanned the surrounding area, his mind racing with new ideas. "You know what, Michael? I think we need to try something different," he said, a hint of determination in his voice. Michael raised an eyebrow, his chest still heaving with exhaustion. "What did you have in mind?" "Parkour," Jasiah said, a mischievous glint in his eye. "We can try to incorporate our elemental powers into our movements. Maybe that's what we need to tap into them." Michael's face lit up with excitement. "That's a great idea, Jasiah! Let's do it!" The two boys set off, racing towards the nearby parkour course.

They vaulted over obstacles, leaped across gaps, and sprinted up walls. Their movements were fluid and agile, their bodies honed from years of martial arts training. But despite their best efforts, their elemental powers remained elusive. Jasiah's flames refused to manifest, and Michael's water powers remained dormant. The two boys stumbled and fell, their bodies crashing to the ground. They groaned, rubbing their sore heads and bruised egos. "Well, that didn't work either," Michael said, his voice laced with disappointment.

Jasiah grinned, a competitive spark in his eye. "Hey, let's make it a competition then.

Whoever can complete the course the fastest wins." Michael's eyes flashed with determination. "You're on, Jasiah. But I'm not going to go easy on you." The two boys took off, racing through the course with reckless abandon. They flipped and spun, their bodies a blur of movement. But despite their speed and agility, their elemental powers remained stubbornly silent. In the end, they crossed the finish line simultaneously, their bodies exhausted and their elemental powers still elusive.

Jasiah grinned, his face flushed with exertion. "I guess we're evenly matched, Michael." Michael nodded, his eyes sparkling with amusement. "Yeah, but we still didn't manage to harness our elemental powers."

CHAPTER 6

LESSONS BEGIN!

As the two boys parted ways, Jasiah trudged back to his dorm, his exhaustion catching up with him. He flopped onto his bed, his eyes drooping shut as soon as his head hit the pillow. The next morning, a loud bell pierced the air, jolting Jasiah awake. "Huh, what the-?!" he exclaimed, rubbing his eyes groggily. The sound of the bell was followed by an announcement, echoing through the stone walls of the ancient building. "All Elemental wielders! Report to class 302, please! Classes start in 20 minutes!" Jasiah's eyes widened as he sat up, still disoriented from the sudden wake-up call. "Who would've thought...? A stone place would be so high tech..." he muttered to himself, throwing off his covers. He quickly got dressed, opting for a plain white shirt and blue jeans.

He navigated through the labyrinthine corridors, he realized he had no idea where he was going. The building's stone walls seemed to stretch on forever, with identical-looking doors and staircases leading to who-knew-where. Just as Jasiah was starting to feel like he was lost in a maze, he spotted Camilla and Neveah walking down a nearby hallway. Camilla, with her hair bouncing and confident stride, seemed to know exactly where she was going. Jasiah decided to follow her, hoping she would lead him to class 302. As he approached the girls, Neveah turned around, her bright blue eyes sparkling with recognition. "Ooh, hey Jah!" she said, waving enthusiastically. Camilla turned around, her eyes scanning Jasiah from head to toe. "Damn, who's that cutie?"

she joked, her voice dripping with sarcasm. Jasiah's face scrunched up in confusion. "Uh... cute...?" he asked, unsure how to respond. Neveah chuckled, rolling her eyes good-naturedly. "Oh, Jasiah's my friend," she said, as if explaining something obvious.

Camilla grinned, her Chocolate brown curly hair bobbing up and down. "Well, in that case, let's get to class. You don't want to be late on your first day." As they walked, Jasiah's eyes wandered around the corridor, taking in the intricate paintings on the walls. They depicted scenes of elemental wielders harnessing their powers, their movements fluid and graceful. Jasiah felt a pang of envy, wishing he could control his flames as effortlessly. He turned back to Camilla and Neveah, his mind still stuck on the idea of classes. "Hey, uhm, Camilla? If there's class, does that mean there's math or...?" he asked, his voice trailing off uncertainly.
Camilla's grin grew even wider as she cut him off. "Nope! No math or anything. It's mainly about misc abilities and elemental powers!" she exclaimed, her chocolate brown curly hair bobbing up and down with excitement. Neveah's eyes widened in surprise, mirroring Jasiah's own expression. "Wait, so Mr. Kamar wasn't lying when he said we won't have normal education?" she asked, her voice laced with skepticism. Camilla chuckled, her eyes sparkling with amusement. "Not one bit, newbies! That geezer never lies!" she said, using a term that made Jasiah raise an eyebrow. Jasiah's gaze drifted back to Camilla, his mind still reeling from the news. "He doesn't even look that old, I mean, he has brown hair and I didn't see a spec of gray hair in his head," he commented, trying to process the information. Camilla added, "Oh, he's twenty-seven," as if that explained

everything. Jasiah's eyes narrowed, his curiosity getting the better of him. "Then why did you call him a geezer?" he asked, only to be cut off by Camilla once again. "Because it's funny!" she replied, her grin still plastered on her face. Neveah rolled her eyes good-naturedly. "Camilla, you're such a goofball," she said, shaking her head in amusement. As they approached the classroom, Jasiah's curiosity grew. The door swung open, revealing a space that was unlike any he had ever seen.

Fancy lights adorned the ceiling, casting a warm glow over the room. Five large windows lined one side of the classroom, allowing natural light to pour in and illuminate the space. Two additional windows were situated at the back of the room, providing a view of the surrounding landscape. Jasiah's eyes widened as he took in the seating arrangement. A small, wooden staircase was attached to a U-shaped platform that circumnavigated the classroom. Each desk was designed to accommodate three people, with plenty of space to spread out. At the front of the class, a raised platform stood, where Mr. Kamar would likely stand to address the students. As Jasiah made his way to an empty desk, he noticed Hanuel and Michael already seated, sitting across from each other. Michael looked tired, his eyes still bearing the exhaustion of their sparring match from the previous day. Jasiah flashed him a friendly smile and took a seat on the left side of the desk. Neveah claimed the right side, her eyes sparkling with amusement. "Hey!" Jasiah said, trying to break the silence. Michael responded with a tired nod, his voice barely above a whisper. Neveah teased, "Seems like someone's quiet for once," her eyes flicking towards Michael. Jasiah rolled his eyes "Well, someone did get their ass kicked last night ," his voice dripping with sarcasm.

Michael shot her a mock offended look, but couldn't help but chuckle. "Hey, that was just a warm-up," he said, grinning. Camilla's eyes lit up with mischief, her face contorting in a mixture of shock and amusement. "Wait... ass kicking...? Last night, whoa guys!" she exclaimed, her voice filled with disdain. Jasiah, oblivious to the implication, looked at her with confusion. "I don't get it...?" he asked, his innocence radiating like a beacon. Michael, on the other hand, gagged and choked on air, his face turning a deep shade of crimson. He knew exactly what Camilla was insinuating, and he was mortified. Neveah, too, looked devastated, her eyes wide with embarrassment.

Camilla's grin grew even wider, her eyes sparkling with amusement. "Oh, come on, guys! You didn't think I'd let that slip by, did you?" she teased, her voice dripping with sarcasm. Jasiah's face scrunched up in confusion, still not grasping the situation. "What's going on? What did I miss?" he asked, looking around at the others. Michael's face was still red, and he looked like he was about to implode from embarrassment. Neveah, too, looked like she wanted to crawl under a rock and hide. Camilla, on the other hand, was having the time of her life, reveling in the awkwardness she had created. Mr. Kamar, sensing the tension in the room, cleared his throat to get everyone's attention.

"Alright, alright, let's focus, shall we?" he said, his voice firm but gentle. The room fell silent, with all eyes fixed on Mr. Kamar. Jasiah, still confused, looked around at the others, hoping someone would fill him in on what had just happened. Michael and Neveah, on the other hand, looked like they wanted to disappear, while Camilla was still grinning from ear to ear, clearly pleased with herself. As Mr. Kamar's words hung in the air, the room remained silent, the only sound being the soft hum of the fluorescent lights overhead.

Jasiah's eyes darted between Michael and Neveah, trying to decipher what had just transpired. Camilla, still grinning, seemed to be savoring the awkwardness she had created. Mr. Kamar, undeterred by the tension, began to take attendance. "Alright, let's get started.

Hanuel, please?" he called out, his eyes scanning the room. Hanuel, seated across from Michael, nodded in response. "Here, sir," he said, his voice low and smooth. Mr. Kamar nodded, his eyes moving to the next student. "Jasiah?" Jasiah, still confused, hesitated for a moment before responding. "Here," he said, his voice barely above a whisper. Neveah, seated beside him, nodded in response to Mr. Kamar's questioning gaze.

"Here, sir," she said, her voice soft and hesitant. Michael, still red-faced, managed a weak "Here" in response to Mr. Kamar's call. Camilla, still grinning, responded with a cheerful "Present and accounted for, sir!" her voice dripping with sarcasm. As Mr. Kamar finished taking attendance, the room remained silent, the only sound being the scratching of his pen on paper. The tension was palpable, with Michael and Neveah still looking like they wanted to disappear, and Camilla still basking in the aftermath of her mischief. Jasiah, still confused, looked around at the others,

hoping someone would finally fill him in on what had just happened.

It seemed that no one was willing to broach the subject, at

least not yet.

As Mr. Kamar finished taking attendance, he turned to face the class, a hint of a smile on his face. "Alright, now that we've got everyone accounted for, let's move on to today's lesson," he said, his eyes sparkling with excitement. He walked over to a large, wooden cabinet at the back of the room, adorned with intricate carvings of various weapons. With a flourish, he opened the cabinet, revealing a vast array of weapons that seemed to glint in the light. "Today, we're going to explore the world of elemental weapons," Mr. Kamar announced, his voice filled with enthusiasm. "From small kunai's to cool-shaped swords, we'll be covering it all." Jasiah's eyes widened as he took in the sight before him. He had never seen so many weapons in one place before, and he couldn't wait to learn more about them.

Mr.Kamar began by holding up a small, curved kunai. "This is a basic kunai, used for close combat and quick attacks," he explained, demonstrating a few swift moves with the weapon. Next, he pulled out a sleek, silver sword with an intricately designed hilt. "This is a wind-based sword, capable of slicing through the air with ease," he said, holding the sword up to the light. As the lesson progressed, Mr. Kamar brought out an array of weapons, each one more fascinating than the last. There were scythes with curved blades, perfect for harvesting elemental energy; bows and arrows infused with fire, ice, and lightning; and even a few exotic weapons that Jasiah had never seen before. Throughout the lesson, Mr. Kamar provided detailed explanations of each weapon, demonstrating their uses and capabilities.

He also emphasized the importance of mastering each weapon, stressing that it was not just about wielding a powerful tool, but about understanding the elemental forces infused with fire, water, and earth;

As Mr. Kamar concluded the lesson on elemental weapons, he paused, surveying the room with a thoughtful gaze. "Now, class, I'd like to discuss a crucial aspect of your training," he began, his voice taking on a more serious tone. "You all possess a unique energy, known as Aerthys Energy.

This energy is the key to unlocking your true potential as elemental warriors," he explained, his eyes sparkling with intensity. Jasiah's curiosity was piqued, and he leaned forward, his eyes fixed on Mr. Kamar. "What is Aerthys Energy, exactly?" he asked, his voice filled with wonder. Mr. Kamar smiled, pleased with Jasiah's inquisitive nature. "Aerthys Energy is a manifestation of your connection to the elemental forces. It's a vital force that resides within each of you, waiting to be harnessed and mastered," he replied, his hands gesturing animatedly as he spoke. "As you progress in your training, you'll discover that Aerthys Energy can be categorized into three tiers: Novice, Adept, and Master," Mr. Kamar continued, his eyes scanning the room to ensure everyone was paying attention. "At the Novice level, you'll have access to basic abilities, such as enhanced jumping and speed. As you progress to the Adept level, you'll unlock intermediate abilities, including flash stepping and wall running," he explained, his voice filled with excitement. Jasiah's eyes widened as he imagined the possibilities. "That sounds amazing!" he exclaimed. Mr. Kamar nodded, a hint of a smile on his face. "And at the Master level, you'll be able to tap into advanced Aerthys Energy capabilities, such as water and air walking, and even manipulate the energy to create complex, dynamic movements," he said, his voice filled with awe.

Neveah raised her hand, her eyes sparkling with curiosity. "How do we access these abilities, Mr. Kamar?" she asked.
"Ah, excellent question, Neveah," Mr. Kamar replied, his eyes lighting up with enthusiasm. "As you continue to train and meditate , you'll begin to unlock your Aerthys Energy potential. It's a process that requires dedication, discipline, and practice, but the rewards are well worth the effort," he said, his voice filled with encouragement. "This is important to the newbies, especially since Camilla and Hanuel already know how to use their elemental powers and have a grasp of Aerthys energy," Kamar said, his eyes scanning the room to ensure everyone was paying attention. "Everyone to the training grounds!" Kamar spoke, his voice firm and commanding, before he got up and walked out of the classroom. The class followed, with Hanuel leading the way, Camilla behind him, Michael behind her,
Jasiah behind him, and Neveah at the back. As they made their way down the stone stairs, the air grew thick with the scent of old parchment and dust. The stairs seemed to circle downward, leading them deeper into the heart of the ancient building. Finally, they reached the last floor, where rows of shelves lined the walls, filled with an assortment of tools, medicines, and raw food. The shelves seemed dirty and old, but the food looked untouched, as if preserved for centuries. At the far end of the room, a huge door loomed, adorned with intricate carvings of elemental symbols.
When it opened, a dojo area unfolded before them, looking like any other dojo anyone would see. "Alright, newbies! Get on the mat!" Hanuel barked in a strict tone,
his eyes gleaming with a hint of amusement. Jasiah quickly

complied, settling onto the mat with a quiet determination. Neveah, however, shot Hanuel a dirty look as she reluctantly sat down, her eyes flashing with resentment. Michael, on the other hand, spoke up, his voice laced with annoyance. "Why should I listen to you? Last time I checked, you're not the teacher," he said, his gaze flicking to Hanuel with a hint of defiance. Hanuel's expression turned cold, his eyes narrowing. "And last time I checked, I could use my poison energy on you, and you couldn't do anything about it," he said bluntly, his voice dripping with disdain. Neveah's eyes widened in shock, while Jasiah let out a low whistle, impressed by the severity of the insult. "You can talk once you know how to use your water energy. Until then, you're nothing but a mutt to me," Hanuel said, his harsh tone making Michael's pride wounded.

Hanuel's words hung in the air, heavy with condescension. "Now, go meditate with your other two friends," he said, his gaze dismissing Michael.

Michael's face darkened, his eyes flashing with anger, but he remained silent, his pride smarting from the insult. With a huff, he settled onto the mat, his movements stiff with resentment. Neveah and Jasiah exchanged a worried glance, their eyes filled with concern for their friend. As they began to meditate, the air was thick with tension, the only sound being the soft hum of Aerthys energy coursing through the room.

As the trio settled into their meditation, they began to focus their minds, quieting their thoughts and syncing their breathing with the gentle hum of Aerthys energy. The air was still, the only sound being the soft rustle of their clothing as they sat cross-legged on the mat. Camilla, who had been observing them with an air of amusement, suddenly appeared beside them, a mischievous glint in her eye. Without warning, she began to place books and items on their heads, her movements swift and silent.

The first to react was Michael, who let out a startled shout as a heavy tome landed on his crown. "Hey, what the hell?!" he exclaimed, his eyes snapping open in surprise. Jasiah and Neveah, who had been deep in their meditation, were abruptly jolted out of their focused state.

They blinked in confusion, their eyes scanning the room as they tried to process what was happening. On Jasiah's head, a small, ornate vase teetered precariously, while Neveah had a stack of parchment scrolls balanced on her crown. The trio looked at each other in dismay, their faces a picture of surprise and annoyance. Camilla, however, was unfazed, her expression serene and innocent. "Just a little test, my friends," she said, her voice sweet and melodious. "I wanted to see how well you could maintain your focus in the face of distraction."

Hanuel, who had been observing the scene with an air of detachment, suddenly spoke up. "Well, it seems they failed miserably," he said, his voice dry and amused. Michael, still fuming, glared at Camilla. "That was not cool, Camilla," he said, his voice low and angry. "What if I had been in a deep meditative state? You could have hurt me."

Camilla's response was a fit of giggles, her eyes sparkling with amusement. "Well, do you think you're going to remain untouched during battles with other people?" she asked, her voice barely above a whisper, but laced with a hint of sarcasm. Michael's face darkened further, his eyes flashing with anger.

"That's not the point, Camilla," he said, his voice low and

menacing. "The point is that you shouldn't be disturbing us during our meditation." Camilla's giggles subsided, but her smile remained, her eyes still sparkling with mischief. "Oh, I'm sorry, Michael. I didn't mean to disturb you. But let's get back to the exercise, shall we?" she said, her voice sweet and innocent.

Without waiting for a response, Camilla began to place scrolls on their heads, stacking them one by one. The trio, still wary, hesitated for a moment before returning to their meditation, their eyes closed, their breathing slow and deliberate. As Camilla continued to stack the scrolls, the trio remained focused, their minds quiet, their bodies still. Jasiah had eight scrolls stacked on his head, Neveah had seven, and Michael had six. Camilla kept adding more, her movements swift and silent.

But at the ninth scroll, Michael's eyes snapped open, his face contorted in frustration. "Aaargh!" he exclaimed, his voice loud and explosive. "Camilla, stop! This is ridiculous!" Camilla's smile faltered, her eyes narrowing in disappointment. "Michael, you failed again," she said, her voice soft but firm. "You need to learn to maintain your focus, no matter what distractions come your way." Jasiah and Neveah, who had been observing the scene, slowly opened their eyes, their faces calm and serene. "It's okay, Michael," Jasiah said, his voice soothing.

"We'll get there eventually." Neveah nodded in agreement, her eyes filled with encouragement. "We just need to practice more, that's all," she said, her voice gentle.

As Jasiah and Neveah spoke, their voices calm and reassuring, Michael's anger began to dissipate, replaced by a sense of determination. He took a deep breath, his eyes closing as he refocused on his meditation. The trio sat in silence, their breathing slow and deliberate, their minds quiet and focused. The air was still, the only sound being the soft rustle of the scrolls on their heads. As the minutes ticked by, a subtle change began to take place. Jasiah's body began to glow with a warm, orange and gold aura, giving him a fiery, energetic feeling.

His eyes, still closed, seemed to burn with an inner intensity, as if his very soul was igniting. Neveah, too, began to radiate an aura, her body surrounded by a soft, blue and lighter blue glow. The color was calming, soothing, and seemed to wash over her like a gentle wave. Her eyes, closed in concentration, seemed to reflect the serenity of the ocean. Michael, the last to exhibit an aura, was enveloped by a dark, black and green glow. The color was intense, mysterious, and seemed to connect him to the very heart of nature. His eyes, still closed, seemed to absorb the energy of the earth, as if he was channeling the power of the land itself. The auras surrounded each of them, a vibrant display of color and energy. For a moment, they sat in perfect harmony, their bodies glowing with an otherworldly light.

CHAPTER 7
STRICTLY TRAINING SESSION

In an instant, the auras vanished, leaving the trio feeling invigorated, yet oddly bereft. They opened their eyes, their gazes locking in a shared moment of understanding. Camilla, who had been watching the scene unfold, nodded her head in approval. "Well done, my friends," she said, her voice filled with pride. "You're making progress. Keep practicing, and you'll soon be able to activate your
elemental powers." Hanuel's expression was a picture of boredom, his eyes fixed on the trio with a mixture of disdain and disinterest. "Whatever," he said, his voice laced with sarcasm. "Now it's time for some physical training." Jasiah, who had been basking in the glow of their successful meditation, stood up, his eyes narrowing in curiosity. "Oh? What are we going to do then?" he asked, his voice tinged with skepticism.
Hanuel's smirk grew wider, his eyes glinting with amusement. "On at a time, you will fight me," he said, his voice dripping with confidence. Jasiah's face fell, his eyes widening in alarm. "That isn't even fair," he protested, his voice laced with dismay. "You have a lot more knowledge than us, and poison... while we still have no clue how to use our elemental powers. Know what? Count me out." Jasiah's words trailed off, his shoulders slumping in defeat. But Neveah and Michael were not ones to back down from a challenge. Neveah's eyes flashed with determination, her face set in a fierce expression.

"I'll do it," she said, her voice firm and resolute. Michael, too, stood up, his eyes fixed on Hanuel with a fierce intensity. "Yeah, I'm in," he said, his voice steady and calm. Hanuel's smirk grew even wider, his eyes glinting with excitement. "Excellent," he said, his voice dripping with anticipation. "Let's see how you three fare against me. But don't say I didn't warn you..." Michael stepped forward, his eyes fixed on Hanuel with a fierce determination. "I'll go first," he said, his voice steady and calm.

Hanuel's smirk grew even wider, his eyes glinting with excitement. "Excellent," he said, his voice dripping with anticipation. "Let's see how you fare against me. But don't say I didn't warn you..." Michael charged forward, his fists clenched, but Hanuel was nowhere to be seen. He had used Aerthys Energy to jump back a far distance, leaving Michael to stumble forward, confused and disoriented. But Hanuel was not done yet. He took a deep breath and exhaled a stream of poison gas, which reached a great distance and enveloped Michael in a purple, poisonous fog.

Michael held his breath, trying to get out of the fog, but it was too dense, too suffocating. "Breathe and you'll be poisoned," Hanuel said, his voice echoing through the fog, making Michael's skin crawl. Just as Michael thought he was going to collapse from lack of air, Hanuel materialized behind him, a kunai pressed to his neck, his arm held in a tight grip. "Running are we?" Hanuel said, his voice low and menacing. Michael's pride was wounded, his self-doubt kicking in. He was defeated that easily...? He didn't even get a single blow in... Not only that, he couldn't even use his water element yet... Hanuel scoffed, walking away, leaving Michael to stew in his own disappointment. Michael's eyes fell, his shoulders slumping in defeat. Just then,. Kamar came bounding over, his brown orange hair standing out like a beacon. "Hey, hey, no need to be sad, boy!" he said, ruffling Michael's pink curly hair. "There's no way you could've won! Hanuel's been training here for at least two years, so there's nothing to be ashamed of. And if you fought Camilla, you'd still lose, since she's been training for three years!" Kamar's words were meant to be reassuring, but Michael just scoffed. "Whatever..

Kamar's face fell, his expression concerned. "Hey, Michael, don't be too hard on yourself. You've only been here for a day, and you're already showing great potential. You just need to keep practicing, and you'll get there!"

Kamar's face fell, his expression concerned. "Hey, Michael, don't be too hard on yourself. You've only been here for a day, and you're already showing great potential. You just need to keep practicing, and you'll get there!" Michael's scoff was all the response Kamar got, and he sighed, shaking his head. But before he could say anything else, Hanuel's voice cut through the air. "Your next," he said, his eyes fixed on Jasiah with a stoic expression. "Come on." Jasiah's eyes widened, his face pale. "Wait, but I don't wanna fight you," he stammered, taking a step back. Hanuel's expression didn't change, but his voice was laced with contempt. "Hmp. So we got an egotistical shit and a coward," he spat out, making Neveah give him a dirty look. Michael's fist clenched, his face twisted with anger. "Bastard!" he shouted, rushing over to Hanuel with a punch.

But Hanuel was too quick, too skilled. He swiftly sidestepped out of the way, and Michael almost stumbled forward to the ground. Just as he was regaining his balance, Hanuel's foot shot out, kicking him in the back and sending him crashing to the ground. Hanuel stepped on Michael's head, his eyes glinting with a cold, hard light. "See what I mean by egotistical shit?" he said, his voice dripping with disdain. Michael's face was red with rage, his eyes blazing with fury. Neveah's eyes were flashing with anger, her hands clenched into fists.

Jasiah looked like he was about to pass out, his eyes fixed on Hanuel with a mixture of fear and loathing. The air was thick with tension, the atmosphere charged with hostility. It seemed like things were about to escalate further, but then Camilla's voice cut through the air, her words calm and soothing. "Enough, Hanuel. You've made your point," she said, her eyes fixed on Hanuel with a firm expression. Hanuel raised an eyebrow, his foot still pressed to Michael's head. "Oh, I've just begun," he said, his voice dripping with menace. Camilla's words seemed to hang in the air, a palpable tension building as Hanuel's gaze locked onto hers. For a moment, it seemed like he was going to defy her, to continue his brutal assault on Michael and Jasiah. But then, his foot lifted off Michael's head, and he turned to Jasiah with a cold, calculating gaze. "Tch ," he said, his voice dripping with malice. Jasiah's eyes widened, his face pale and sweaty. He took a step back, his hands raised in a defensive gesture, as if to ward off the impending attack. Hanuel sneered, his eyes flashing with contempt. "You think you can defend yourself against me?" he taunted, his voice dripping with disdain. Jasiah nodded, his jaw set in a determined expression. He raised his fists, his eyes fixed on Hanuel with a fierce intensity. But it was clear that he was no match for the older boy's skill and strength. Hanuel charged forward, his movements lightning-fast and deadly precise.

Jasiah tried to defend himself, but Hanuel's blows rained down on him like a storm, each one landing with precision and power.

Jasiah stumbled back, his eyes wide with fear, his face pale and clammy. But then, in a moment of desperation, Jasiah managed to land a weak punch on Hanuel's jaw. It was a glancing blow, hardly enough to cause any real damage, but Hanuel's eyes flashed with anger all the same. He retaliated with a vicious kick, sending Jasiah crashing to the ground. The younger boy lay there, dazed and defeated, as Hanuel loomed over him, his eyes blazing with fury. "You shouldn't have tried to think you belong here ," Haneul spat, his voice dripping with malice. "You're nothing but a pathetic little coward." Jasiah's eyes filled with tears, his face twisted with pain and fear. Neveah's eyes were flashing with anger, her hands clenched into fists.

Michael's face was red with rage, his eyes blazing with furyThe air was thick with tension, the atmosphere charged with hostility. It seemed like things were about to escalate further, but then Camilla's voice cut through the air, her words calm and soothing.

As the group began to disperse, Michael suddenly managed to stand , his movements shaky and unsteady. He coughed, his chest heaving with exertion, and then glared at Hanuel with a fierce intensity. "Aye, Hanuel, watch," Michael said, his voice sharp and annoyed. "When I get stronger, I'll make you pay for what you did today." Hanuel raised an eyebrow, his expression unreadable. But Michael didn't back down, his eyes blazing with determination. "You think you're tough, don't you?" Michael spat, his words laced with venom. "You think you can just bully and intimidate everyone, and no one will stand up to you?" Hanuel shrugged, his expression still unyielding.

"I'm just showing you all what it takes to survive in this world," he said, his voice cold and detached. Michael's face twisted with anger, his eyes flashing with fury. "You're not showing us anything except how to be a coward," he said, his voice dripping with disdain.

Jasiah's eyes widened, his face still twisted with pain and fear. But Michael ignored him, his gaze fixed on Hanuel with a fierce intensity. "I'll make sure you pay for what you did today," Michael repeated, his voice sharp and menacing. "You just wait and see." Hanuel smiled, his eyes glinting with amusement. "I'm shaking in my boots," he said, his voice dripping with sarcasm. The tension between the two boys was palpable, the air thick with hostility. Neveah's eyes were flashing with anger, her hands clenched into fists. Kamar's face was twisted with concern, his eyes fixed on Michael with a worried expression. Just as it seemed like the situation was about to escalate further, Kamar's voice cut through the air, his words calm and soothing. "Hey, hey, let's not do this," he said, his eyes fixed on Michael and Hanuel with a worried expression. But Michael and Hanuel didn't back down, their faces still twisted with anger and determination. Kamar's face fell, his eyes flashing with concern. He knew he had to do something, and fast, before things got out of hand.

Without hesitation, Kamar raised his hands, and a warm, golden light began to emanate from his body.

The air around him began to vibrate with energy, and a powerful aura began to radiate from his very being. The effect was immediate. Michael and Hanuel, still locked in their fierce stare-down, suddenly felt their knees buckle, their bodies weakened by the sheer force of Kamar's spiritual energy. They stumbled, their eyes widening in shock, as they struggled to stay upright.

Neveah, Jasiah, and Camilla, who had been watching the exchange with bated breath, also felt the effects of Kamar's aura. They stumbled, their eyes flashing with surprise, as they too struggled to remain standing. The air was thick with Kamar's energy, a palpable force that seemed to suffocate the very breath from their lungs. It was as if the very fabric of reality had been warped and distorted, bending to Kamar's will. As the group struggled to regain their footing, Kamar's eyes flashed with a fierce intensity. "Enough," he said, his voice low and commanding. "We're not going to let our emotions get the best of us. We're a group, and we need to work together if we're going to survive." The group slowly began to rise to their feet, their faces pale and drained. Michael and Haneul, still locked in a fierce stare-down, slowly backed away from each other, their eyes flashing with anger and resentment.

as they backed away from each other, the air was thick with animosity, the tension between them palpable. Michael's eyes blazed with fury, his face twisted in a scowl. Hanuel's expression was equally venomous, his eyes flashing with resentment. The group watched in silence, their faces grave with concern.

 They knew that the situation was volatile, that one wrong move could spark a full-blown confrontation. Neveah's eyes were fixed on Michael, her face etched with worry. She knew that he was still reeling from Hanuel's brutal words, that his emotions were raw and exposed. She took a step forward, her hand reaching out in a calming gesture. "Michael, it's okay," she said, her voice soft and smoothing.

"Let it go. We need to focus on the bigger picture." But Michael shook her off, his face twisted in anger. "No, Neveah, I won't let him get away with this," he said, his voice low and menacing. "He needs to pay for what he did." Hanuel sneered, his eyes glinting with malice. "You think you can take me down, Michael?" he said, his voice dripping with contempt. "I'll crush you like the insignificant insect that you are." Michael's eyes blazed with fury, his face red with rage. He took a step forward, his fists clenched at his sides. But before he could do anything, Kamar intervened, his voice calm and authoritative.

"Enough," he said, his eyes fixed on Michael and Hanuel. "We're not going to resolve anything with violence and aggression. We need to talk this through, to find a way to work together." The group fell silent, their faces somber with determination.

They knew that Kamar was right, that they needed to find a way to put their differences aside and work together.

As the days passed, Jasiah, Michael, and Neveah continued to meditate, determined to master their elemental powers. They sat cross-legged on the ground, their eyes closed, their breathing slow and deliberate. But despite their best efforts, none of them could focus. Their minds were a jumble of thoughts and emotions,

their concentration wavering like a fragile reed in the wind. Jasiah's mind was a maelstrom of anxiety and fear, his thoughts consumed by the specter of Hanuel's brutal training methods. He couldn't shake the feeling of vulnerability, of being at the mercy of a classmate. Michael's mind was a cauldron of anger and resentment, his thoughts seething with bitterness towards Hanuel. He couldn't forgive the older boy for his cruel words and actions, his heart still raw and wounded.

Neveah's mind was a labyrinth of confusion and doubt, her thoughts torn between her loyalty to her friends and her growing unease about Hanuel's motives. She couldn't shake the feeling that something was off, that Hanuel's intentions were not entirely pure. As they meditated, their minds wandered, their focus fragmented and scattered. They couldn't seem to quiet their minds, to still the turbulent waters of their thoughts and emotions. Their auroras faltered, their elemental powers flickering like dying embers. They couldn't sustain the energy, their connection to the elements tenuous and fragile. Camillia's voice was laced with indignation, her gentle brown eyes hardening as she gazed at Hanuel's indifferent face. "What the hell was that?" she demanded, her words echoing off the stone walls of the hallway outside the dojo. "You completely broke their spirits! They're our new classmates, for crying out loud!" Hanuel's black eyes remained unyielding, his expression a mask of cold calculation.

"I don't care," he said bluntly, his voice devoid of emotion. "They're clearly not ready for the real world."

Camillia's face twisted in disgust, her lips curling in revulsion. "The real world?" she repeated, her voice dripping with sarcasm. "You call this a simulation of the real world? You're just trying to break them, to see how much they can take before they crack."

Hanuel shrugged, his shoulders barely rising off his chest. "If they can't handle a little pressure, then they're not worthy of being here," he said, his tone devoid of empathy.

Camillia's eyes flashed with anger, her hands clenching into fists at her sides. "That's not the point," she said, her voice low and even. "The point is to teach them, to guide them, not to break them. You're supposed to be a role model , not a torturer."

Hanuel's expression remained unchanged, his face a mask of indifference. "I'm preparing them for the worst," he said, his voice cold and detached. "If they can't handle me, then they'll never survive in the real world."

Camillia's face twisted in frustration, her eyes burning with anger. "You're not preparing them for anything," she said, her voice rising.

"You're just trying to prove some twisted point, to show them who's boss. Well, newsflash, Hanuel: you're not God. You can't just play with people's lives like they're pawns in some sick game."

Hanuel's eyes narrowed, his face darkening with anger. "You don't know anything about me," he said, his voice low and menacing. "You don't know what I've been through, what I've had to do to survive. So don't lecture me about morality, Camillia. You don't have a clue." The air was thick with tension, the words hanging in the air like a challenge. Camillia's face was set in a fierce determination, her eyes blazing with defiance. Hanuel's face was a mask of cold anger, his eyes glinting with a malevolent intensity.

Just as it seemed like the tension between Camillia and Hanuel was about to boil over, the bell rang through the stone walls, signaling breakfast time. The sound was like a release valve, diffusing the pressure and allowing the air to return to a sense of normalcy. Hanuel scoffed, a derisive

sound that seemed to sum up his opinion of the entire situation. He turned on his heel, walking up the stone stairs to the kitchen room with a deliberate slowness, as if daring anyone to follow him. As he climbed the stairs,
Hanuel couldn't help but feel a twinge of guilt for his behavior earlier. But he squashed the feeling, refusing to admit it even to himself. He was Hanuel, after all - the toughest, the strongest, the one who always came out on top. Michael, Jasiah, and Nevaeh followed him, their footsteps quiet and reluctant. They didn't want to sit next to Hanuel at all, but they knew they had to eat.

The kitchen room was already bustling with activity, the long tables laden with a variety of breakfast dishes. There were boiled eggs, scrambled eggs, and even some fried hotdogs and boiled ones, served alongside toast and bowls of cereal. The drinks table was stocked with orange, grape, and apple juice, as well as pitchers of milk and water.

The smell of freshly brewed coffee wafted through the air, enticing and rich. Camillia entered the kitchen room last, her eyes fixed on Hanuel's back as he took a seat at the far end of the table. She felt a surge of anger and frustration, but she pushed it down, determined to focus on the task at hand. The breakfast table was a sea of faces, all chatting and laughing as they dug into their meals. Michael, Jasiah, and Nevaeh stuck together, clustering at one end of the table as they tried to avoid Hanuel's gaze. As they ate, Jasiah, Michael, and Nevaeh stuck together, clustering at one end of the table as they tried to avoid Hanuel's gaze.

They chatted quietly among themselves, their conversation a gentle hum of laughter and shared memories. "I'm telling you, Michael, the best video game of all time is still 'Epic

Quest,'" Jasiah said, his eyes shining with enthusiasm. "I mean, who doesn't love a good old-fashioned fantasy RPG?" Michael chuckled, his mouth full of toast. "You're crazy, Jasiah. Galactic Odyssey' is where it's at. The space battles are so sick!" Nevaeh giggled, her eyes sparkling with amusement. "You guys are so silly, I'm more of a 'Fantasy Frenzy' kind of girl myself. I mean, who doesn't love a good puzzle game?" Camillia, who had been quietly observing the trio, couldn't help but smile. "I'm a bit of a retro gamer myself," she said, her voice warm and inviting. "Give me a good old-fashioned game of 'Pac-Man' any day." The group laughed, their conversation flowing easily as they swapped stories and jokes about their favorite childhood games. It was a welcome respite from the tension and drama of the previous day, a chance to relax and just be themselves. As they chatted, Camillia couldn't help but notice the way Michael's eyes lit up when he talked about his favorite games. She saw the way Nevaeh's face softened when she spoke about her love of puzzle games.

She saw the way Jasiah's entire demeanor changed when he was talking about something he was passionate about. It was a moment of pure connection, a moment that transcended the petty squabbles and rivalries of the dojo. For a brief, shining moment, they were all just kids again, laughing and joking and having the time of their lives. But as the breakfast period drew to a close, the group reluctantly began to disperse. Hanuel, who had been quietly observing the group from the far end of the table, pushed back his chair and stood up, his eyes cold and unforgiving.

"It's time to get back to work," he said, his voice dripping with malice. "You all have a lot to learn, and I'm not going to go easy on you." The group exchanged nervous glances, their smiles and laughter forgotten in the face of Hanuel's brutal reminder. They knew that the real work was only just beginning, and that the road ahead would be long and arduous.

For one brief, shining moment, they had forgotten all about that. They had forgotten about the drama and the tension, and had just been themselves. And that, Camillia thought, was a beautiful thing.

The group reluctantly filed out of the kitchen room, their stomachs full but their spirits dampened by Hanuel's ominous warning. They made their way back to the dojo, their footsteps echoing off the stone walls. As they entered the dojo, Kamar was waiting for them, a large array of weapons spread out before him. "Alright everyone," he said, stepping aside to reveal the selection. "You will choose an weapon that seems fit for you.

You'll be given shurikens and katanas later, but for now, choose wisely." Neveah went first, her eyes scanning the array of weapons with a discerning gaze. "Hmm, I'll go with this one," she said, picking up an axe with a cool gray design on it. The axe was heavy and sturdy, its weight feeling solid in her hands. After Neveah, Michael stepped forward, a confident smirk on his face. "This is way too easy," he said, picking up the golden and green spear that had a slight glow to it. The spear felt light and agile in his hands, its balance perfect for his quick and agile fighting style. Finally, Jasiah didn't even have to think about it.

He walked straight over to a sword, its black blade adorned with a purple line that ran down the center to the tip.

"A sword really?

That's so basic!" Michael teased playfully, rolling his eyes. "Hey, shut up!" Jasiah retorted, grinning good-naturedly. "I like what I like, and this sword feels right." Kamar watched the group with a discerning eye, his expression unreadable. "Very well," he said, once they had all made their choices. "Now that you have your weapons, let's move on to the next stage of your training." The group exchanged nervous glances, their hearts racing with anticipation.

They knew that the real work was only just beginning, and that the road ahead would be long and arduous. But they were ready. They were ready to face whatever challenges lay ahead, armed with their new weapons and their determination to succeed.

Not anyone in the trio had ever held a weapon like this before, and the weight of it in their hands was both exhilarating and intimidating. They fidgeted with excitement, their fingers adjusting to the feel of the weapons as they waited for Kamar's next instruction. "Alright everyone, pick a sparring partner," Kamar spoke up, a hint of humor in his voice. "Hanuel will be the judge, since he's a little...harsh." He chuckled, but no one found it funny. The mention of Hanuel's name was enough to sober them up, and they exchanged nervous glances. Michael didn't hesitate, instantly saying, "Come on, Jah, let's go against each other!"

He held up his spear, a confident grin spreading across his face. Jasiah looked at his friend, then nodded hesitantly. "Oh, uh, okay!" He gripped his sword tightly, trying to hide his nervousness. Meanwhile, Camilla threw her arm around Neveah's shoulder, a mischievous glint in her eye. "Come on, let's spar! I'll go easy on you, since you're new...unlike Mr. Grumpy over there." She glanced over at Hanuel, who was scowling at her, and Neveah chuckled. "I can hear you, you know!" Hanuel spoke up, his voice low and menacing. "Well, then shut up!" Camilla yelled back, her tone laced with amusement. She winked at Neveah, who giggled and playfully rolled her eyes.

The group began to pair off, their weapons at the ready. The air was electric with tension, their hearts pounding in anticipation of the battles to come. Hanuel watched them with a critical eye, his face unyielding as he waited for the sparring to begin. Kamar, on the other hand, seemed almost relaxed, a small smile on his face as he watched his students prepare to face off against each other. He nodded encouragement, his eyes sparkling with approval.

"Remember, this is just a training exercise," he said, his voice carrying across the room. "The goal is to learn, not to win. So, let's get started!"

The first sparring match was Neveah vs Camilla, and the two women faced off against each other with determined expressions. Neveah gripped her axe tightly, its weight feeling unfamiliar in her hands. Camilla, on the other hand, wielded a scythe with ease, its curved blade glinting in the light.

The match began, and Neveah charged forward with a loud whoop, swinging her axe in a wide arc. But she quickly realized her mistake - the axe was much heavier than she had anticipated, and her swing faltered mid-air. The axe slipped from her grasp, clattering to the floor with a loud thud. Neveah's face flushed with embarrassment as she quickly picked up her axe, her heart racing with excitement. Camilla, on the other hand, barely batted an eyelash, her expression calm and collected. "Good try, Neveah," Camilla said, her voice gentle but firm. "But maybe you should focus on your footwork instead of trying to muscle the axe." Neveah nodded, taking a deep breath as she reset her stance. She charged forward again, this time more cautiously, her axe at the ready.

Camilla waited patiently, her scythe poised for a strike. The two girls clashed, their weapons ringing out as they exchanged blows. Neveah's axe bit deep into the wooden floor, but Camilla's scythe sliced through the air with deadly precision, its curved blade whispering close to Neveah's ear. Neveah stumbled back, her eyes

wide with surprise, as Camilla pressed her advantage. Her scythe flashed in the light, its blade glinting with a deadly intensity that made Neveah's heart skip a beat. Despite her best efforts, Neveah found herself on the defensive, her axe struggling to keep up with Camilla's lightning-fast strikes. She stumbled, her footing unsure, as Camilla landed a series of quick jabs that sent Neveah stumbling back.

Neveah gritted her teeth, her determination renewed as she faced off against Camilla once more. She focused on her opponent's movements, watching as Camilla's scythe flashed in the light, its blade glinting with a deadly intensity that made Neveah's heart skip a beat. Despite her best efforts, Neveah found herself on the defensive, her axe struggling to keep up with Camilla's lightning-fast strikes.

She stumbled, her footing unsure, as Camilla landed a series of quick jabs that sent Neveah stumbling back. But Neveah refused to give up. With a sudden burst of energy, she launched herself forward, her leg coiling into a powerful kick that aimed straight for Camilla's stomach. Camilla, caught off guard, stumbled backward as

Neveah's kick connected with a loud thud.She quickly followed up, her axe at the ready as she ducked beneath Camilla's retaliatory scythe strike. The blade whizzed mere inches above her head, its deadly intent clear, but Neveah was already moving, her eyes fixed on Camilla's vulnerable moment. With a swift, economical motion, Neveah swung her axe in a low, sweeping arc, aiming to catch Camilla off guard. But Camilla was no novice, and she saw the attack coming.

With a lithe, agile movement, she jumped backward, avoiding the axe's deadly path by mere inches. Neveah's axe bit into the wooden floor, the impact jarring her arm, but she barely had time to register the missed attack before Camilla counterattacked. The scythe flashed in the light, its blade glinting with a renewed intensity as Camilla unleashed a flurry of strikes that sent Neveah stumbling backward. The battle raged on, the two women exchanging blows in a flurry of movement and sound. Neveah's axe clashed with Camilla's scythe, the weapons ringing out as they danced across the dojo floor. The air was thick with tension, the outcome of the match hanging precariously in the balance.

As the battle raged on, the two women exchanging blows in a flurry of movement and sound, Jasiah and Michael watched from the sidelines, their eyes fixed on the intense match. They cheered Neveah on, their voices ringing out across the dojo floor as they urged her to victory. "Come on, Neveah! You got this!" Jasiah shouted, his voice hoarse from yelling. "Yeah, take her down!" Michael added, his eyes shining with excitement.

But Hanuel, standing off to the side, looked unimpressed. His face wore a disapproving scowl, his arms crossed over his chest as he watched the match with a critical eye. "This is amateur hour," he muttered to himself, shaking his head in disgust. "She's not even using proper form." Neveah, however, was too focused on the match to notice Hanuel's disapproval. She was completely absorbed in the battle, her ax clashing with Camilla's scythe as they danced across the dojo floor. The air was thick with tension, the outcome of the match hanging precariously in the balance. Camilla, meanwhile, was starting to tire. Her movements were beginning to slow, her scythe strikes losing their precision as Neveah's relentless pressure wore her down.

Neveah sensed her opportunity and pounced, unleashing a flurry of axe strikes that sent Camilla stumbling backward. The crowd gasped, Jasiah and Michael cheering loudly as Neveah gained the upper hand. Hanuel, on the other hand, looked even more disapproving, his face twisted into a scowl of displeasure. "This is a disaster," he muttered to himself, shaking his head in disgust. "She's not even following proper technique." But Neveah didn't care. She was too busy fighting for victory, her axe clashing with Camilla's scythe as they battled on. The outcome of the match was far from certain, but one thing was clear: only one woman could emerge victorious.

As the battle raged on, Camilla's experience and skill began to tell. She landed a series of swift and precise strikes, her scythe slicing through the air with deadly accuracy. Neveah stumbled backward, her axe faltering as she struggled to keep up with Camilla's lightning-fast movements. Finally, with a swift and merciless strike, Camilla knocked the axe from Neveah's hand, sending it clattering to the floor.

Neveah stumbled back, her chest heaving with exhaustion, as

Camilla stood over her, her scythe poised for the final blow. Kamar called out, "Hold! Match over!" and Camilla lowered her scythe, a triumphant smile spreading across her face. Neveah, despite her defeat, smiled back, her eyes shining with admiration.

"You won," she said, her voice breathless. "You're amazing." Camilla chuckled, reaching out to help Neveah to her feet. "You're not so bad yourself," she said, her eyes warm with approval. "You've got heart, and that's what matters." Together, the two women walked off the dojo floor, their arms around each other's shoulders as they laughed and joked. Hanuel, still looking disapproving, shook his head in disgust, but Kamar smiled, his eyes shining with pride.

"Well done, Camilla," he said, clapping her on the back. "You're a true warrior. And Neveah, don't be discouraged. You've got potential, and with practice, you'll be a formidable opponent in no time."

As the two women walked off the dojo floor, Kamar's voice boomed out, calling the next match.

"And now, the second and final match will be Jasiah vs Michael!" he exclaimed, his eyes shining with excitement. Jasiah and Michael, who had been watching the previous match with bated breath, stepped forward, their faces set with determination. They walked onto the dojo floor, their footsteps echoing off the walls as they faced each other. Camilla and Neveah, still chatting and laughing, moved to the sidelines, their eyes fixed on the two boys as they prepared to face off. Hanuel, standing off to the side, looked disapproving, his arms crossed over his chest as he watched the two boys assume their stances. Jasiah clenched his sword, his grip tight as he held the weapon at the ready.

Michael, meanwhile, grasped his spear, his hands shaking slightly as he tried to find his balance. But it was clear to everyone watching that neither boy had ever used a weapon before.

Their forms were off, their movements sloppy and uncoordinated. Hanuel let out a disapproving look, his face twisting into a scowl of displeasure. "This is a travesty," he muttered to himself, shaking his head in disgust. "They're not even holding their weapons correctly." But Kamar, undeterred by the boys' lack of skill, called out, "Begin!" and the match started. Jasiah and Michael circled each other, their eyes locked in a fierce stare.

They lunged and parried, their movements awkward and unpracticed, but they refused to back down. The clash of their weapons echoed through the dojo, the sound of metal on metal ringing out as they battled on. Camilla and Neveah watched with bated breath, their eyes fixed on the two boys as they struggled to gain the upper hand. Hanuel, meanwhile, looked like he was about to have a heart attack, his face red with frustration as he watched the two boys stumble and fumble their way through the match.

The awkwardness of the match continued, with Jasiah and Michael stumbling over each other, tripping over their own feet, and generally making a mess of things. It was like watching two clumsy puppies trying to fight, with neither one quite sure what they were doing. Camilla and Neveah couldn't help but giggle at the spectacle, their eyes shining with amusement as they watched the two boys struggle to gain the upper hand.

Hanuel, on the other hand, looked like he was about to have a heart attack, his face red with frustration as he watched the two boys stumble and fumble their way through the match. But despite their embarrassment, Jasiah and Michael couldn't help but laugh too. They were so bad at fighting that it was almost comical, and they couldn't help but find the humor in it. They exchanged sheepish grins, their eyes sparkling with amusement as they continued to clash in a flurry of awkward movements. "I think I just tripped over my own feet," Jasiah said, laughing, as he stumbled backward.

"Yeah, I think I just poked myself with my own spear," Michael replied, chuckling, as he awkwardly tried to regain his balance. The two of them burst out laughing, their embarrassment momentarily forgotten as they enjoyed the absurdity of the situation.

Even Hanuel couldn't help but crack a smile, his face softening slightly as he watched the two boys have the time of their lives. The match continued, with Jasiah and Michael stumbling and fumbling their way through it, but it was clear that they were having the time of their lives. They were laughing, joking, and generally having a blast, and it was infectious. Even Camilla and Neveah were laughing now, their earlier amusement giving way to full-blown hilarity. It was, without a doubt, the most entertaining match Kamar had ever seen. And as the two boys finally managed to somehow, miraculously, land a blow on each other, the crowd erupted into cheers and applause.

Kamar, grinning from ear to ear, stepped forward to declare the match a tie. "And the winner is... no one!" he exclaimed, holding up his hands in a gesture of mock surrender. "Jasiah and Michael, you both fought valiantly, but in the end, it's clear that neither of you was willing to give up. Congratulations, gentlemen, on a match that will be remembered for years to come!" The group cheered and whistled, as Jasiah and Michael stumbled forward, grinning from ear to ear, to accept their congratulations. Camilla and Neveah rushed over to hug them, laughing and joking as they celebrated the absurdity of it all. As the group hugged and high-fived, Hanuel shook his head, a wry smile on his face. "I never thought I'd see the day when a match would end in a tie," he muttered to himself, "but I suppose it's fitting, given the... creative approach these two took to combat." Kamar, overhearing, chuckled and clapped Hanuel on the back. "Ah, come on, Hanuel," he said. "Lighten up. It's just a bit of fun. And who knows? Maybe this is the start of a new trend. Maybe we'll start seeing more ties in the future." Hanuel raised an eyebrow, his expression skeptical. "I doubt it," he said, "but I suppose stranger things have happened."

CHAPTER 8
BURDENED AND BOUND

"Alright, rookie trio," Kamar said, referring to Jasiah, Michael, and Neveah. "Follow me to the track and field zone." The three of them followed Kamar as he walked through the hallway, their footsteps echoing off the stone walls. As they emerged from the building, they were surprised to find that the structure was actually a huge monastery, sprawling across the mountainous terrain. Jasiah's eyes widened in awe as he took in the sight.

"Whoa..." he breathed, his voice barely audible. Michael and Neveah shared his shock, their eyes scanning the sprawling complex. The monastery was mostly made of stone, with vines crawling up the walls and a stone pathway that wound its way up the mountain. As they made their way to the back of the monastery, they were greeted by a huge track with obstacles and training equipment scattered across it.

Neveah let out a whistle of amazement. "It must suck for whoever has to walk all the way up here," she said, laughing.
"But why would anyone want to?" Jasiah asked, his curiosity getting the better of him. Kamar chuckled, leading them onto the track. "This is where the real training begins," he said. "This is where you'll learn to push your limits, to test your

strength and endurance. And trust me, it's not going to be easy." As he spoke, Jasiah noticed that the track was surrounded by a series of obstacles,
including hurdles, ropes, and even what looked like a mini-maze.

There were also various stations set up, each with its own unique challenges. "You guys have to run all 100 meters," Kamar said, his eyes sparkling with a mischievous glint. Jasiah's and Neveah's jaws dropped in unison, their eyes widening in shock. "Are you kidding me?" Jasiah asked, his voice laced with incredulity. But Michael, ever the proud one, was undaunted. "Alright then!" he said, getting into a running position, his feet flexed and his hands clenched into fists.

Kamar chuckled, a sly smile spreading across his face. "Not so fast, Michael," he said, producing three heavy backpacks from seemingly nowhere. "There you go," Kamar said, strapping the backpacks onto their shoulders.

Jasiah's eyes widened in horror as he felt the weight of the backpack settle onto his shoulders. "What the...?" he exclaimed, his voice trailing off in shock. Neveah looked like she was about to cry, her eyes brimming with tears. "This is insane," she muttered, her voice barely audible. But Michael, still proud, still defiant, looked like he was ready to take on the world. "Bring it on," he said, his teeth gritted in determination. And then, before they could even react, Kamar blew the whistle, the sound piercing the air like a gunshot.

The three of them took off, their feet pounding the ground in unison as they struggled to make their way across the

100-meter track. The backpacks weighed them down, making every step feel like a struggle. Jasiah's legs felt like lead, his lungs burning as he gasped for air. Neveah stumbled, her foot catching on the edge of the track, and Michael's pace faltered as he struggled to maintain his momentum.

As they trudged along, the backpacks seemed to grow heavier, the weight of them pulling them down like anchors. Jasiah's legs felt like they were wading through quicksand, every step a labored effort as he struggled to make progress.

His lungs burned, his chest heaving as he gasped for air, his mouth dry and parched. Neveah stumbled again, her foot catching on the edge of the track, and Michael's pace faltered he reached out to grab her arm, pulling her back up to her feet. "Come on, Neveah!" he shouted, his voice hoarse from exertion. But despite their efforts, they were nowhere close to the finishing line.

The track seemed to stretch out before them like an endless expanse of torture, the 100 meters feeling like an eternity. Jasiah's gaze was fixed on the horizon, his eyes scanning the track for any sign of relief, but there was none. Sweat dripped down their faces, their bodies drenched in perspiration as they labored under the weight of the backpacks. Neveah's eyes were fixed on the ground, her vision blurring as she struggled to keep her footing. Michael's face was set in a grimace, his teeth clenched in determination he pushed himself to the limit. As they struggled on, the sounds of the monastery echoed around them - the distant chanting of monks, the rustling of leaves in the wind, and the distant clang of a bell tolling the hour. But to Jasiah, Neveah, and Michael, it was all just background noise, their focus fixed on the task at hand.

As they struggled on, the sounds of the monastery echoed around them - the distant chanting of monks, the rustling of leaves in the wind, and the distant clang of a bell tolling the hour, But to Jasiah, Neveah, and Michael, it was all just background noise, their focus fixed on the task at hand. Neveah's eyes were fixed on the ground, her vision blurring she struggled to keep her footing. Her legs were trembling, her body weakened by the weight of the backpack. Suddenly, she stumbled, her knees buckling beneath her.

She fell to the ground, her body crashing onto the track with a thud. Michael, oblivious to Neveah's struggles, continued to push forward, his face set in a grimace, his teeth clenched in determination. He was nearing the 30-meter mark, his body heaving with exhaustion. He huffed and puffed, his chest rising and falling with each labored breath. Meanwhile, Jasiah had noticed that Neveah was no longer running. He glanced back, his eyes scanning the track until they landed on Neveah's crumpled form.

Without hesitation, he turned back, his feet pounding the ground as he ran towards her. As he reached her side, he dropped to his knees, his hands grasping for her arms. "Neveah, come on!" he shouted, his voice urgent with concern. Neveah looked up at him, her eyes glassy with exhaustion, her face pale and drained. With a Herculean effort, Jasiah hauled Neveah to her feet, her body swaying unsteadily as she struggled to regain her balance. He wrapped his arm around her waist, holding her close as they started to walk, their feet dragging along the track.

They were no longer running, their bodies too weak to sustain the effort. But they refused to give up, their spirits unbroken despite the exhaustion that threatened to consume them. They walked, their feet shuffling along the track, their bodies supported by each other as they struggled towards the finish line.

They walked, their feet shuffling along the track, their bodies supported by each other as they struggled towards the finish line. The weight of the backpacks seemed to grow heavier with each step, their legs trembling with fatigue as they pushed forward. But they refused to yield, their determination and perseverance driving them forward despite the overwhelming exhaustion that threatened to consume them. Their breathing was labored, their chests heaving with each ragged gasp of air.

Their faces were set in determined masks, their eyes fixed on the horizon as they struggled to reach the finish line. The track seemed to stretch out before them like an endless expanse of torture, the 100 meters feeling like an eternity. But they refused to give up, their spirits unbroken despite the exhaustion that threatened to consume them.

They drew strength from each other, their bond and camaraderie fuelling their efforts as they struggled towards the finish line. Jasiah's arm was wrapped tightly around Neveah's waist, holding her close as they walked, their bodies swaying together like two people in a slow dance. The sounds of the monastery grew louder, the chanting of the monks, the rustling of the leaves, and the tolling of the bell echoing around them. But to Jasiah and Neveah, it was all just background noise,their focus fixed on the task at hand. They were like two machines, their bodies driven by a single-minded focus on reaching the finish line, no matter what it took. As they approached the 20-meter mark,

As they approached the 20-meter mark, they could see the finish line in the distance, a bright yellow line that seemed to stretch out before them like a beacon of hope. Their hearts lifted, their spirits buoyed by the sight of the finish line, they summoned up their last reserves of strength and energy. Meanwhile,Michael was at the 45-meter mark, his body pumping furiously as he sprinted towards the finish line. He wasn't bothering to look back at his two friends, his focus fixed solely on the task at hand. He was driven by a fierce determination not to lose to Jasiah, his pride and ego fueling his efforts as he pushed himself to the limit. His face was set in a grimace, his teeth clenched in concentration as he pounded the ground with his feet. He could feel the weight of the backpack digging into his shoulders, but he refused to let it slow him down. He was like a machine, his body driven by a single-minded focus on reaching the finish line first.

As they approached the 20-meter mark, they could see the finish line in the distance, a bright yellow line that seemed to stretch out before them like a beacon of hope. Their hearts lifted, their spirits buoyed by the sight of the finish line, they summoned up their last reserves of strength and energy. Meanwhile, Michael was at the 45-meter mark, his body pumping furiously as he sprinted towards the finish line.

He wasn't bothering to look back at his two friends, his focus fixed solely on the task at hand. He was driven by a fierce determination not to lose to Jasiah, his pride and ego fueling his efforts as he pushed himself to the limit. His face was set in a grimace, his teeth clenched in concentration as he pounded the ground with his feet. He could feel the weight of the backpack digging into his shoulders, but he refused to let it slow him down. He was like a machine, his body driven by a single-minded focus on reaching the finish line first.

Michael approached the 52-meter mark, he could feel his body screaming for mercy, his legs burning with fatigue, his lungs heaving with exhaustion. But he refused to yield, his pride and ego driving him forward like a whip, urging him to reach the finish line before Jasiah and Neveah. Meanwhile, Jasiah and Neveah were still struggling to make progress, their bodies moving at a slow, laborious pace. They were only at the 29-meter mark, their faces contorted with effort, their bodies swaying unsteadily as they fought to stay upright. But Michael didn't look back, didn't bother to glance over his shoulder to see how his friends were doing. He was too focused on his own goal, too driven by his desire to win. He was like a bullet, propelled forward by his own momentum, his body moving with a singular purpose. As he approached the 60-meter mark, he could feel his energy starting to flag, his body beginning to slow down.

He refused to give in, refused to let his exhaustion get the better of him. He dug deep, finding a hidden reservoir of strength and energy that he didn't know he possessed. With a fierce cry, he surged forward, his body pumping furiously as he sprinted towards the finish line. He could feel the wind rushing past his face, his heart pounding in his chest like a drum. He was like a force of nature, unstoppable and unyielding. As he approached the 80-meter mark, he could see the finish line in the distance, a bright yellow line that seemed to beckon him forward like a siren's call. He could feel his body screaming for relief, his muscles burning with fatigue, but he refused to yield.

With one final burst of energy, he crossed the finish line, his body collapsing in exhaustion as he
let out a triumphant cry. He had done it, he had reached the 100-meter mark, his pride and ego swelling with satisfaction. He stood there, gasping for air, he finally allowed himself to look back at his friends. He gazed out at the track, his eyes scanning the distance until they landed on Jasiah and Neveah. They were still struggling to make progress, their bodies moving at a slow, laborious pace.
Michael's gaze lingered on them for a moment, a slight smile spreading across his face as he took in the sight. He couldn't help but feel a sense of superiority, a sense of pride and accomplishment that he had beaten his friends to the finish line. He took a deep breath, feeling a sense of relaxation wash over him as he gazed out at the track. He leaned forward, his hands on his knees, and let out a low chuckle. It was a soft, amused sound, one that was born of exhaustion and triumph. "Wow," he muttered to himself, shaking his head in disbelief. "They're really struggling back there." He stood up straight,

his chest heaving with exhaustion, and looked out at the track again. Jasiah and Neveah were still a good 30 meters behind him, their bodies moving slowly and painfully towards the finish line.

Michael's smile grew wider, his eyes crinkling at the corners as he gazed out at his friends. He felt a sense of pride and accomplishment, a sense of superiority that he had beaten them to the finish line.

Michael gazed out at his friends, he could see the determination etched on their faces. Neveah, in particular, looked like she was summoning up every last ounce of energy to make it to the finish line. Her face was pale, her eyes sunken, but her jaw was set in a fierce determination. "I'm okay to run now, thanks, Jah," Neveah said, her voice barely above a whisper. But as she spoke, she took a deep breath, and suddenly her body seemed to transform. Her legs straightened, her arms pumped, and she launched herself forward, her feet pounding the ground with a newfound vigor. Jasiah, not wanting to be left behind, quickly followed suit. "Wa-" he started to say, but his words were cut off as he too began to run.

His body was a blur of motion, his legs pumping furiously as he sprinted towards the finish line. Michael watched in amazement as his friends suddenly found new energy, their bodies moving with a speed and agility that belied their exhaustion. He could feel a sense of pride and admiration for them, his friends who refused to give up even when the going got tough.

As Neveah and Jasiah drew closer to the finish line,

Michael could see the strain etched on their faces. Their bodies were screaming for relief, their muscles burning with fatigue, but they refused to yield. They were determined to cross that finish line, no matter what it took. As Neveah and Jasiah crossed the finish line, their bodies collapsing in exhaustion, Michael grinned, feeling a sense of pride and admiration for his friends. They had done it, they had pushed themselves to the limit and come out on top. But their moment of triumph was short-lived, as Kamar's voice cut through the air, his eyes gleaming with a stern intensity. "Good!" he said, his voice firm but approving. "Now you guys must do that 40-meter obstacle course." The trio groaned in unison, their faces falling as they gazed up at Kamar. They had been dreading this moment, had been hoping against hope that they could avoid this particular challenge. But Kamar was unforgiving, his expression unyielding. "You've made it this far," he said, his voice firm. "Now it's time to see if you can overcome the ultimate test of endurance." Neveah's eyes dropped, her face pale with exhaustion.

Jasiah's shoulders slumped, his body language screaming surrender. Michael's face set in a determined mask, his jaw clenched in resolve. The obstacle course loomed before them, a daunting gauntlet of challenges that would push them to their limits. There were walls to climb, ropes to swing, and hurdles to jump. It was a course designed to test their strength, their agility, and their endurance. Kamar was not one to be swayed by their doubts and fears. "You've come this far," he said, his voice firm. "Now it's time to see if you can go the distance." With a deep breath, the trio steeled themselves for the challenge ahead. They knew it wouldn't be easy, but they were determined to see it through. They would push themselves to the limit, would give it everything they had, and would emerge victorious on the other side.

With a deep breath, the trio steeled themselves for the challenge ahead. They knew it wouldn't be easy, but they were determined to see it through. They would push themselves to the limit, would give it everything they had, and would emerge victorious on the other side. As they approached the obstacle course, they could feel their hearts pounding in their chests. The course stretched out before them, a seemingly endless gauntlet of challenges that would test their strength, their agility, and their endurance. The first obstacle was a series of hurdles, each one higher and more daunting than the last.

Neveah, Jasiah, and Michael approached the first hurdle, their heavy backpacks weighing them down like anchors. They knew they had to clear the hurdle, but the weight of their packs made their jumps lower and less powerful than they normally would be.

Neveah went first, her legs pumping furiously as she sprinted towards the hurdle. She launched herself into the air, her backpack straining against her shoulders, but she barely cleared the bar. She landed awkwardly, her ankle twisting beneath her, but she refused to give up. Jasiah followed close behind, his face set in a determined mask. He leaped into the air, his backpack threatening to pull him back down, but he managed to clear the hurdle by a hair's breadth. He landed heavily, his knees buckling beneath him, but he struggled back to his feet, his eyes fixed on the next obstacle. Michael brought up the rear, his backpack weighing him down like a leaden shroud. He sprinted towards the hurdle, his legs pumping furiously, but he stumbled mid-air, his pack throwing him off balance. He crashed to the ground, his body rolling awkwardly as he struggled to regain his footing.

As Michael struggled to regain his footing, Jasiah and Neveah paused to help him up, their faces etched with concern. They knew that the obstacle course was taking a toll on their bodies, but they refused to give up, refused to let their exhaustion get the better of them. With a grunt of effort, Michael hauled himself to his feet, his backpack weighing him down like an anchor.

He nodded grimly to his friends, his eyes fixed on the next obstacle. The trio set off once more, their bodies moving in tandem as they tackled the next challenge. The obstacle course seemed to stretch on forever, a never-ending gauntlet of hurdles, walls, and ropes that tested their strength, their agility, and their endurance. The trio refused to yield, refused to let their fatigue get the better of them. They climbed over walls, their backpacks scraping against the rough concrete. They swung over ropes, their hands burning with friction. They crawled through tunnels, their bodies crawling through the dirt like worms. But despite the obstacles, despite the exhaustion that threatened to overwhelm them, the trio pressed on, driven by their determination to see it through. They knew that the finish line was within reach, that all they had to do was push themselves just a little bit further. They pushed, their bodies screaming in protest, their minds fixed on the goal ahead. They stumbled, they staggered, but they refused to fall. They were a team, united in their determination to overcome the obstacle course and emerge victorious on the other side.

Approaching the final stretch, the trio was greeted by the most daunting obstacle of all: a towering rock climb that seemed to touch the sky. The rock face was a sheer wall of granite, its surface slick with dew and treacherous with hidden handholds. The trio gazed up at the rock, their eyes widening in awe at its imposing height. But they didn't hesitate.

With a deep breath, they began their ascent, their bodies straining against the rock as they sought out the tiniest footholds. Neveah led the way, her hands and feet finding hidden crevices in the rock that seemed invisible to the naked eye. Jasiah followed close behind, his powerful arms hauling him up the rock face with ease. Michael brought up the rear, his backpack weighing him down like an anchor, but he refused to yield. As they climbed, the rock face seemed to grow steeper and more treacherous, the handholds dwindling to nothing more than tiny ledges of stone.

The trio's bodies were slick with sweat, their muscles screaming in protest as they hauled themselves up the rock. But they refused to give up, their minds fixed on the summit above. The air was thick with tension as they climbed, the only sound the scraping of their hands and feet against the rock. The sun beat down on them, its fiery rays burning into their skin like a branding iron.

But the trio didn't falter, their determination driving them onward like a relentless drumbeat.

Despite their determination, the trio was still a long way from the top. They had barely covered a quarter of the rock face, and the summit seemed to mock them, its peak disappearing into the clouds like a mirage. Neveah's hands were raw and blistered, her fingers numb from gripping the rock. Jasiah's arms were trembling with fatigue, his muscles screaming in protest.

Michael's backpack seemed to weigh heavier with every step, his legs buckling beneath him like a collapsing column. The rock face seemed to stretch on forever, a never-ending expanse of granite that threatened to swallow them whole. The trio's bodies were drenched in sweat, their clothes clinging to their skin like wet rags. The sun beat down on them, its rays burning into their skin like a branding iron, leaving behind a trail of blisters and sunburn.

As they climbed, the trio's progress slowed to a crawl. They were no longer moving with the confidence and purpose of before, their steps now hesitant and uncertain. Neveah's foot slipped, and she barely caught herself, her heart racing with fear. Jasiah's handhold gave way, and he fell, his body crashing against the rock face with a sickening thud. Michael's backpack shifted, throwing him off balance, and he stumbled, his arms flailing wildly as he struggled to regain his footing. Despite their struggles, the trio refused to give up. They knew that they had come too far to turn back now, that the only way to overcome the obstacle course was to push through the pain and the fear.

They climbed on, their bodies screaming in protest, their minds fixed on the summit above But as they climbed, the trio couldn't shake off the feeling that they were getting nowhere. The rock face seemed to stretch on forever, its peak disappearing into the clouds like a mirage. They were still at the bottom, their bodies exhausted, their spirits flagging.
The obstacle course seemed to be winning, its challenges too great, its obstacles too insurmountable.

As the trio struggled to make progress, the rock face seemed to stretch on forever, its peak disappearing into the clouds like a mirage. They were still at the bottom, their bodies exhausted, their spirits flagging. The obstacle course seemed to be winning, its challenges too great, its obstacles too insurmountable. Jasiah refused to give up. He gritted his teeth, his eyes fixed on the wall above, and began to climb with a newfound determination. His hands and feet moved with a precision and speed that belied his exhaustion, his body seeming to find hidden reserves of energy and strength. Neveah and Michael watched in awe as Jasiah began to pull ahead, his lead growing with every handhold and foothold. They knew that they had to keep up,that they couldn't let Jasiah get too far ahead, but their bodies seemed to be made of lead, their movements slow and labored.

Jasiah climbed, the rock face seemed to come alive around him, the granite walls shimmering and glistening like a living thing. The air was electric with tension, the sound of Jasiah's breathing and the scrape of his hands and feet against the rock face the only sounds in a world that seemed to have been muted. Neveah and Michael struggled to keep up, their bodies screaming in protest as they hauled themselves up the wall.

They were like two worn-out machines, their movements jerky and stiff, their faces contorted with effort. But Jasiah was a machine, a well-oiled engine that seemed to be fueled by his determination to win.

He climbed with a precision and speed that left Neveah and Michael in the dust, his body seeming to defy gravity as he soared up the wall. As he climbed, the rock face seemed to narrow, the walls closing in around him like a vise. The air grew hotter and more oppressive, the sun beating down on him like a hammer. But Jasiah didn't falter, his eyes fixed on the top of the wall, his heart pounding in his chest like a drum. Jasiah ascended the wall, the rock face seemed to converge around him, the granite slabs closing in like a vice, exerting a crushing pressure on his already-strained body.

The air grew thick and heavy, like a dense fog that threatened to suffocate him, and the sun beat down on him with a relentless ferocity, its fiery rays searing into his skin like a branding iron. But Jasiah didn't waver, his eyes fixed on the top of the wall with an unyielding determination, his heart pounding in his chest like a drum, its rhythmic beat echoing through his veins like a battle cry. His muscles screamed in protest, his fingers aching with fatigue, but he refused to yield, his willpower and resilience forging a path through the sea of obstacles that threatened to engulf him. As he climbed, the rock face seemed to shift and writhe around him, like a living entity that sought to shake him off its surface. The holds grew smaller and more precarious, the granite crumbling beneath his fingers like sand, threatening to send him tumbling to the ground in a cascade of rocks and dust. But Jasiah adapted, his fingers closing around the holds with a precision and strength that belied their exhaustion, his body contorting into impossible shapes as he navigated the treacherous terrain. His breathing grew ragged, his lungs burning with the effort, but he refused to stop, his eyes fixed on the summit, his heart pounding with a fierce and unyielding determination.

CHAPTER 9
UNEXPECTED CHALLENGE

As Jasiah adapted to the treacherous terrain, his fingers closing around the holds with a precision and strength that belied their exhaustion, his body contorting into impossible shapes as he navigated the rock face.
His breathing grew ragged, his lungs burning with the effort, but he refused to stop, his eyes fixed on the summit, his heart pounding with a fierce and unyielding determination. Finally, after what seemed like an eternity, the trio reached the summit of the wall climb, their bodies exhausted, their spirits drained. But as they gazed out at the breathtaking view below, they saw a zipline that stretched out before them, its steel cables glinting in the sunlight like a silver snake.

Michael grinned, his eyes shining with excitement, as he gazed out at the zipline. "BET! Now we're talking!" he exclaimed, grabbing onto the zipline and launching himself down the cable with a whoop of joy. "Wait up!" Jasiah called out, grabbing onto the second zipline and following Michael down the cable. Neveah, forgetting her exhaustion, got on the last zipline, her eyes shining with a newfound energy. As they zipped down the cable, the wind rushing past their faces, the trio felt a rush of exhilaration, their spirits soaring with the thrill of the ride. And when they finally reached the ground, Kamar was waiting for them, a broad smile on his face as he removed the heavy backpacks from their shoulders.

Jasiah let out a sigh of relief, his body sagging with exhaustion as he fell to the ground. "Ah, sweet mercy," he groaned, his eyes closing in bliss as he savored the feeling of solid ground beneath his feet.

Neveah collapsed beside him, her eyes closing in exhaustion, a smile still on her face. Michael dropped down beside them, his grin still plastered on his face, his eyes shining with the thrill of the ride.

As Kamar spoke, the group stood up, their muscles still sore from the endurance training. They walked back to the front of the monastery, then made their way to another floor upstairs. Kamar led them to a door, where he input a passcode and opened it, revealing an armory filled with Ninja robes in various colors. Each robe was encased in a glass display, adorned with an elemental symbol. The red robe, with golden outlines and kneepads, gray pants, and brown boots, had a unique fire symbol emblazoned on its chest. The blue robe, with silver outlines and kneepads, shone with a water symbol.

The black robe, with silver outlines and kneepads, had a more feminine design, featuring a rock symbol. "I'll be sending you guys on your first quest, so put on those uniforms," Kamar announced, his eyes sparkling with excitement. Neveah protested, "But we don't even know how to use our elemental power yet, nor Aerthys Energy, while Camillia and Hanuel do. Why not tell them?" Kamar replied, "Because maybe there's a chance you will indeed be able to use your elemental power during the mission." Before he could continue, Michael nodded enthusiastically, "I call the blue one!" he exclaimed.

Kamar chuckled, "Calm down, you were already gonna get the blue one anyway, Michael." "And Jasiah will get the red one, while Neveah gets the black one," Kamar declared, a smile spreading across his face. Jasiah's eyes lit up as he opened the glass door for the red robe. "Sweet!" he exclaimed, his fingers tracing the golden outlines and kneepads. Neveah walked over to the black robe, her eyes fixed on the rock symbol. "This one's nice," she said, her hands running over the silver outlines. Michael, meanwhile, was already slipping on the blue robe, his face beaming with excitement. "This is awesome!" he exclaimed, his eye shining with anticipation.

As they changed into their new uniforms, the trio felt a sense of camaraderie and purpose wash over them.

They knew that their first quest was just around the corner, and they were ready to face whatever challenges lay ahead.

With their elemental robes now donned, they felt an added layer of confidence and determination. The three friends made their way downstairs to the dojo, their footsteps echoing off the wooden floorboards. As they walked out of the monastery, the warm sunlight greeted them, casting a golden glow over the serene landscape.

Kamar waited for them outside, a nod of approval on his face. "You three look ready for battle," he said, a hint of pride in his voice. "Now, for your mission..." Kamar tossed them a map, which Jasiah caught with a quick reflex. "Huh, what's this for?" Jasiah asked, examining the parchment.

"It's for your mission," Kamar explained.

"It'll show you where the unforeseen cave temple is located. Be careful, though - there's a lot of bad men there, so stay safe." The trio nodded solemnly, their eyes locked on the map. They knew that this was it - their first real test as Ninja-in-training. Michael's eyes scanned the map, his mind racing with strategies and tactics. Neveah's gaze was fixed on the cave temple's location, her thoughts centered on the unknown dangers that lay within. Jasiah, meanwhile, was already planning their route, his mind mapping out the most efficient path to their destination.

With the map in hand, the trio set off on their mission, They walked away from the monastery, the trio felt a sense of excitement and trepidation. They were about to embark on a journey that would test their skills, their courage, and their wits. But they were not alone - they had each other, and together, they would face whatever challenges the unforeseen cave temple had in store for them. For a while, they walked in silence, their footsteps echoing off the mountain walls.
The air was crisp and clean, with a hint of earthy scent from the surrounding vegetation. As they descended further, the trees grew taller and the path narrowed, forcing them to walk in single file.
Michael led the way, his eyes scanning the terrain for any signs of danger. Neveah followed closely behind, her senses on high alert as she kept watch for any potential threats.
 Jasiah brought up the rear, his gaze fixed on the map as he navigated their route. As they reached the bottom of the mountain, the trio found themselves at the entrance of a

winding pathway. The trees grew denser here, casting deep shadows that made it difficult to see more than a few feet ahead. They exchanged a nervous glance, then began their journey through the pathway.

Meanwhile, back at the monastery, Camillia and Hanuel watched from afar as the trio disappeared into the trees. Camillia turned to Hanuel, a look of concern etched on her face. "Mr. Kamar, are you sure it was a good idea to send them on the mission so early? I mean, isn't it only their second day?" Kamar's expression was unyielding, his eyes fixed on the distant trees. "Yup! But they will never learn if they're not at risk. They think life is a game; they've had it too easy." Hanuel nodded in agreement, his brow furrowed in thought. "I see what you mean, Kamar. But what if they're not ready? What if they fail?"

Kamar's smile was enigmatic, his eyes glinting with a hint of mischief. "Failure is not the opposite of success, Hanuel. It's a stepping stone to success. And besides, I have faith in them. They've got this far, haven't they?" Camillia and Hanuel exchanged a skeptical glance, but Kamar's confidence was infectious. They knew that the trio was in good hands, and that Kamar would not send them on a mission unless he was certain they were ready. As they continued to watch, the trees seemed to swallow the trio whole, leaving only the faintest whisper of their presence.

The air was heavy with anticipation, and Camillia and Hanuel knew that the fate of the trio hung precariously in the balance. The journey had begun, and only time would tell if the trio would emerge victorious - or if they would succumb to the dangers that lay ahead. As they continued to walk, the trio's footsteps echoed through the silent forest, the only sound breaking the stillness of the air. The trees loomed above them, their branches creaking softly in the gentle breeze.

The path wound its way through the forest, leading them deeper into the heart of the mountains. Michael spoke up, his voice breaking the silence. "I bet we're going to show whoever the bad men are a lesson!" he said with a grin, his eyes sparkling with confidence. Jasiah looked unamused, his brow furrowed in concern. "Can't you please be serious for once?" Jasiah asked, his voice tinged with frustration.

Before Michael could respond, Neveah interrupted, her voice booming through the forest. "For once, Michael is right!" Neveah exclaimed, her eyes flashing with determination. "We're gonna kick ass!" Neveah said, her fists clenched at her sides. Michael's grin broadened, and he high-fived Neveah. "That's the spirit!" he cheered, his enthusiasm infectious. Jasiah rolled his eyes, but a small smile played on his lips. The trio continued to walk, their banter and laughter echoing through the forest. They were a team, united in their quest to complete their mission and prove themselves as worthy Ninja.

They walked, the trees seemed to close in around them, the shadows deepening and darkening. As they strolled through the forest, their conversation flowed effortlessly, touching on everything from their favorite foods to their childhood memories.

Michael regaled them with stories of his mischievous

younger brother, making Neveah giggle with his impressions. Jasiah chimed in with tales of his family's traditional cooking, his eyes lighting up as he described the intricate recipes.

The trees seemed to fade into the background, the only sound being the gentle rustle of leaves and the trio's laughter. The air was alive with the scent of blooming flowers, and the warm sun cast dappled shadows on the forest floor. "I'm telling you, the secret to making the perfect ramen is all about the broth," Jasiah insisted, his hands gesticulating emphatically. "Oh, come on, Jasiah," Michael teased, "you can't serious about that. It's all about the noodles!" Neveah chuckled, her eyes sparkling with amusement.

"You guys are so silly. It's all about the toppings, obviously."

The trio continued to bicker good-naturedly, their banter flowing easily as they delved into a heated debate about the best way to eat a sandwich. Michael advocated for the classic combination of turkey and avocado, while Jasiah swore by the simplicity of peanut butter and jelly. Neveah, meanwhile, claimed that the only way to eat a sandwich was with crispy bacon and melted cheddar.

As they walked, the forest seemed to stretch on forever, the trees growing taller and the underbrush thicker. The air grew cooler, the shadows deepening into dark, mysterious pools.

The trio didn't notice, too caught up in their own conversation and camaraderie. They were a team, united in their quest to complete their mission and prove themselves as worthy Ninja. But for now, they were just three friends, enjoying each other's company and the beauty of the forest.

The mission could wait; for now, they were content to

simply be, to soak in the peaceful atmosphere and enjoy each other's company. As they walked, the forest grew quieter, the only sound being the soft rustle of leaves and the trio's gentle laughter. The trees seemed to lean in, as if listening to their conversation, their branches creaking softly in the breeze. The air was alive with the scent of blooming flowers, and the warm sun cast dappled shadows on the forest floor. The trio continued to talk, their conversation flowing effortlessly as they delved into a discussion about their favorite books. Michael waxed poetic about the classics, while Jasiah advocated for the latest bestsellers. Neveah, meanwhile, claimed that the only books worth reading were the ones with dragons and magic. As they walked, the forest seemed to grow darker, the shadows deepening into dark, foreboding pools

Walking continuously, the forest grew denser, the underbrush thicker and more treacherous. The trio navigated the path with ease, their senses on high alert as they scanned their surroundings. "How much longer is this going to take?" Neveah asked, her voice tinged with frustration. She was getting tired, her legs aching from the long walk. Jasiah looked down at the map, his brow furrowed in concentration. "Uh, like two miles left?" he asked, his tone casual as if he was asking about the weather. Michael and Neveah exchanged a skeptical glance. Two miles? That was still a long way to go, especially considering the treacherous terrain they had to navigate.

They didn't say anything, merely nodded and continued to walk. The forest loomed above them, the trees towering like giants in the fading light. As they walked, the silence grew thicker, the only sound being the rustle of leaves and the soft crunch of gravel beneath their feet. The air was heavy with anticipation, the trio's senses on high alert as they scanned their surroundings. They knew they were getting close, that the unforeseen cave temple was just around the corner.

They could feel it, a thrumming energy that pulsed through the air. But they didn't let it deter them, merely pressed on with determination. They were Ninja, after all, and they were not about to let a little thing like treacherous terrain stand in their way.

As they walked, the forest grew darker, the shadows deepening into dark, foreboding pools. But the trio didn't notice, too focused on their mission and their own conversation. As they walked, the forest grew darker, the shadows deepening into dark, foreboding pools.

The trio didn't notice, too focused on their mission and their own conversation. They were a well-oiled machine, their footsteps synchronized as they navigated the treacherous terrain. But suddenly, without warning, a strong gust of wind swept through the forest, making Jasiah quickly pull out his sword and Michael pull out his spear.

Neveah, meanwhile, grasped her axe tightly, her eyes scanning the surroundings for any signs of danger. The wind grew stronger, its force intensifying to tornado-like strength. "What the-!?" Michael exclaimed, his voice barely audible over the howling gale. Before they knew it, they were all separated from each other, the wind tossing them about like rag dolls. Jasiah stumbled backwards, his sword slipping from his grasp as he struggled to regain his balance. Michael was blown off his feet, his spear flying out of his hands as he crashed to the ground. Neveah, meanwhile, was swept up in a whirlwind of debris, her axe clattering to the ground as she tumbled through the air.

The map that Kamar had given to Jasiah was snatched from his grasp, the wind carrying it away like a confetti of paper scraps. Jasiah watched in horror as the map disappeared into the distance, his heart sinking with despair. When the wind finally died down, the trio found themselves scattered across the forest, each one isolated from the others. Jasiah called out, his voice hoarse from the wind, "Guys??" But there was no response.

The forest was silent, the only sound being the distant rustling of leaves and the creaking of branches. Jasiah's heart raced with anxiety as he scanned his surroundings, his eyes straining to see any sign of his friends. He was alone, the darkness closing in around him like a suffocating shroud. The forest loomed above him, its trees towering like giants in the fading light.

Jasiah took a deep breath, his mind racing with thoughts of his friends. Were they okay? Had they been hurt? And what about the map? Without it, they were lost, adrift in a sea of uncertainty. He called out again, his voice louder this time, "Michael! Neveah! Guys, can you hear me?" But the only response was the silence of the forest, a silence that seemed to swallow him whole.

With a heavy heart, Jasiah grabbed his sword from the

ground and started walking. He had to keep moving, had to find his friends and get out of this forest. But as he started walking, he saw some men with daggers and ski masks emerging from the shadows.

Jasiah's instincts kicked in, his hand tightening around the hilt of his sword. He had no skill, no experience, and no progress to speak of during his training today. But he wasn't about to back down, not when his friends were still out there.

The men in ski masks saw him, their eyes gleaming with malice. "Oh, so there's the so-called fire wielder!" one of them sneered, his voice dripping with contempt. Jasiah knew he couldn't use his elemental power yet, not with his lack of training and control. So he took a step back, his sword at the ready. "No, you don't," the second guy said, using his gravity element to pull Jasiah back. Jasiah's eyes widened in shock as he felt himself being pulled towards the men. "THE HELL?!" he yelled out, his sword flashing in the fading light. The men closed in, their daggers glinting with deadly intent. Jasiah swung his sword wildly, but he was no match for their skill and experience.

He stumbled backward, his sword clattering to the ground as the men overpowered him.

Jasiah's vision began to blur, his head spinning from the blows. He was losing, and he knew it. The men were too strong, too fast, and too skilled.

Jasiah was just a novice, a rookie with no chance of winning. As the men closed in for the kill, Jasiah closed his eyes and prayed for a miracle. He was going to die, and he knew it.

But he refused to give up, refused to surrender to the

darkness that surrounded him. With a final burst of energy, Jasiah swung his sword up, the blade flashing in the fading light. But it was too little, too late. The men were too strong, and Jasiah was no match for them. As the darkness closed in, Jasiah knew he was doomed. He was going to lose, and he was going to die.

In a different part of the forest, Michael was fighting for his life. He was surrounded by the ski-masked men and women, their daggers and swords glinting in the fading light. Michael swung his scythe with all his might, but he was no match for the sheer number of his attackers. One of the men, a burly figure with a cruel grin, snatched Michael's scythe from his grasp and slammed it into the ground. Michael stumbled backward, his eyes widening in shock as the man raised the scythe and slashed him across the chest. Michael cried out in agony as the blade bit deep into his flesh.

The men and women closed in, their blows raining down on him like a torrent of pain. Michael stumbled, fell, and was beaten mercilessly, his screams echoing through the forest. Meanwhile, in another part of the forest, Neveah was in a desperate struggle for survival.

She was surrounded by the ski-masked women, their daggers flashing in the dim light. Neveah swung her axe with all her might, but she was no match for the sheer number of her attackers. One of the women, a lithe figure with a cruel smile, grabbed Neveah from behind and held her in place. Neveah struggled, kicked, and screamed, but the woman's grip was like a vice. The other women closed in, their daggers raised high, ready to strike. Neveah's eyes were wide with fear as she realized she was about to meet her end. She was trapped, helpless, and at the mercy of her attackers. The woman holding her in place leaned in close,

her hot breath whispering in Neveah's ear, "You're going to pay for what you've done." And with that, the woman raised her dagger, ready to deliver the killing blow. Neveah's eyes went wide, Neveah's eyes went wide, her pupils dilating in terror as she stared up at the dagger poised above her. The woman's hand was steady, her arm tense with anticipation. Neveah's life was about to end, and she knew it. But then, something strange happened.

At the spot of the forest where Jasiah lay beaten and battered, a faint orange glow began to emanate from his chest. It was a soft, pulsing light, like the warmth of a candle flame. At the same time, in the distant part of the forest where Michael lay bleeding and broken, a blue glow began to emanate from his chest.

The light was stronger than Jasiah's, pulsating with an otherworldly energy. And in the very spot where Neveah was about to meet her end, a green glow began to emanate from her own chest. The light was vibrant, alive, and seemed to pulse with a fierce determination.

The ski-masked attackers froze, their eyes fixed on the glowing lights. What did it mean? Were the trio finally going to be able to use their elemental powers? Neveah's eyes locked onto the dagger still poised above her, but her gaze was distant, unfocused. She felt something stirring inside her, a power that had been dormant for so long. The woman holding her in place hesitated, her grip relaxing ever so slightly. Neveah took advantage of the momentary distraction, using all her strength to break free.

She stumbled backward, the green glow around her chest intensified, illuminating the dark forest like a beacon of hope. The ski-masked attackers took a step back, their eyes wide with uncertainty. What was happening? Was Neveah finally awakening to her elemental power? And what about Jasiah and Michael? Were they too about to unlock their Elemental energy? The fate of the trio hung in the balance, as the forest seemed to hold its breath in anticipation of what was to come...

CHAPTER 10
OLD LEGACY REAWAKENED

As the ski-masked attackers took a step back, their eyes wide with uncertainty, Jasiah suddenly stood up, his movements swift and fluid. Smoke began to emit from his hands, curling around his fingers like a living entity. The attackers' eyes widened in terror as they instinctively backed away from Jasiah. Jasiah's smirk was taunting, his voice dripping with confidence. "What's wrong? Why you running now?" he said, his words laced with a hint of amusement.

The ski-masked attackers felt a strange presence emanating from Jasiah, a palpable energy that seemed to crackle with power. They backed up further, their eyes fixed on Jasiah's hands, which now held a small, orange majestic flame. The flame danced in the air, its warmth and light illuminating the dark forest. The attackers' attempts to flee were awkward and panicked, their movements hindered by their own fear. Jasiah's eyes gleamed with a mischievous light as he raised his hand, the flame growing larger and more intense. With a swift motion, Jasiah launched a fireball at one of the attackers, striking him with a burst of flame that sent him stumbling back.

The attacker cried out in pain, clutching at his chest as the flames licked at his clothes. Before the attacker could recover, Jasiah conjured up another fireball, this time targeting a second attacker. The flame struck the attacker with precision, leaving a burn mark on his back and a circle of ripped fabric where the flames had singed his shirt. The attackers were now in full retreat, their panicked cries echoing through the forest as they stumbled over each other in their desperate bid to escape. Jasiah's smirk grew wider, his eyes gleaming with a fierce satisfaction as he watched his enemies flee.

The attackers stumbled backward, Jasiah pressed his advantage, launching a barrage of fireballs that rained down upon the fleeing figures. The flames erupted in a burst of light and heat, illuminating the dark forest with a fiery glow.
The attackers, desperate to escape, began to fight back, but their blows were wild and uncoordinated. Jasiah, fueled by his newfound power, parried each strike with ease, his movements swift and precise. With each passing moment, Jasiah's flames grew stronger, his control over the element more refined. He danced through the forest, his feet bare and his clothes tattered, but his spirit unbroken.
The ski-masked attackers, however, were beginning to falter. Their blows lacked strength, their movements slow and labored. It was as if they were fighting against a tide of fire, their bodies weakened by the relentless barrage of flames.
 But one attacker, the one with the gravity element, seemed different. He stood tall, his eyes fixed on Jasiah with an unnerving intensity. As Jasiah launched another fireball, the attacker raised his hand, and a strange force seemed to bend the flames back upon themselves. The fireball, weakened by

the attacker's gravity, faltered and died, its flames extinguished by an unseen force. Jasiah's eyes narrowed, his brow furrowed in concentration. He knew that his flames were still weak, freshly awakened from their slumber.

The attacker's gravity element was disrupting his control, making it harder for him to maintain the flames. But Jasiah was determined to push on, to overcome the obstacles that stood in his way. He summoned all his strength, focusing his will upon the flames. Slowly, the fire began to grow, its power coursing through Jasiah's veins like liquid gold. The flames danced and swirled, their warmth and light illuminating the dark forest. The battle raged on, the attackers stumbling backward as Jasiah's flames grew stronger.

The air was thick with smoke and ash, the smell of burning wood and flesh hanging heavy over the forest. And in the midst of it all, Jasiah stood tall, his eyes blazing with a fierce determination. He was a warrior, awakened to his true potential, and he would stop at nothing to protect his friends and defeat his enemies...

As Jasiah's flames grew stronger, the air was thick with smoke and ash, the smell of burning wood and flesh hanging heavy over the forest. The trees, once green and vibrant, now stood as charred and blackened sentinels, their branches like skeletal fingers reaching towards the sky.

In the midst of it all, Jasiah stood tall, his eyes blazing with a fierce determination. He was a warrior, awakened to his true potential, and he would stop at nothing to protect his friends and defeat his enemies. But as the battle raged on, a figure in a hoodie watched from afar, a smirk playing on their lips. They stood at the edge of the forest, their features obscured by the shadows, their eyes fixed on Jasiah with an unnerving intensity.

The fight continued, the figure vanished into the trees, leaving behind only a faint whisper of their presence. The ski-masked attackers, however, were too caught up in their own struggle to notice. "How can you not beat this damned kid!" one of the ski-masked members yelled out, stomping his feet in frustration. "He's just a rookie, for crying out loud! We're the ones with the experience, the skills, and the power!" The other attackers nodded in agreement, their faces twisted with anger and frustration. They had never encountered an opponent like Jasiah before, one who seemed to tap into a deep well of power and determination. As they launched another attack, Jasiah parried each blow with ease, his flames dancing and swirling around him like a fiery aura. The attackers stumbled backward, their movements growing more desperate and erratic.

But despite their best efforts, neither side could gain the upper hand. The battle raged on, the flames and smoke engulfing the forest in a vortex of chaos and destruction.

in the midst of it all, Jasiah stood tall, his eyes burning with an unyielding determination. He was a warrior, awakened to his true potential, and he would stop at nothing to emerge victorious...

However, Jasiah's flames were weakening, their intensity waning as the fight wore on. The ski-masked attacker, sensing his chance, prepared to strike once more, his gravity element at the ready. But just as he was about to unleash his attack, Jasiah suddenly vanished, only to reappear behind the attacker in a flash of orange Aepthy energy.

His legs glowed with an ethereal light, his speed and agility enhanced to supernatural levels. The ski-masked attacker, caught off guard, stumbled forward, his gravity element faltering as Jasiah struck. With a swift and deadly motion, Jasiah slashed across the attacker's back and arm, his blade biting deep into the flesh. Blood gushed out from the wounds, spouting from the attacker's back like a crimson fountain. The attacker cried out in agony, his body crumpling to the ground as Jasiah's blade continued to dance in the air, its orange glow illuminating the dark forest. "Die," Jasiah said bluntly, his voice devoid of emotion, his eyes burning with a fierce intensity. The attacker's gravity element, once so formidable, now lay dormant, its power spent as the attacker's life force ebbed away.

The forest was silent once more, the only sound the dying attacker's ragged gasps for air. Jasiah stood tall, his chest heaving with exhaustion, his eyes fixed on the fallen attacker with a cold, calculating gaze.

The silence was short-lived, as the other ski-masked member,his eyes wide with horror, stumbled forward, his hands raised in a desperate plea for mercy. "W-wait, kid! I got candy! I'll buy you the newest iPhone!" the ski-masked member stammered, his voice trembling with fear. Jasiah's gaze didn't waver, his expression unyielding as he regarded the pleading attacker. For a moment, it seemed as though he might show mercy, that the ski-masked member's words might have some effect. But then, Jasiah's face twisted into a fierce snarl, and he summoned another fireball, its flames burning bright with an intense, orange light. With a swift motion, he cocked his arm back, and then threw the fireball at the ski-masked member like a football, its trajectory true and deadly.

The fireball struck the ski-masked member with a loud whoosh, the flames engulfing him in a blaze of orange and yellow. The member's screams were drowned out by the roar of the flames, his body stumbling backward as he tried to flee. It was too late. The fireball's impact had already been felt, its power coursing through the ski-masked member's body like a deadly poison. He crumpled to the ground, his screams silenced as the flames consumed him, leaving nothing but a charred and smoldering husk in their wake.

Meanwhile, back where Michael was in the forest, he was fighting off the other ski-masked attackers with his newly awakened water abilities. The air was filled with the sound of rushing water, as Michael summoned wave after bullets of liquid fury to crash down upon his foes. The attackers , stumbled backward as Michael's water attacks rained down upon them. They tried to defend themselves, but Michael's powers were too strong, too relentless. Michael showed no empathy, no mercy, as he unleashed his elemental fury upon the hapless attackers.

His eyes gleamed with pride, his face set in a fierce and determined expression, as he reveled in the sheer power coursing through his veins. With a wave of his hand, he summoned a massive wave of water to crash down upon the attackers, sending them tumbling to the ground. They struggled to rise, but Michael was relentless, his water attacks pinning them down, refusing to let them escape. As the battle raged on, Michael's pride and confidence grew. He was finally demonstrating his true strength, his true power. And he was determined to make the most of it, to show the world what he was capable of.

The attackers, realizing they were no match for Michael's elemental fury, turned to flee. But Michael would have none of it. With a swift motion, he summoned a wall of water to block their escape, trapping them in a watery prison.

Then, with a cruel smile spreading across his face, Michael began to toy with his captives. He manipulated the water, creating whirlpools and eddies that sent the attackers tumbling about, their cries of fear and panic echoing through the forest.

Michael was no longer fighting to defend himself. He was simply bullying his opponents, reveling in his newfound power and the fear it inspired in others.His pride and arrogance had reached new heights, as he reveled in the sheer dominance he had achieved over his enemies...

His pride and arrogance had reached new heights, as he reveled in the sheer dominance he had achieved over his enemies. He was the master now, the one in control, and he would make sure they knew it. "You should have never attacked me" Michael sneered, his voice dripping with contempt as he gazed at the cringing attackers. "You should have just got a job at Mcdonalds." He raised a hand, and the water around the attackers began to churn and froth, sending them tumbling about like rag dolls. Michael laughed, a cold, mirthless sound, as he watched his enemies struggle to escape his watery grasp. "You're no match for me," he taunted, his voice echoing through the forest. "I'm the one with the power now. I'm the one who's going to win." The attackers, their faces pale and frightened, gazed up at Michael with a mixture of fear and loathing.

They knew they were no match for his elemental fury, knew that they were at his mercy. And Michael, reveling in his dominance, was determined to make them suffer.

He was determined to make them pay for daring to cross him, for daring to challenge his authority. With a wave of his hand, he sent a massive wave of water crashing down upon the attackers, sending them tumbling to the ground. And then, as they struggled to rise, he unleashed a torrent of water, pinning them down, refusing to let them escape. The attackers, their bodies battered and bruised, lay helpless on the ground, their cries of pain and despair echoing through the forest.

Michael stood over them, his chest heaving with exertion, his eyes blazing with a fierce and elemental power. "Are we seriously losing to a fourteen-year-old!?" one of the attackers exclaimed, his voice laced with incredulity and frustration. Michael's smile grew wider, his eyes glinting with amusement as he gazed at the hapless attackers. With a flick of his wrist, he summoned a barrage of water bullets, each one striking its target with precision and force. "This is what happens when you mess around and find out," Michael said, his voice dripping with arrogance as he blew on his finger, mimicking the action of firing a gun. The attackers cried out in pain, their bodies jerking and twitching as the water bullets struck them. Michael laughed, a cold and mirthless sound, as he watched his enemies squirm and struggle. The forest was silent, the only sound the cries of the attackers and the gentle rustling of the trees. Michael stood tall, his chest heaving with exertion, his eyes blazing with a fierce and elemental power.

As the attackers lay helpless on the ground, Michael began to circle around them, his eyes fixed on them with a cold and calculating gaze. He was the predator now, the hunter, and they were his prey. And Michael, reveling in his triumph, was determined to make them suffer.

He was determined to make them pay for daring to challenge his authority, for daring to cross him.

With a wave of his hand, he summoned another wave of water, sending it crashing down upon the attackers. They cried out in pain, their bodies battered and bruised, their spirits broken. Michael laughed, a cold and mirthless sound, as he watched his enemies suffer. He was the master now,

In another part of the forest, Neveah was exacting her own brand of revenge upon the ski-masked members who had dared to mess with her curly brown hair. Her earth elemental powers were on full display as she summoned a series of massive boulders to crash down upon her foes. The sound of crushing rocks and screams of pain filled the air as Neveah's enemies were pummeled into submission. Her open-minded and easy-going personality had given way to a fierce determination to protect herself and her friends. "You shouldn't have messed with my hair," Neveah said, her voice laced with a pleasant difficulty, as she gazed at the battered and bruised attackers. "Now, you're going to pay the price." With a flick of her wrist, Neveah summoned a massive trench to open up beneath the attackers, swallowing them whole.

The earth closed in around them, trapping them in a prison of stone and soil. Neveah's envious streak had taken over, and she was determined to make sure her enemies suffered for their transgressions.

Her brash and clever nature had given way to a cold and calculating logic, as she carefully planned out her next move. As the attackers struggled to free themselves from their earthen prison, Neveah began to taunt them, her voice dripping with sarcasm. "You should have stayed out of this," she said, her words laced with a pleasant malice. "But you didn't, and now you're paying the price." The earth trembled beneath their feet as Neveah summoned another wave of boulders to crash down upon her enemies. They cried out in pain, their bodies battered and bruised, their spirits broken.

With a final flourish, Neveah summoned a massive boulder to crash down upon the ski-masked woman, trapping her beneath its crushing weight.

The earth shook with the impact, and the woman's cries of pain were silenced as the boulder pinned her to the ground. Neveah dusted off her hands, a satisfied smile spreading across her face. "Well, that's them now," she said, her voice tinged with a sense of accomplishment. "Time to find Michael and Jasiah." Without hesitation, Neveah set off in a random direction, her brown boots crunching against the forest floor.

She didn't really know where she was going, but she had a feeling that her friends might be heading towards the Unforeseen Temple, a mysterious structure rumored to hold ancient secrets and powerful artifacts. As she walked, Neveah's thoughts turned to her friends, wondering if they were safe, if they had encountered any dangers on their own. Her pleasant and easy-going nature had given way to a sense of worry and concern, her mind racing with all the possible scenarios that could have unfolded. "Maybe they're already at the Unforeseen Temple or something," Neveah muttered to herself, her voice barely above a whisper.

She quickened her pace, her senses on high alert as she navigated the treacherous forest terrain. The trees seemed to close in around her, their branches tangling above her head like skeletal fingers. Neveah shivered, despite the warmth of the day, her intuition telling her that she was being watched.
She glanced around, her eyes scanning the shadows, but saw nothing out of the ordinary. Undeterred, Neveah pressed on, her determination to find her friends driving her forward.
She would not rest until she had located Michael and Jasiah, until she knew they were safe and sound.
The sun began to set, casting a warm orange glow over the forest, Neveah decided to take a break. She had been walking for hours, and her earthy boots were starting to feel heavy and cumbersome. She spotted a clearing up ahead, surrounded by a ring of towering trees, and made her way towards it. The air was filled with the sweet scent of blooming flowers, and the soft chirping of birds provided a soothing background melody.

Neveah collapsed onto the soft grass, her body exhausted from the day's exertions. She closed her eyes, letting the peaceful atmosphere wash over her, and took a deep breath. Meanwhile, Jasiah was searching for Neveah and Michael, but he couldn't find them anywhere. He had been scouring the forest for hours, his eyes scanning the trees and underbrush for any sign of his friends. But they were nowhere to be found. Growing increasingly worried, Jasiah decided to wait by a tree, hoping to catch a glimpse of Neveah and Michael as they passed by.

He leaned against the trunk, his eyes fixed on the horizon, and waited. The minutes ticked by, each one feeling like an eternity. Jasiah's anxiety was growing, his mind racing with worst-case scenarios. Had they gotten lost? Been captured by the ski-masked thugs? Or worse? As the sun dipped below the horizon, casting the forest in a dark, ominous shadow, Jasiah's hopes began to dwindle. He had been waiting for what felt like hours, there was still no sign of his friends.

As the minutes ticked by, Jasiah's anxiety gave way to boredom. He had been standing by the tree for what felt like an eternity, scanning the horizon for any sign of Neveah and Michael. But they were nowhere to be found. To pass the time, Jasiah reached for his sword, its familiar weight a comforting presence in his hand. He began to draw slow, deliberate slits on the trunk of the tree, the metal slicing through the bark with ease.

The sound of the sword scraping against the wood was soothing, a rhythmic pattern that seemed to calm Jasiah's racing thoughts. He drew more slits, each one precise and deliberate, as he lost himself in the simple task. The tree trunk began to resemble a canvas, with Jasiah's sword strokes creating a intricate pattern of lines and shapes.

The slits grew longer and more complex, as Jasiah's boredom gave way to a sense of creative expression.

CHAPTER 11
ELEVEN STRANGE NIGHT

As the darkness deepened, Jasiah's sword continued to weave a mesmerizing pattern on the tree trunk, the metal slicing through the wood with ease. The sound of the sword scraping against the wood grew louder, a haunting melody that echoed through the forest.

Jasiah's movements became more fluid, his sword strokes growing longer and more intricate as he lost himself in the rhythmic motion. The tree trunk began to resemble a canvas, with Jasiah's sword strokes creating a masterpiece of lines and shapes. But as the minutes ticked by, Jasiah's sense of creative expression began to wane.

The repetitive motion of his sword strokes, which had initially been so calming, now seemed monotonous and dull. The eerie shadows cast on the forest floor, which had once been so fascinating, now seemed tedious and uninteresting.

Jasiah's boredom, which had been momentarily assuaged by his creative endeavor, began to creep back in. He found himself yawning, his eyelids growing heavy as the sword strokes became more mechanical and less inspired. Despite his best efforts, Jasiah couldn't shake off the feeling of ennui that had settled over him. He continued to draw slits on the tree trunk, his sword strokes growing more listless and lackluster with each passing minute. The sound of the sword scraping against the wood, which had once been so hypnotic, now seemed like a dull, repetitive drone. Jasiah's mind began to wander, his thoughts drifting away from the task at hand as he struggled to stay focused.

As the darkness deepened, Jasiah's sword strokes slowed to a crawl, his boredom and frustration growing with each passing moment. He was trapped in a cycle of tedium, with no escape in sight...

The darkness deepened, Jasiah's sword strokes slowed to a crawl, his boredom and frustration growing with each passing moment. He was trapped in a cycle of tedium, with no escape in sight. The sound of the sword scraping against the wood, which had once been so soothing, now seemed like a monotonous drone, echoing through the forest. Finally, Jasiah couldn't take it anymore.

He dropped his sword, the metal clattering against the forest floor, and slumped against the tree trunk. He let out a deep sigh, his chest heaving with exhaustion. As he sat there, his stomach began to rumble, protesting the lack of food and nourishment. Jasiah's eyes fluttered closed, his mind foggy with fatigue. He was too tired to even think about food, let alone get up and search for some. The fight with the ski-masked thugs had taken a lot out of him, and Jasiah's body was still recovering from the exertion.

His muscles ached, his joints creaking with every movement He felt like he'd been put through a wringer, and the thought of getting up and doing anything more was almost too much to bear. Jasiah's head nodded forward, his chin dipping towards his chest. He was on the verge of drifting off to sleep, his body craving rest and relaxation. The forest around him grew quiet, the only sound the distant rustling of leaves in the wind. As he sat there, Jasiah's thoughts began to wander, his mind slipping into a state of semi-consciousness.

He dreamed of food, of hot meals and warm bread, of savory flavors and satisfying crunches. His stomach growled in protest, his body crying out for sustenance.
Jasiah's thoughts drifted further into the realm of fantasy, his body began to feel the chill of the night air. The forest, which had seemed so warm and inviting just hours before, now seemed dark and foreboding. The rustling of leaves in the wind took on a menacing tone, and Jasiah's skin prickled with gooseflesh. Suddenly, he was jolted back to reality by a loud rumble of thunder. The sky above had darkened, and a storm was brewing.

Jasiah's heart raced as he realized he was completely unprepared for the impending weather. With a surge of adrenaline, Jasiah struggled to his feet, his tired muscles protesting the sudden movement. He looked around, his eyes scanning the forest floor for any signs of shelter or protection. There was none to be found. Without hesitation, Jasiah reached into his backpack and pulled out a small pouch of matches.He had always been prepared for emergencies, and this was no exception. With a few quick strikes, a small flame erupted from the match, casting a warm glow over the surrounding forest. Jasiah smiled to himself as he gazed into the flames.
The fire was small, but it was enough to keep him warm and

dry in the face of the approaching storm. He added a few dry twigs and branches to the fire, watching as it grew and crackled in the silence. As Jasiah's thoughts drifted further into the realm of fantasy, his body began to feel the chill of the night air. The forest, which had seemed so warm and inviting just hours before, now seemed dark and foreboding. The rustling of leaves in the wind took on a menacing tone, and Jasiah's skin prickled with gooseflesh. Suddenly, he was jolted back to reality by a loud rumble of thunder.

The sky above had darkened, and a storm was brewing. Jasiah's heart raced as he realized he was completely unprepared for the impending weather. With a surge of adrenaline, Jasiah struggled to his feet, his tired muscles protesting the sudden movement. He looked around, his eyes scanning the forest floor for any signs of shelter or protection But there was none to be found. Without hesitation, Jasiah reached into his backpack and pulled out a small pouch of matches. He had always been prepared for emergencies, and this was no exception. With a few quick strikes, a small flame erupted from the match, casting a warm glow over the surrounding forest. Jasiah smiled to himself as he gazed into the flames. The fire was small, but it was enough to keep him warm and dry in the face of the approaching storm.

He added a few dry twigs and branches to the fire, watching as it grew and crackled in the silence. Jasiah's thoughts began to wander. He remembered the countless times he had struggled to start a fire, using cumbersome matches and flint. He remembered the frustration and disappointment that had come with each failed attempt. And then, he remembered his elemental power. The power of fire that coursed through his veins, waiting to be unleashed.

Jasiah's eyes narrowed as he focused his thoughts, calling upon the ancient magic that lay within him. Suddenly, a spark of flame erupted from his fingertips, dancing in the air before him. Jasiah's eyes gleamed with excitement as he watched the spark grow, fed by his elemental power. The flames grew larger and more intense, until they were blazing with a fierce intensity. Jasiah's heart raced with excitement as he gazed into the fire. He had never felt so alive, so connected to the natural world. The power of fire coursed through his veins, a fierce and primal force that seemed to pulse with every beat of his heart.|

With a wave of his hand, Jasiah sent the flames dancing across the forest floor, casting a warm glow over the surrounding trees. The storm raged on outside, but Jasiah was warm and dry, protected by the fire that burned within him. As he sat by the fire, Jasiah felt a sense of peace wash over him. He knew that he was safe, that he had the power to protect himself from the dangers of the storm. The fire elemental power that coursed through his veins was a reminder of his strength and his resilience, a symbol of his connection to the natural world.For a long time, Jasiah sat by the fire, lost in thought.

The flames danced and crackled, casting a hypnotic spell over him. The storm raged on outside, but Jasiah was safe, warm, and protected. He was one with the fire, one with the natural world.

Jasiah sat by the fire, the warmth and comfort of the flames began to lull him into a deep sleep. His eyelids grew heavy, his head nodding forward as he succumbed to the exhaustion of the day. As he drifted off, Jasiah's mind began to wander, carrying him away on a tide of memories and emotions. He found himself back in his childhood, on his eighth birthday, standing in the doorway of his family's small apartment.

Jasiah's eyes were fixed on his father, a faceless figure packing up his belongings in a small suitcase. The memory was hazy, but the emotions that came with it were vivid and intense. "Daddy, please don't go!" Young Jasiah pleaded, his voice trembling with fear and desperation. His father's response was cold and cruel. "Shut up, brat!" he growled, his face twisted in anger. "You're just like your mother, always whining and complaining." Jasiah's eyes stung as he remembered the sting of his father's words. He had felt so small and powerless, unable to stop his father from leaving. "Please... stay!" Jasiah pleaded, his voice cracking with emotion.

"If it's because of me, I'm sorry!" But his father's response was a slap across the face, the pain and shock of it still echoing in Jasiah's mind. "I said shut up, brat!" his father snarled, his voice filled with anger"I'm taking your brother with me. He's the only likable one in this stupid house!" Jasiah's heart still ached from the memory of that day.

He had felt so abandoned and rejected, left behind with a mother who was struggling to cope with her own emotions.

As Jasiah relived the memory, he felt the same sense of desperation and fear that he had felt on that day. He remembered grabbing his father's hand, pleading with him to stay, but his father just shoved him off with a rough push. "Shut up, you stupid kid!" his father yelled out at him, his face red with anger. "You're just a burden, a constant reminder of your mother's mistakes!" Jasiah's heart still ached from the memory of those harsh words. He felt like he was reliving the pain and rejection all over again.

Just as his father was about to turn and leave, Jasiah's older brother Scott came downstairs. Like his father, Scott's face was a blur, a featureless visage that Jasiah couldn't quite recall. "Dad, stop!" Scott spoke out, his voice calm and firm. "Leave Jasiah alone! He's just a kid, he doesn't understand. Jasiah's father just sneered at Scott, his eyes flashing with anger. "You're just like your mother, always sticking up for this little brat," he spat out. "You're just as useless as she is!" Scott's face remained calm, but Jasiah could sense the tension in his brother's body. He was trying to defend him, to stand up to their father's cruelty. "Please, Dad," Scott said, his voice still calm. "Don't do this. Don't leave us like this." But Jasiah's father just laughed, a cold, mirthless sound. "You're too late, Scott," he said, his voice dripping with malice. "I've made up my mind. I'm leaving, and I'm taking you with me." As Jasiah relived the memory, he felt the same sense of helplessness and despair that he had felt on that day. He was trapped in a nightmare, reliving the pain and rejection of his childhood...

As Jasiah relived the memory, he felt the same sense of helplessness and despair that he had felt on that day. He was trapped in a nightmare, reliving the pain and rejection of his childhood. But suddenly, he was jolted back to reality by the sound of voices calling his name. "Jasiah, wake up! Oh, we found you and you're alive!" Michael's voice was loud and unworried, but Neveah's tone was laced with concern and relief. Jasiah's eyes fluttered open, and he saw his friends standing over him, their faces etched with worry and exhaustion.

He sat up, rubbing his eyes, trying to shake off the remnants of the nightmare. "We found the temple," Michael said, his eyes sparkling with excitement. "So let's go! This will be a piece of cake since we all know how to use our elemental energy now!" Michael took off, running towards the temple, and Neveah sighed and followed, her eyes fixed on Jasiah with a mixture of concern and encouragement. Jasiah quickly got up, his heart was still racing from the nightmare, and followed his friends, his legs stiff from the long sleep.

Jasiah followed his friends, he couldn't help but feel a sense of trepidation. The temple was still far away, its towering spires and grand façade a distant silhouette on the horizon. The journey was going to be long and arduous, and Jasiah's legs still felt stiff from the long sleep.

He quickened his pace, trying to keep up with Michael and Neveah, who seemed to be fueled by a sense of excitement and adventure. The air was thick with an otherworldly energy, and Jasiah could feel his elemental power stirring, responding to the call of the temple. As they walked, the landscape around them began to change. The dense forest gave way to a barren wasteland, the earth dry and cracked, the sky a deep, foreboding crimson.

The air grew hotter, the sun beating down upon them like a relentless hammer. Jasiah's throat was parched, his canteen almost empty. He glanced at his friends, who seemed to be faring no better. Michael's face was set in a determined expression, his eyes fixed on the temple, while Neveah's eyes darted back and forth, scanning the horizon for any signs of danger.

"We need to find shelter," Neveah said, her voice low and urgent. "This heat is unbearable, and we don't know what dangers lie ahead." Michael nodded, his eyes scanning the horizon. "I see something," he said, pointing to a cluster of rocks in the distance. "Let's head there. We can rest and regroup before we continue."

Jasiah nodded, his legs aching with exhaustion. He followed his friends, his heart pounding with anticipation, as they made their way towards the rocks, the temple still a distant dream on the horizon... As they approached the rocks, Jasiah looked around, confused. "Huh? But it isn't hot at all. It's warm," Jasiah asked, scratching his head. "It's not even that hot." Neveah's eyes widened in surprise. "HOW THE HELL?" she exclaimed, her voice loud and incredulous.

 Michael shrugged, not really caring. "It's probably cause of his fire energy," he said, his tone nonchalant.|
"You know, heat resistance and all that." Jasiah's eyes narrowed, still looking confused. "But I don't understand," he said, his brow furrowed. "I can feel the heat, but it's not bothering me like it is you two." Neveah's eyes sparkled with curiosity. "That's really interesting," she said, her voice filled with excitement. "We should study this further. Maybe your fire energy is more powerful than we thought." Michael rolled his eyes. "Yeah, yeah, science stuff," he said, his tone

dismissive. "Can we just focus on getting to the temple first?" Jasiah nodded, his mind still reeling from the discovery. He had always known that he had a special connection to fire, but he had never realized that it could give him heat resistance.

They rested and regrouped, Jasiah couldn't help but wonder what other secrets his fire energy held. He looked at his friends, who were busy arguing over the best route to take to the temple. "Hey, guys?" Jasiah said, his voice interrupting their conversation. "Do you think my fire energy could be useful in some way?" Neveah's eyes lit up with excitement. "Oh, definitely," she said, her voice filled with enthusiasm. "We could use your heat resistance to our advantage. Maybe you could-" Michael cut her off, his voice rough. "Look, let's just focus on getting to the temple, okay? We can worry about Jasiah's fire energy later."

Michael continued, his voice dripping with confidence. "My water energy is better anyway, plus water beats fire. We don't need to rely on Jasiah's heat resistance." Neveah's eyes narrowed, her voice taking on a defensive tone. "That's not fair, Michael. Jasiah's fire energy is just as powerful as your water energy. And who says water always beats fire?" Michael snorted, his expression dismissive. "Elementary school science, Neveah. Water extinguishes fire. It's basic." Jasiah's face fell, his eyes stinging from Michael's harsh words. He knew that his fire energy was powerful, but he also knew that it had its limitations.

He didn't want to be a liability to his friends.

Neveah was quick to defend him. "That may be true in the

physical world, Michael, but we're not dealing with ordinary fires and waters here. We're dealing with elemental energies, and Jasiah's fire energy is a powerful tool."

Jasiah argued back, his voice rising in frustration. "Oh well, what are you gonna do with water, Mike? Pour me a glass of water?" Michael scoffed, his expression disgusted. "Hell no, I'm not filling you a cup." Michael rolled his eyes, his body language radiating annoyance.

Neveah watched them bicker, her eyes darting back and forth between them. She knew exactly what to say to shut them up, and she didn't hesitate. "Can y'all shut up and kiss?" Neveah said bluntly, her words dropping like a bombshell. Jasiah and Michael both side-eyed her, their faces twisted in disgust. "Ew, I'm not kissing HIM!" they said at the same time, their voices overlapping in perfect harmony. Neveah just shrugged, a mischievous glint in her eye. "Well, it usually works in any argument. You two are just too caught up in your own egos." Jasiah and Michael looked at each other, their faces still twisted in distaste. But then, something strange happened. They both burst out laughing, their argument forgotten in the face of Neveah's ridiculous suggestion. "Oh man, Neveah," Jasiah said, wiping tears from his eyes. "You're such a weirdo."

Neveah watched them, a satisfied smile on her face. She knew that her friends were prone to arguing. It took a ridiculous suggestion to get them to stop most of the time

CHAPTER 12
THE CHASE

The long extended walk to the landscape seemed to stretch on forever, with no sign of the unseen Temple in sight. The trio's spirits began to flag, their energy waning in the face of the unforgiving environment. But then, suddenly, Michael stepped over a string, and the ground seemed to fall away beneath them. The trio's stomachs lurched as they plummeted downwards, their screams echoing off the walls of the cavity they were falling into.

Time seemed to slow as they fell, their minds racing with thoughts of what lay below. Would they land safely, or would they crash to their deaths on the unforgiving rock? Finally, they landed with a thud, the impact jarring their bones. Dazed and disoriented, they struggled to their feet, looking around in wonder at their surroundings. They found themselves in a massive cave, the ceiling lost in darkness. The air was cool and damp, and the sound of dripping water echoed through the cavern. But it was not the cave itself that caught their attention - it was the small, cave-like structures that dotted the landscape, each one glowing with a soft, ethereal light. In the center of the cave, a small river flowed, its crystal clear waters reflecting the light of the caves. The river seemed to pulse with a life of its own, its gentle flow a soothing balm to their frazzled nerves.

They looked around, they realized that they had stumbled into an underground city, hidden away from the world above. The caves were neatly arranged, each one seeming to serve a specific purpose. There were dwellings, stores, and even what appeared to be a grand, crystal-encrusted palace at the heart of the city.

"Where are we?" Jasiah asked, his voice laced with a hint of frustration. "Bold of you to assume that we magically know where," Michael spoke in a dismissive tone, his eyes rolling in exasperation. "Well, for starters, we're in a cave," Michael said, stating the obvious. Neveah spoke up, looking around with a sigh. "Well, no shit we are," she said, her voice dripping with sarcasm. Michael spoke up again, his tone annoyed.

"Well, tell us something we don't know," he said, his arms crossed over his chest. Jasiah shook his head, his brow furrowed in concentration. "I mean, what's the purpose of this underground city? Who built it? And why?" he asked, his curiosity getting the better of him. Neveah nodded in agreement, her eyes sparkling with interest. "Yeah, and what's with the palace in the center? Is that where the rulers of this city live?" she asked, her voice full of wonder. Michael snorted, his expression skeptical. "Rulers? You mean like, some kind of underground kingdom?" he asked, his tone dripping with disdain. Jasiah shrugged, his shoulders rising and falling. "Why not? We've stumbled into an underground city, for crying out loud. Anything's possible at this point," he said, his voice firm.

They continued to speculate about the rulers of the city, the trio began to start walking, looking for an exit from the underground metropolis. The soft glow of the luminescent caves provided an eerie light, casting long shadows on the walls as they moved. Suddenly, Neveah let out a shrill cry, jumping back in surprise. "Guys, IT'S A BAT!" she exclaimed, her eyes fixed on the small, winged creature flitting around the cave. Jasiah chuckled, a warm smile spreading across his face. "Aww, how cute! It's a bat!" he said, his eyes shining with amusement. Neveah shot him a disgusted look, her nose wrinkling in distaste. "It's not cute, idiot!" she said, her voice dripping with sarcasm. "Hey, you're going to hurt its feelings!" Jasiah teased, his voice rising in mock outrage. Neveah glared at him, her eyes flashing with annoyance. "I don't care.

You're only saying that because you're just as ugly as it," she retorted, her voice laced with venom. Jasiah's eyes narrowed, his face darkening with anger. "Ugly where!?" he exclaimed, his voice rising in indignation. Neveah smirked, her eyes glinting with amusement. "I mean, your two-toned dreads play a huge part in that," she teased, her voice dripping with sarcasm.

Jasiah side-eyed her, his expression unimpressed. "Oh, whatever," he muttered, crossing his arms over his chest. Michael, who had been watching the exchange with amusement, spoke up, his voice dry. "You know, guys, we're still lost in an underground city. Maybe we should focus on finding a way out instead of bickering about bats and hair," he said, his tone laced with exasperation.

 Michael's words of wisdom fell like a cold splash of water on the trio's banter, silencing them instantly. They exchanged sheepish glances, their faces flushing with embarrassment. "Yeah, you're right," Jasiah muttered, his voice laced with regret. "We need to find a way out of here." Neveah nodded, her eyes scanning the surrounding caves. "But where do we even start? We've been walking for what feels like hours, and we still haven't found an exit." Michael shrugged, his expression grim. "We'll just have to keep searching. We can't give up now."

The trio trudged on, their footsteps echoing through the cavernous space. The air was thick with tension, their senses on high alert as they navigated the winding tunnels.

On the walk, the silence between them grew thicker, like a physical presence. The only sound was the soft dripping of water, echoing off the walls like a slow, mournful beat. Neveah shivered, her eyes darting nervously around the darkness. "Guys, do you feel that?" she whispered, her voice barely audible.

Jasiah and Michael exchanged a puzzled glance. "Feel what?" Jasiah asked, his voice low. Neveah hesitated, her eyes fixed on some invisible point in the distance. "I don't know...it's just a feeling. Like we're being watched." Michael's expression turned skeptical. "We're probably just spooked from being down here too long," he said, his voice reassuring. But Jasiah's eyes were fixed on Neveah, his face set in a determined expression. "I think we should keep moving," he said, his voice firm. "We can't let fear get the best of us." The trio pressed on, their hearts pounding in unison as they delved deeper into the unknown.

The darkness seemed to closing in around them, like a suffocating shroud. And yet, they moved forward, driven by a desperate desire to escape the underground city... as they continue to walked, the silence grew thicker, the air more oppressive. It was as if they were walking into a trap, a trap from which there was no escape. And still, they pressed on, their footsteps echoing through the darkness, like a slow, mournful march towards doom...

Their footsteps seemed to reverberate through the cavernous space, echoing off the walls in a slow, funereal rhythm. The air was heavywith anticipation, like a physical weight that pressed down upon them. As they turned a corner, the trio was confronted with a labyrinthine tunnel, its entrance shrouded in darkness. The air that wafted out was stale and musty, reeking of decay and neglect.

Neveah's eyes widened, her gaze fixed on the tunnel's mouth. "What's that smell?" she whispered, her voice trembling. Michael's expression was grim. "I don't know, but I don't like it," he muttered, his eyes scanning the tunnel's entrance. Jasiah's hand instinctively went to the Sword he carried, his fingers closing around its reassuring weight. "Let's just get this over with," he said, his voice low and determined. As they stepped into the tunnel, the darkness seemed to envelop them like a living entity.

The air was thick with the stench of rot and corruption, making their stomachs churn with nausea. Their footsteps echoed through the tunnel, the sound waves bouncing off the walls in a maddening rhythm. It was as if they were being herded towards some unknown fate, trapped in a nightmare from which they couldn't awaken.

Suddenly, Neveah's hand shot out, grasping Jasiah's arm in a death grip. "Wait," she whispered, her eyes fixed on something ahead.

Jasiah's heart skipped a beat as he followed her gaze. In the distance, a faint, flickering light seemed to pulse with a malevolent energy, like a beacon calling them towards some ancient, forgotten horror... And still, they pressed on,
their hearts pounding in their chests, as they stumbled towards the unknown, driven by a desperate desire to escape the underground city...

Every step they took seemed to echo through the tunnel, the sound waves bouncing off the walls in a maddening rhythm that sent shivers down their spines. The silence between them grew thicker, like a physical presence that pressed down upon them, making it hard to breathe.

Minutes ticked by, each one feeling like an eternity as they stumbled through the darkness. Suddenly, Jasiah's hand shot up, his palm cupped around a flickering flame that danced in the darkness. The trio gasped in unison as the fire illuminated the tunnel, casting eerie shadows on the walls. And then, they saw it. A living skull wolf, its eyes glowing with a malevolent crimson energy, its teeth stained with blood. The creature's presence seemed to fill the tunnel, its aura of death and decay washing over them like a cold, dark wave.

Corpses littered the ground around it, their empty eyes staring up into the darkness. Neveah's scream was the first to shatter the silence, her voice echoing off the walls as she stumbled backward in terror.

Michael's eyes were fixed on the creature, his face white with fear. Jasiah's grip on his fire energy faltered, the flame dying as he took a step back, his eyes wide with horror. And then, they turned and ran, their footsteps pounding through the tunnel as they desperately sought to escape the living nightmare that pursued them.

The skull wolf's howl echoed through the tunnel, its voice like a rusty gate scraping against the walls of their sanity. The trio didn't dare look back, their hearts pounding in their chests as they sprinted through the darkness, driven by a desperate desire to escape the underground city and the horrors that lurked within...

Their footsteps pounded out a frantic rhythm on the cold, damp stone, echoing off the walls as they fled from the skull wolf's unholy howl. The sound seemed to pursue them, its mournful wail piercing their eardrums and shredding their nerves.

Neveah's breath came in ragged gasps, her chest heaving with exhaustion as she stumbled through the darkness. Michael's eyes were fixed on some unknown
 point ahead, his face set in a determined grimace as he drove himself forward. Jasiah's fire energy flickered fitfully, casting eerie shadows on the walls as he struggled to maintain a steady flame. The darkness seemed to closing in around them, like a suffocating shroud that threatened to snuff out their lives.

Despite their desperate efforts, the trio found themselves lost in a labyrinthine maze of tunnels, their twists and turns seemingly designed to confound and disorient. Every door they burst through led only to more darkness, more twisted corridors that seemed to stretch on forever.

Their hearts pounded in their chests, their pulses racing with fear as they stumbled through the underground city. The skull wolf's howl still echoed through the tunnels, its voice like a ghostly refrain that haunted their every step. But still, they pressed on, driven by a desperate desire to escape the horrors that lurked within the underground city. They had to find a way out, no matter what terrors lay in wait for them.

Yet, as they ran, the tunnels seemed to shift and twist around them, like a living, breathing entity that sought to trap them forever. And with every step, they felt themselves being pulled deeper into the heart of the underground city, further and further from the safety of the surface.

Their screams echoed through the tunnels, lost in the darkness as they stumbled through the endless labyrinth, pursued by the skull wolf's malevolent presence...

The screams grew hoarse, their throats raw from the constant shrieking as they stumbled through the darkness. The skull wolf's howl seemed to grow louder, its voice like a deafening drumbeat that pulsed through their very being.

Suddenly, Michael spun around, his eyes flashing with determination. With a swift motion, he raised his hands, and a jet of water shot out, striking the skull wolf's glowing eyes. The creature let out a pained yelp, its howl faltering for a brief moment. The trio took advantage of the distraction, their footsteps pounding out a frantic rhythm as they sprinted forward.

Like a beacon of hope, they saw it. A canoe, half-hidden in the shadows, its wooden hull creaking softly in the silence. "Quick, in there!" Michael shouted, his voice echoing off the walls. Jasiah was the first to respond, his long legs carrying him swiftly towards the canoe.

He leapt in, his movements fluid and practiced, as if he'd been born to navigate treacherous waters. Neveah followed close behind, her eyes fixed on the canoe as if it were her only salvation. She tumbled in, her body crashing against the wooden hull as she scrambled to find a secure foothold. Finally, Michael leapt in, his body landing with a thud as he grasped the canoe's edges, his knuckles white with tension.

The trio huddled together, their chests heaving with exhaustion, their eyes fixed on the darkness behind them. The skull wolf's howl still echoed through the tunnels, its voice like a mournful cry that pierced their hearts.

The canoe glided smoothly across the dark, glassy waters, the trio's paddles dipping in and out of the surface with a rhythmic intensity. They didn't dare look back, their hearts still racing from the close call with the skull wolf. But then, without warning, the silence was shattered by the sound of splashing water. The trio's heads snapped around, their eyes scanning the darkness behind them. And then, they saw it.

The skull wolf, its bony body undulating through the water with an unnatural grace. Its eyes glowed with an otherworldly energy, its jaws open in a perpetual snarl as it pursued them with a relentless determination.

"WOLVES MADE OUT OF BONES CAN SWIM NOW!?" Neveah exclaimed, her voice trembling on the edge of hysteria. "This is insane!" The canoe wobbled violently as Jasiah and Michael paddled with all their might, their muscles straining against the resistance of the water.

No matter how hard they paddled, the skull wolf kept pace with them, its bony body slicing through the water with an eerie silence. The trio's breathing grew ragged, their chests heaving with fear as they watched the skull wolf's relentless approach. Its eyes seemed to burn with an unholy intensity, its very presence seeming to draw the life force out of them.

"We're not going to make it," Neveah whispered, her voice barely audible over the sound of their paddling. "It's going to catch us." Michael's face was set in a grim determination, his eyes fixed on the darkness ahead. "We can't give up," he growled. "We have to keep going." But as they paddled, the skull wolf's presence seemed to grow stronger, its malevolent energy washing over them like a cold, dark wave. The trio's hearts pounded in their chests, their screams echoing through the darkness as they desperately sought to outrun the monster that pursued them...

The canoe's wooden hull creaked and groaned under the strain, the trio's frantic paddling sending it hurtling through the dark waters. But no matter how fast they went, the skull wolf kept pace, its bony body undulating through the water with an unnatural ease. With the air was heavy with tension, the trio's screams and the sound of their paddling echoing off the walls of the underground cavern. The skull wolf's presence seemed to grow stronger, its malevolent energy washing over them like a cold, dark wave.

Suddenly, the canoe lurched violently, throwing the trio off balance. Neveah's scream was cut short as she fell forward, her hands grasping wildly for the canoe's edges. The skull wolf had managed to plant its claws on the back of the canoe, its grip like a vice. Jasiah's eyes went wide with terror as the wolf's jaws snapped shut mere inches from his face. But then, in a flash of inspiration, Jasiah remembered his fire energy. With a swift motion, he raised his hand, and a blast of flame erupted from his palm.

The skull wolf's eyes widened in surprise as Jasiah blasted a fireball directly into its face. The wolf's howl of pain echoed through the cavern, its claws releasing their grip on the canoe as it stumbled backward. "Nice!" Michael exclaimed, his voice full of admiration. But their relief was short-lived. The skull wolf recovered quickly, its bony body undulating through the water as it launched itself at the canoe once more. This time, its jaws closed around one of Jasiah's dreads, the wolf's teeth snapping shut with a sickening crunch.

Jasiah's scream of pain and fear echoed through the cavern as the wolf's grip tightened.
Neveah's eyes went wide with horror as she watched the skull wolf's jaws close around Jasiah's dread. Her mouth hung open in shock, her face pale and drained of all color. Jasiah's
scream of pain and fear echoed through the cavern, the sound waves bouncing off the walls and ceiling. The skull wolf's grip tightened, its teeth sinking deeper into Jasiah's dread. In a swift, brutal motion, the skull wolf bit Jasiah's dread right off. A trickle of blood dripped from Jasiah's scalp, the crimson liquid mingling with the dark waters of the cavern. Before the skull wolf could do anything more, Jasiah pulled out his sword, the blade flashing in the dim light of the cavern.

With a swift, desperate motion, he struck the skull wolf,

the blade biting deep into its bony flesh. But to their horror, the sword had no effect. The skull wolf didn't even flinch, its bony body seeming to absorb the blow. Jasiah's eyes widened in disbelief as he struck the wolf again and again, but it was like hitting a statue. The skull wolf's response was to bite Jasiah's sword to bits, the metal shattering and splintering beneath its jaws. The sound of crunching metal echoed through the cavern, the trio's hearts sinking in despair. Jasiah's eyes went wide with shock and fear, his sword arm falling limp and useless.

The skull wolf's jaws opened wide, its teeth glinting in the dim light as it prepared to strike again. The trio's hearts were racing, their bodies tense with fear as they awaited the inevitable. But just as the wolf was about to attack, Michael's keen eyes scanned the horizon, his gaze fixed on the water ahead.

His expression changed from fear to surprise, and then to alarm. "Everyone, hold tight! There's a drop!" Michael informed his friends, his voice low and urgent. "Sorry, WHAT?!" Neveah yelled out, her voice piercing the air as she turned to stare at Michael in disbelief. "You mean, like, a waterfall or something?!" "Yes, exactly!" Michael replied, his eyes fixed on the water ahead. "We're approaching the end of the river, and it's a dead end. We have to hold on for dear life!"

The trio's eyes went wide as they took in the sight before them. The river was indeed coming to an end, and it was a steep drop into the unknown.

The sound of rushing water grew louder, the air filling with the misty spray of the falls. Jasiah's eyes were still fixed on the skull wolf, which was still clinging to the canoe's edge. But Michael's warning had given them a new priority - survival.

The canoe was picking up speed, hurtling towards the edge of the falls with a deadly momentum. The trio's hearts were in their throats as they clung to each other, their screams echoing through the cavern as they plummeted towards the unknown. The waterfall loomed ahead, its misty veil shrouding the abyss below.

The sound of rushing water grew deafening, a thunderous roar that threatened to consume them whole. Jasiah's eyes never left the skull wolf, its bony grip still clinging to the canoe's edge. But even the wolf's malevolent presence was forgotten in the face of their impending doom. The canoe's wooden hull creaked and groaned, the sound of splitting wood echoing through the cavern as they approached the edge.

Thier screams reached a fever pitch, their bodies tense with fear as they braced for impact. And then, in an instant, they were over the edge. The canoe plummeted downwards, its occupants weightless and helpless as they fell towards the churning water below. The trio's screams were cut short as they hit the water, the shock of the impact knocking the wind out of them. They sank beneath the surface, the water closing over their heads like a cold, dark shroud. The skull wolf, still clinging to the canoe, was dragged down with them, its bony body disappearing into the depths of the water.

The canoe, its wooden hull shattered and splintered, sank slowly beneath the surface, leaving behind a trail of bubbles and debris. The trio's fate was unknown, their bodies lost in the dark, churning waters of the underground river. Had they survived the fall, or had they succumbed to the deadly forces that lurked beneath the surface? Only time would tell...

CHAPTER 13

ENDANGERED TEMPLE

High above the chaotic waters, a masked man stood atop one of the rock platforms, his piercing gaze fixed on the spot where the trio had vanished. He was clad in a long, flowing robe, its dark fabric billowing behind him like a shadow. In his hand, he grasped a spear, its tip glinting in the dim light of the cavern. The man's eyes gleamed with approval as he gazed out at the scene before him. "You have done well, my Skull Wolf," he murmured, his voice low and gravelly. With a satisfied nod, the man turned to depart, his footsteps echoing off the walls of the cavern as he vanished into the darkness.

His parting words hung in the air, however, leaving a sense of foreboding in their wake. "Now, time to get the scroll from the temple and kill the Wind Elemental," the man's voice drifted back, his tone dripping with malevolence. "Then, I'll get the Wind Kyrium." The man's gaze flicked back to the pool of water where the trio had fallen, a calculating glint in his eye. "Maybe I'll take their Kyriums too..." he mused, his voice dripping with avarice. "And get their elemental powers after I'm done with my target." With that, the man turned and walked away, leaving behind a sense of unease that lingered in the air like a shadow.

The Skull Wolf, still lurking beneath the surface, seemed to sense its master's departure, its bony body sinking deeper into the darkness as it awaited its next command.

The man continued to walk, his footsteps echoing off the walls of the cavern as he made his way through the winding tunnels. He moved with a sense of confidence, his strides long and purposeful. "This should be easy," the man spoke to himself, a hint of scoffing in his voice. He had been searching for the temple for what felt like hours, but he knew it was only a matter of time before he found it.

As he turned a corner, the man's eyes fell upon the stone temple, its cracked and weathered facade looming before him like a ancient sentinel. The temple's entrance was a large, stone door, adorned with intricate carvings of elemental symbols.

The man's gaze swept over the door, his eyes lingering on the symbols of wind, water, earth, and fire. A cold, calculating smile spread across his face as he reached out a hand to push the door open. The door creaked and groaned, its ancient hinges protesting the movement.

The man stepped inside, his eyes adjusting to the dim light within. Musty and stale, filled with the scent of age and decay. As the man stepped inside, his eyes scanned the dimly lit interior of the temple, taking in the musty air and the scent of decay.

The room was vast, with a high, vaulted ceiling that seemed to disappear into the darkness. But what caught the man's attention was the huge hole in the middle of the temple, a massive void that seemed to yawn open like a chasm.

And on the other side of the hole, he saw it - the scroll, lying on a pedestal, its parchment glowing with an otherworldly light. "Easy enough," the man said to himself, a confident smile spreading across his face. He took a step forward, his eyes fixed on the scroll. But just as he was about to take another step, a figure suddenly jumped into his path, blocking his way. The man's eyes narrowed, his hand instinctively reaching for the spear at his side.

The boy who stood before him was young, no more than fifteen years old. He had a jet-black, curly afro, and a vertical scar above his right eye, with a smaller one on his lip. His prominent features were set in a fierce determination, and he wore a black Polo shirt and gray Athletic shorts. In his hand, he grasped a silver dagger, its blade glinting in the dim light. "Not another step!" the boy shouted, his voice echoing off the walls of the temple.

The man chuckled, a cold, mirthless sound. "Ahh, so you're the Wind Wielder, aren't you?" he said, his eyes gleaming with interest. The boy's face twisted in anger. "No! I'm not, but what do you want with my brother?" he demanded, his voice trembling with emotion. The man's eyes narrowed, his smile growing wider. "Ahh, so you're his brother," he said, his tone dripping with amusement. "How... convenient."

The boy's face twisted in anger, his eyes blazing with fury. Without hesitation, he rushed the masked man, his dagger flashing in the dim light of the temple.

The man didn't seem to care, his eyes gleaming with amusement as he watched the boy's attack.

The boy's movements were swift and deadly, but the man dodged and weaved with effortless ease, avoiding each strike with a precision that was almost supernatural. The boy's attacks grew more frantic, his breathing ragged as he tried to land a hit, but the man was a ghost, always one step ahead. "Hm, how pitiful," the man said, his tone dripping with condescension.

"Do you even have any type of elemental power?" he sneered, his voice like a slap to the boy's face.

The boy's anger boiled over, his face red with rage. With a fierce cry, he threw his dagger at the man, hoping to catch him off guard. But the man was too quick, his reflexes too sharp. He caught the dagger with his two fingers, the blade hovering in mid-air as he regarded the boy with a dismissive gaze. "Weak," the man said, his voice like a cold wind. The boy's dagger trembled in the air, suspended by the man's fingers, before he casually tossed it aside, the blade clattering to the stone floor. The boy's eyes widened in shock, his face pale with fear.

He had never seen anyone move like that before, with a speed and agility that was almost inhuman. For a moment, he was frozen, unsure of what to do next. But the man didn't give him a chance to regroup. With a sudden movement, he reached out and grasped the boy's wrist, his grip like a vice. The boy struggled to free himself, but the man's hold was unyielding.

The boy's eyes were fixed on the man's, his gaze paralyzed by the intensity of the man's stare. He tried to speak, but his voice was caught in his throat, unable to escape the grip of fear that had taken hold of him. The man's grip on his wrist tightened, the boy's bones creaking in protest. The boy's vision began to blur, his eyes feeling like they were about to pop out of his head as the man's grip constricted. The air was thick with tension, the silence between them oppressive and heavy. The boy's heart was racing, his pulse pounding in his ears like a drumbeat of doom.

The man's face was inches from the boy's, his hot breath washing over him like a wave of fear. The boy's skin crawled, his flesh rippling with goosebumps as the man's gaze seemed to bore into his soul.

The man then whispered in his ear, his voice like a snake slithering through the grass. "What if I just killed you?" he said, his tone smug, self-assured. The boy's heart stopped, his breath catching in his throat. He felt like he was staring into the abyss, with no safety net to catch him if he fell. The man's words hung in the air, suspended like a guillotine's blade, waiting to drop and sever the boy's life. The boy's eyes were frozen on the man's, his mind racing with thoughts of death, of oblivion, of nothingness.

The seconds ticked by like hours, each one stretching out into an eternity of fear and uncertainty. The boy's fate hung in the balance, his life teetering on the edge of a precipice. Would the man spare his life, or would he snuff it out like a candle flame? The boy didn't know, but he knew one thing - he was running out of time.

    The boy's eyes remained fixed on the man's, his mind reeling with the implications of his own mortality. The seconds ticked by like hours, each one stretching out into an eternity of fear and uncertainty. The boy's fate hung in the balance, his life teetering on the edge of a precipice. Suddenly, the man's eyes seemed to flash with an other worldly energy, his pupils constricting into pinpricks of intensity. He raised his hand, and a gleaming silver sign materialized out of thin air, hovering above his palm. The sign pulsed with a strange, pulsating power, its surface etched with intricate runes that seemed to shift and writhe like living serpents. The boy's eyes widened in terror as the man's fingers closed around the sign, his grip like a vice.

And then, in a movement that seemed almost casual, the man raised his hand, and a Tear ripped through the fabric of space, unleashing a slashing wave of distorted energy that cut through the air like a scythe. The boy's scream was drowned out by the sound of his own arm being severed, the limb torn from his body with a wet, sickening crunch. He stared in horror as his arm dropped to the ground, the fingers still twitching and spasming like a dying creature. Blood fountained from the stump, spattering the stone floor in a gruesome parody of a Jackson Pollock painting.

The boy's vision began to blur, his eyes streaming with tears as he stared at the ruin of his own body. He felt a wave of nausea wash over him, his stomach churning with a mix of fear and pain.

The man's face seemed to loom over him, a grim and unforgiving mask of cruelty.

The boy's mind reeled in shock, his thoughts reduced to a jumbled mess of fear and panic. He was unable to process the sheer horror of what was happening, his brain numb with the knowledge that he was about to die.

And yet, even as the darkness closed in around him, the boy's eyes remained fixed on the man's, his gaze burning with a fierce and desperate hatred. He knew that he was about to meet his maker, but he refused to go quietly into the night. With a surge of adrenaline, the boy launched himself at the man, his remaining arm flailing wildly as he sought to strike back at his tormentor. But it was too late. The man's grip was already closing around his throat, squeezing the life from his body like a python crushing its prey. The boy's vision began to fade, his eyes growing dim as the darkness closed in around him. He knew that he was about to die, and that the man would escape, free to wreak havoc on the world once more. But even in death, the boy's hatred would endure, a

burning flame of fury that would fuel his spirit as it passed into the great beyond.

With a surge of adrenaline, the boy launched himself at the man, his unscathed hand clenched into a fist as he threw a wild punch. But the man was too quick, too skilled, and too ruthless. With a movement that seemed almost casual , he raised his hand, and a slashing wave of distorted energy cut through the air, its trajectory aimed directly at the boy's head. The boy's eyes went wide with terror as he realized that he was about to meet his maker. He tried to duck, to dodge, to escape the killing blow, but it was too late.

The man's attack was too swift, too deadly, and too merciless. Slashing energy struck the boy's head with a wet, sickening crunch, the sound echoing through the chamber like a crack of thunder. The boy's eyes went dark, his vision fading to black as his head was severed from his body in a gruesome, bloody arc. The boy's decapitated corpse slumped to the ground, his limbs twitching and spasming in a macabre dance of death.

The man stood over him, his eyes blazing with a malevolent intensity, his chest heaving with exertion as he surveyed the carnage he had unleashed. The air was thick with the stench of blood and death, the Temple echoing with the sound of the boy's screams as they faded into the abyss of eternity. The man's face was a mask of cruelty, his eyes burning with a fierce and unholy pleasure as he gazed upon the ruin of his victim.

To add a final touch of horror to the scene, the man reached down and picked up the boy's severed head, his fingers closing around the bloody scalp like a vice.

He gazed into the dead eyes, a sick and twisted smile spreading across his face as he savored the triumph of his victim's destruction. The boy's head hung limp and lifeless in the man's grasp, a gruesome trophy to his brutality and power. The man's eyes seemed to burn with an otherworldly energy, his gaze piercing the very soul of the chamber as he reveled in the horror he had unleashed.

The man's eyes gleamed with a malevolent intensity as he gazed into the dead eyes of his victim. A sick and twisted smile spread across his face, his lips curling upwards in a grotesque parody of pleasure. The boy's head hung limp and lifeless in his grasp, a gruesome trophy to his brutality and power.

For a moment, the man seemed to savor the triumph of his victim's destruction, his eyes burning with an otherworldly energy as he reveled in the horror he had unleashed. And then, with a sudden movement, he tossed the head aside, its lifeless eyes staring blankly into the distance as it bounced and rolled across the stone floor.

The man turned his attention to the scroll, his eyes fixed on the ancient parchment with an unblinking gaze. He reached out a hand, his fingers closing around the scroll with a grasping intensity. But as he did, a sudden burst of energy erupted from the walls of the temple, a hail of arrows firing out of hidden compartments with deadly precision. The man's eyes narrowed, his gaze flashing towards the source of the attack. But he was too quick, too skilled, and too powerful . With a flick of his wrist, he summoned an Aurora Shield, its shimmering surface flashing into existence with a burst of light and energy.

The arrows struck the shield, their deadly tips deflected and repelled by the man's defenses. The shield glowed with a fierce, pulsing light, its energy dissipated slowly as the arrows fell harmlessly to the ground. The man's eyes gleamed with a cold, calculating intensity as he surveyed the Temple.

"Hm, smart defenses," he thought to himself, "but not smart enough. Now, where is the Wind Wielder?" His eyes scanned the room, his gaze probing every corner and crevice as he searched for any sign of his quarry.
His lips curled into a cold, cruel smile as he contemplated the fate of his next victim.
"I'll find you," he whispered to himself, his voice barely audible over the sound of his own breathing. "And when I do, you'll suffer the same fate as this boy
. You'll beg for mercy, but it will be too late. I'll make sure of it." The man's eyes glowed with an unnatural energy, his very presence seeming to fill the chamber with an aura of menace and dread. He was a force of destruction, a bringer of death and chaos, and he would stop at nothing to achieve his goals. The man's eyes glowed with an unnatural energy, his very presence seeming to fill the temple with an aura of menace and dread. He was a force of destruction, a bringer of death and chaos, and he would stop at nothing to achieve his goals. With a cold, calculating smile, the man reached out and grasped the scroll, his fingers closing around it with a sense of triumph.

"Heh, yes," he snickered, his eyes flashing with amusement as he examined the symbol etched onto the parchment. The earth elemental symbol stared back at him, its intricate lines and curves seeming to dance across the surface of the scroll. The man's smile grew wider, his eyes gleaming with a malevolent intensity as he realized the truth. "Way too easy,"

he said, his voice dripping with contempt. "Guess the boss lied. The Wind Wielder isn't even here." The man's eyes narrowed, his gaze flashing towards the chamber's entrance as if searching for some hidden trap or deception. But there was none. The room was empty, the only sound the man's own heavy breathing and the soft rustle of the scroll in his hand. The man's face twisted into a scowl, his brows furrowing in annoyance. He had been played, duped into believing that the Wind Wielder was hiding in this very Unforeseen temple. But it was all a ruse, a clever trap designed to waste his time and resources.

The man's own heavy breathing and the soft rustle of the scroll in his hand were the only sounds that broke the silence of the temple. The man's face twisted into a scowl, his brows furrowing in annoyance as he realized he had been played. He had been duped into believing that the Wind Wielder was hiding in this very Unforeseen temple, but it was all a ruse, a clever trap designed to waste his time and resources. The man's eyes blazed with anger, his grip on the scroll tightening as he crushed it in his hand.

He was furious, his mind racing with the implications of this deception. Who was behind this trap? And what was their ultimate goal? As he stood there, seething with rage, a voice rang out behind him. "Hey." The voice was flat, devoid of emotion, but there was a hint of anger lurking beneath the surface. It was as if something was playing with his life, toying with his very existence. The man's head snapped towards the sound, his eyes scanning the chamber with a fierce intensity how ever there was no one in sight. The voice seemed to come from all around him, echoing off the walls and ceiling. "Who's there?" the man growled, his voice low and menacing. There was no response. The silence was oppressive, heavy with tension. The man's eyes narrowed, his gaze darting back and forth as he searched for any sign of movement.

But there was none. He was alone in the temple, surrounded by the oppressive silence. And then, just as suddenly as it had begun, everything was quiet. The voice was gone, leaving the man to ponder the implications of what had just happened. But as he stood there, frozen in uncertainty, he couldn't shake the feeling that he was being watched. That unblinking eyes were fixed on him, waiting for him to make his next move.

CHAPTER 14

TEMPLE BRAWL

There was none. He was alone in the temple, surrounded by the oppressive silence. And then, just as suddenly as it had begun, everything was quiet. The voice was gone, leaving the man to ponder the implications of what had just happened. But as he stood there, frozen in uncertainty, he couldn't shake the feeling that he was being watched. That unblinking eyes were fixed on him, waiting for him to make his next move.

Meanwhile, in the Cavern, Jasiah, Michael, and Neveah lay passed out against a stone wall, their bodies still soaked from falling into the water. The sound of dripping water and the quiet rustling of their own breathing were the only sounds that broke the silence. After a while, Jasiah's eyes flickered open, his gaze blurry and unfocused. He groggily sat up, his head spinning as he took in his surroundings. "Guys...?" he asked, his voice barely above a whisper. Neveah's blue eyes slowly opened, her gaze locked onto Jasiah's as she took in her surroundings. Michael, however, remained out cold, his body limp and still. Neveah's eyes widened as she took in their surroundings, her gaze darting back and forth. "Im awake... We survived falling off that waterfall?" she said, her voice laced with a mix of shock and relief.

Jasiah nodded, his eyes still foggy. "Yea, we did," he replied, his voice still rough from the fall. Neveah's gaze fell onto Michael's still form, her eyes flashing with concern. "Michael?" she called out, her voice soft and gentle. Michael didn't stir, his body remaining motionless as the two friends gazed at him with growing concern Neveah's gaze fell onto Michael's still form, her eyes flashing with concern. "Michael?" she called out, her voice soft and gentle. Michael didn't stir, his body remaining motionless as the two friends gazed at him with growing concern. "I don't think he's waking up anytime soon," Neveah said, her voice laced with a sense of urgency.

"You should go to the temple and get the scroll." Jasiah's eyes widened in surprise, but Neveah continued before he could protest. "I'll stay back and watch over Michael. We can't leave him here alone and vulnerable." Jasiah's expression turned worried, his brow furrowing with concern.

"But what if the Skull Wolf comes back?" he asked, his voice tinged with anxiety. He couldn't shake the feeling that they were being watched, and the thought of Neveah and Michael being left alone in the cavern was unsettling. Neveah smiled, a reassuring smile that seemed to calm Jasiah's nerves.

"Don't worry, I'll be able to handle it," she said, her voice firm and confident. Jasiah nodded, though his eyes still lingered on Neveah and Michael. "Make sure," he said, his voice soft and serious. With a deep breath, Jasiah turned away and began to run through the cavern, his footsteps echoing off the walls as he searched for the Unforeseen temple.

The darkness seemed to swallow him whole, but he pressed on, driven by the need to retrieve the scroll and uncover the secrets it held. As he disappeared into the darkness, Neveah's gaze fell back onto Michael, her eyes filled with a mix of concern and determination. She would protect him, no matter what dangers lay ahead. And she would wait for Jasiah's return as Jasiah ran through the cavern, his footsteps echoed off the walls, the only sound breaking the oppressive silence. He pushed forward, driven by the need to retrieve the scroll and uncover the secrets it held.

As he ran, a nagging feeling began to creep up on him. He Jasiah's hand instinctively went to his back, reaching for his sword, only to remember that it was gone, lost when the Skull Wolf bit it in half. The realization hit him like a ton of bricks, and Jasiah's pace slowed, his chest heaving with exertion.

He sighed, feeling a pang of frustration and disappointment wash over him. He knew he had to rely on his fire powers now, but the thought sent a wave of anxiety through him. He had only just awakened them a few hours ago, and he had no proper training or control over them.

The thought of using them in a high-pressure situation was daunting, to say the least. Jasiah's mind raced with doubts and fears, but he knew he couldn't afford to dwell on them. He had to keep moving, had to find the temple and retrieve the scroll. The fate of his friends, and possibly the entire world, depended on it.

With a deep breath, Jasiah pushed aside his doubts and focused on the task at hand. He kneeled down, his eyes scanning the ground for any materials he could use. His gaze fell upon a cluster of stones, about 20 in total, scattered across the ground. He quickly gathered them up, his mind racing with possibilities.

Perhaps he could use them to create a makeshift weapon, or as a distraction to draw attention away from himself. Or maybe, just maybe, he could use his fire powers to imbue the stones with energy, creating a powerful projectile to aid him in his quest. Jasiah's thoughts swirled with possibilities as he gathered the stones, his determination to succeed growing with every passing moment.

He would find a way to overcome his lack of training and use his powers to his advantage. He had to. The temple, and the secrets it held, were within his reach, and Jasiah was determined to grasp them.

Jasiah pressed on, his determination to succeed growing with every passing moment. He would find a way to overcome his lack of training and use his powers to his advantage. He had to. The temple, and the secrets it held, were within his reach, and Jasiah was determined to grasp them. Finally, after what seemed like an eternity of navigating the treacherous cavern, Jasiah saw the temple come into view. His eyes widened in awe as he took in the stunning architecture, the intricate carvings and imposing pillars that seemed to stretch up to the ceiling. Jasiah stopped in his tracks, his chest heaving with exertion, and took a deep breath. He had made it. He had finally reached the temple.

A sense of pride and accomplishment swelled within him, but he knew he couldn't afford to indulge in it just yet. He still had to retrieve the scroll and uncover its secrets. He took a moment to catch his breath, his eyes scanning the temple grounds for any signs of danger. The air was quiet, the only sound the soft rustling of the wind through the cavern's entrance.

   Jasiah's gaze fell upon the temple's entrance, a grand stone doorway adorned with elemental symbols.

For a moment, he simply stood there, taking in the sights and sounds of the temple. He had never seen anything like it before, and he couldn't help but feel a sense of wonder and awe.

But as the moment passed, Jasiah's focus snapped back into

place. He knew he had to move quickly, before any unwanted attention was drawn to him. With a deep breath, Jasiah steeled himself for what lay ahead. He gripped the stones tightly in his hand, his mind racing with plans and strategies.

He was ready to face whatever lay within the temple, armed with nothing but his wits and his fledgling fire energy.
As he walked into the temple, he felt a strange sensation beneath his feet, as if he was standing on someone. Jasiah's eyes widened in horror as he looked down to see a body without an arm or a head, its torso twisted in a grotesque position. Jasiah's instincts screamed at him to turn around and flee, but his legs seemed rooted to the spot. He tried to take a step back, but it was too late.
A hand clamped down on his shoulder, spinning him around to face the masked man. "Ah, hello," the masked man said, his voice dripping with smugness. "I don't believe we met before." Jasiah's eyes locked onto the masked man's, his heart racing with fear. He tried to speak, but his voice caught in his throat. The masked man's eyes glinted with amusement, as if he knew a secret that Jasiah didn't. "Who are you?" Jasiah managed to stammer, his voice barely above a whisper.

The masked man chuckled,| the sound sending a shiver down Jasiah's spine. "Oh, I'm just a humble guide," he said, his voice dripping with sarcasm. "And you, my friend, are in a world of trouble."
Jasiah's eyes darted around the temple, searching for an escape route, but the masked man seemed to be enjoying the cat-and-mouse game. He held up the scroll, taunting Jasiah with it. "I assume you're looking for this?" the masked man said with amusement in his tone. Jasiah's eyes widened as he nodded, his voice trembling. "Y-yea..." The masked man's

smile grew wider.

"Then... fight me for it. A life or death battle." Jasiah's eyes went wide with horror. "Wait, what- bu-" he stammered, but before he could finish, the masked man kicked him backward, slamming him into the wall of the temple. Jasiah's head spun as he stumbled back to his feet, but the masked man was already upon him, his eyes blazing with a malevolent intensity. Jasiah reacted on instinct, throwing five of his stones at the man's head in a desperate bid to distract him.

The stones flew true, striking the masked man with a loud crack, but he barely flinched. Jasiah didn't wait to see if his attack had any effect - he turned and ran, dashing towards the temple entrance in a desperate bid to escape. As Jasiah turned to flee, the masked man dashed to the entrance, his strides long and menacing. He reached out, his hand closing around Jasiah's wrist like a vice, stopping him from escaping. Jasiah tried to struggle, but the masked man's grip was unyielding. With a cruel smile, he raised his hand, and Jasiah felt himself being pulled down, as if an invisible force was warping the gravity around him. Jasiah's body slammed into the ground, the impact sending shockwaves of pain through his entire being. He grunted, his breath knocked out of him, as the masked man stood over him, his eyes gleaming with sadistic delight. The masked man's foot snapped out, catching Jasiah in the chin with a vicious kick.

Jasiah's body flew backward, his head spinning as he crashed into the temple wall. "Geez, you're quite weak!" the masked man said, his voice dripping with sarcasm as he giggled. "I've seen toddlers put up a better fight than you." Jasiah's vision blurred, his head throbbing with pain as he struggled to get to his feet. But by the time he did, the masked man was already in front of him, his fist cocked back for another blow.

The right hook landed with precision, Jasiah's jaw cracking under the force of the impact. He stumbled backward, his eyes watering as the masked man's laughter echoed through the temple. Jasiah's anger and fear mixed into a potent cocktail, driving him to fight back.

He summoned every last ounce of strength, his hands curling into fists as he prepared to face his enemy.

But the masked man was relentless, his attacks coming in swift and merciless succession. Jasiah stumbled, his defenses crumbling under the onslaught, as the masked man's laughter grew louder, more maniacal... As Jasiah summoned his last ounce of strength, his hands curling into fists as he prepared to face his enemy. The masked man, however, was unfazed, his attacks coming in swift and merciless succession. Jasiah stumbled, his defenses crumbling under the onslaught, as the masked man's laughter grew louder, more maniacal. The temple echoed with the sound of punches and kicks, the air thick with tension and suspense.

The masked man's laughter was beginning to take on a hysterical quality, his eyes gleaming with a madman's intensity. But Jasiah refused to back down. As the masked man paused in his laughing fit, Jasiah saw his chance.

With a swift motion, he grabbed two stones from his pouch and infused them with his flame energy. The flames danced across the stones' surfaces, casting flickering shadows on the temple walls. Jasiah's eyes locked onto the masked man, his gaze burning with determination. With a swift motion, Jasiah threw both stones at the masked man.

The man's eyes widened in surprise as the stones struck him, the flames erupting in a blaze of glory. The masked man glared at Jasiah, his face twisted in a mixture of anger and fascination. "Oh, now this is interesting, BOY," he said, his voice low and menacing.

He chuckled to himself, a cold, mirthless sound. For a moment, the masked man seemed to be savoring the sensation of the flames, his eyes glinting with a madman's delight. Then, his face contorted in a snarl, he raised his hand, preparing to unleash a cosmic blast-like attack. But something seemed to catch his attention, something in Jasiah's eyes that made him freeze. "No way..." the man muttered under his breath, his gaze fixed on Jasiah with an unsettling intensity. Jasiah took advantage of the momentary distraction.

With a fierce cry, he engulfed his fist in flames, the fire roaring to life with a ferocity that seemed to shake the very foundations of the temple. The masked man's eyes widened in surprise as Jasiah landed a solid punch, the flames exploding in a blaze of glory. The man stumbled backward, his eyes flashing with anger and surprise, as Jasiah stood tall, his flames burning bright with a fierce and defiant intensity. Jasiah's hand was still engulfing with flames, his fist clenched and ready to strike again.

He went for another punch, the flames dancing across his skin like living tendrils of fire. But the masked man was not going to go down without a fight.

With a swift motion, the man raised his hand, and a shimmering Aurora field erupted around him, blocking Jasiah's punch. The flames danced against the field, casting a kaleidoscope of colors across the temple walls. Jasiah's eyes widened in shock as his punch was blocked, his flames faltering for a moment.

The masked man took advantage of the hesitation, his eyes flashing with anger and determination.

With a swift backhand, the man struck Jasiah across the face, sending him stumbling backward. Jasiah's flames flickered and died, his vision blurring as he struggled to regain his footing. But the masked man was relentless, his attacks coming in swift and merciless succession. With a cruel smile, he raised his hand, and a cosmic blast of energy erupted from his palm. The blast struck Jasiah with incredible force, launching him across the temple and slamming him into the wall.

The impact was tremendous, the sound of Jasiah's body crashing into the stone echoing through the temple like a thunderclap. The wall cracked and crumbled, the stone shattering under the force of the blast.

Jasiah's body slid to the ground, his vision blurring as he struggled to breathe. The masked man stood over him, his eyes blazing with a fierce and malevolent intensity.

Just as the masked man was about to deliver the finishing blow, Jasiah quickly rolled out of the way, avoiding the attack by a hair's breadth. He jumped back to his feet, creating distance between himself and his opponent.

With a fierce cry, Jasiah summoned a small blast of flames, directing it at the masked man. But the barrier around him simply absorbed the attack, the flames flickering and dying as they hit the shimmering field.

The masked man teleported behind Jasiah, his movements swift and silent. He grabbed Jasiah by the throat, his grip like a vice. "Your flames are weak," he spat, his eyes blazing with contempt. "You're not putting anger or resentment or hatred into them. That's what's going to get you killed." The man's grip tightened, choking Jasiah as he threw him to the ground. Jasiah's vision began to blur as the man punched him in the face multiple times, the blows raining down like a torrent of fury. "And that's WHAT'S GOING TO GET YOU KILLED!" the man shouted, his voice echoing through the temple like a thunderclap. With a cruel smile, the man raised his hand, and a cosmic blast of energy erupted from his palm.

The blast struck Jasiah in the face and chest, sending him flying backward as the temple walls shook and trembled around him.

The masked man's fist connected with Jasiah's face once, twice, three times, the blows landing with precision and power. Jasiah's head snapped back with each impact, his eyes glazing over as the man's rage intensified.

The man's knuckles cracked against Jasiah's cheekbone, the sound echoing through the temple like a gunshot. Jasiah's face contorted in agony as the man's blows rained down, each one landing with pinpoint accuracy. The man's fist smashed into Jasiah's nose, sending a geyser of blood erupting from his nostrils.

Jasiah's eyes watered as he struggled to defend himself, but the man was relentless, his blows coming in swift and merciless succession. The masked man's foot snapped out, catching Jasiah in the stomach with a vicious kick. Jasiah's body doubled over, his breath expelled from his lungs in a painful whoosh.

The man's hand grasped Jasiah's hair, yanking him back up to his feet. Jasiah's eyes blurred as the man's fist connected with his face once more, the blow sending him stumbling backward. The cosmic blast of energy struck Jasiah with incredible force, sending him flying backward as the temple walls shook and trembled around him.

Jasiah's body crashed to the ground, his vision fading to black as the masked man stood over him, his eyes blazing with a fierce and malevolent intensity.

The man's boot came down, striking Jasiah's chest with a sickening crunch. Jasiah's body arched backward, his vision blurring as the man's boot came down again, and again, and again. The masked man's fist came down again, striking Jasiah's face with a vicious crunch.

Jasiah's head snapped back, his eyes glazing over as the man's blows rained down upon him. But Jasiah refused to give up. With a surge of adrenaline, he reached up and caught the man's fist, his grip like a vice. The man's eyes widened in surprise as Jasiah glared at him, a look of pure fury burning in his eyes. It was a look that the man had seen before, a look that he thought he'd never see again. Jasiah's anger was palpable, his eyes blazing with a fierce intensity that seemed to burn hotter than the flames that danced across his skin. The man's smile faltered, his eyes widening in surprise as Jasiah's hand began to heat up.

The air around them seemed to shimmer and distort, the flames erupting from Jasiah's palm with a ferocity that sent the man stumbling backward. The blast of flames was stronger than any of Jasiah's previous blows, the flames roaring to life with a deafening crash. The masked man stumbled backward, his eyes wide with shock and fear as

Jasiah advanced on him, his flames burning brighter and

hotter than ever before.

The temple walls seemed to shake and tremble around them, the air thick with the scent of smoke and ozone. Jasiah's eyes blazed with a fierce and malevolent intensity, his flames dancing across his skin like living tendrils of fire. The masked man raised his hands, summoning a barrier of shimmering energy to protect himself from Jasiah's flames. But Jasiah was undeterred, his flames burning hotter and brighter as he advanced on the man. Jasiah's flames burned with an unprecedented ferocity, the blaze engulfing the air around him like a living entity. The temple walls shook and trembled, the stones cracking and crumbling under the intense heat. The masked man stumbled backward, his eyes wide with shock and fear as Jasiah advanced on him.

The flames danced across Jasiah's skin, casting flickering shadows on the walls as he raised his hands to unleash another blast of fire. The flames erupted from Jasiah's palms, a torrent of blazing energy that threatened to consume the masked man whole.

But the man refused to back down, his eyes flashing with a fierce determination as he raised his hands to defend himself. "I think I've had enough of this!" the man snarled, his voice dripping with malice. With a swift movement, he summoned a Spiritual Slash, a tear in space-time opening up behind him like a gaping wound. A distorted wave of energy erupted from the slash, hurtling towards Jasiah with incredible force. The wave was aimed squarely at Jasiah's left side, the man's intent clear: to sever Jasiah's face in two pieces.

But Jasiah was no ordinary fighter.

With a swift movement, he dodged to the side, his head narrowly avoiding the deadly slash. The wave of energy struck his white dreadlocks instead, the hair severed cleanly as if by a razor-sharp blade. Jasiah's dreadlocks fell to the ground, the severed strands lying limp and lifeless on the stone floor.

Jasiah's eyes flashed with anger and pain as he raised a hand to his head, feeling the sudden absence of his iconic locks. Jasiah's eyes blazed with fury, his flames burning hotter and brighter than ever before. He raised his hands, summoning a blast of fire that threatened to incinerate the masked man whole.

The man was too cunning, too quick. With a sudden flash of movement, he teleported behind Jasiah, his foot cocked back for a vicious kick. Jasiah, however, was not caught off guard. He could feel the man's energy, could sense his movements before they even happened.

With a swift gesture, Jasiah tapped into Aerthys' power, channeling the ancient energy into his own body. In an instant, Jasiah was behind the masked man, his foot flashing out in a flame-wreathed kick that sent the man flying backward.

The man crashed to the ground, his eyes wide with shock and pain as he struggled to catch his breath. "That's enough," the man snarled, his eyes flashing with anger as he raised his hands to summon another attack. But before he could do anything, a figure emerged from the shadows, their movements swift and silent. A booted foot flashed out, striking the man in the neck with incredible force. The man's eyes went wide, his body crumpling to the ground as the figure stood over him, their face hidden behind a mask of shadows.

Jasiah's eyes narrowed, his flames burning brighter as he

gazed upon the mysterious figure. "Who are you?" Jasiah demanded, his voice low and menacing.

The figure turned to Jasiah, their black hair Messy and spiky, their creamy cocoa skin tone a stark contrast to the platinum piercing of their eyes.

Those eyes seemed to shoot daggers into Jasiah's soul, their intensity unnerving. "The question is, who are you?" the figure asked, their voice low and husky, their grip on the masked man's shoulder tightening. Jasiah's confusion was evident on his face, his flames burning brighter as he struggled to comprehend the situation. "Jasiah... Jasiah Adolescence," he spoke, his voice laced with uncertainty. The figure nodded, their piercing eyes never leaving Jasiah's face. "Call me Darius," they said, their voice dripping with an air of nonchalance. Darius's gaze flickered to Jasiah's hair, his eyes narrowing as he noticed the severe asymmetry of Jasiah's locks. "Damn, who the fuck was your barber? They messed you up for real," Darius said, his tone semi-joking, but Jasiah's scoffing response was immediate.

"That masked man did it," Jasiah said, his anger and frustration evident in his voice. Darius stood by Jasiah's side, his eyes flashing with a fierce determination. "Alright, then we gotta get him back for it then," Darius said, his voice low and menacing. The masked man, still restrained by Darius, grinned up at them, his eyes gleaming with a manic intensity. "Ahh, finally, the wind wielder, you're finally here!" he exclaimed, his voice dripping with excitement. Darius's expression darkened, his eyes flashing with irritation.

"Yeah, and I'm not gonna let you get away with killing my brother," he growled, his voice low and deadly. The air was thick with tension, the flames burning brighter as Jasiah and

Darius stood united against the masked man, their determination to exact revenge palpable... The atmosphere was electric, the tension between Darius, Jasiah, and the masked man crackling with anticipation. With a sudden burst of energy, Darius and Jasiah charged at the masked man, their movements fluid and synchronized.

The masked man, however, was no pushover. With a flick of his wrist, he summoned an Aurora Barrier, a shimmering shield of light that deflected Darius's initial blow. The barrier glowed with an ethereal intensity, its presence both mesmerizing and intimidating. Undeterred, Jasiah unleashed a blast of flames, the inferno erupting from his palms with incredible force.

   The masked man raised his hands, and the Aurora Barrier flared to life, absorbing the flames and neutralizing their impact. Darius, meanwhile, had been observing the masked man's tactics, his eyes narrowing as he analyzed the man's defenses. With a sudden burst of speed, Darius darted to the side, his movements a blur as he conjured a whirlwind of air. The whirlwind erupted with incredible force, its winds howling like a banshee as it struck the masked man with incredible ferocity. The Aurora Barrier wavered, its light flickering as it struggled to absorb the sheer power of Darius's attack.The atmosphere was electric, the tension between Darius, Jasiah, and the masked man crackling with anticipation.

With a sudden burst of energy, Darius and Jasiah charged at the masked man, their movements fluid and synchronized. The masked man, however, was no pushover. With a flick of his wrist, he summoned an Aurora Barrier, a shimmering

shield of light that deflected Darius's initial blow. The barrier glowed with an ethereal intensity, its presence both mesmerizing and intimidating.
Undeterred, Jasiah unleashed a blast of flames, the inferno erupting from his palms with incredible force. The masked man raised his hands, and the Aurora Barrier flared to life, absorbing the flames and neutralizing their impact.
Darius, meanwhile, had been observing the masked man's tactics, his eyes narrowing as he analyzed the man's defenses. With a sudden burst of speed, Darius darted to the side, his movements a blur as he conjured a whirlwind of air.
The whirlwind erupted with incredible force, its winds howling like a banshee as it struck the masked man with incredible ferocity.

   The Aurora Barrier wavered, its light flickering as it struggled to absorb the sheer power of Darius's attack. The masked man, however, was far from defeated. With a sudden burst of energy, he unleashed a Cosmic Blast, a blindingly bright beam of energy that hurtled towards Darius and Jasiah with incredible speed. The two boys dodged the attack with ease, their movements swift and fluid as they avoided the blast. Jasiah, however, was not one to hesitate. With a fierce cry, he unleashed another blast of flames, the inferno erupting from his palms with incredible force. But Darius was not impressed.
He gazed at Jasiah's flames with a critical eye, his expression skeptical. "You call that a blast?" he muttered, shaking his head. Jasiah's eyes narrowed, his confusion evident on his face. "Huh?" he asked, his voice laced with uncertainty. Darius didn't bother to respond. Instead, he raised his hands, and a burst of wind erupted from his palms, swirling around

Jasiah's flames.

The fire danced and flickered, its intensity increasing as Darius's wind infused it with new life. Jasiah's eyes widened as he realized what Darius had done. His flames were now faster, stronger, and more potent than ever before. "Now!" Darius shouted, his voice echoing through the temple. "Use your flames now!" The masked man, still reeling from Darius's earlier attack, gazed up at them with blurred vision. His eyes were unfocused, his movements slow and labored.

Jasiah didn't hesitate. With a fierce cry, he unleashed his strengthened flames, the inferno erupting from his palms with incredible force.

The masked man stumbled backward, his eyes wide with shock as he struggled to defend himself against the onslaught. But the man was not one to give up easily. With a sudden burst of energy, he unleashed a blast of Cosmic abilities, the powers of the universe coursing through his veins like a raging tempest...

CHAPTER 15
TERRAKA SCROLL RETRIEVED

The masked man's blast of Cosmic abilities was like a tidal wave of energy, crashing down on Jasiah and Darius with incredible force. The air was filled with the sound of crackling energy, the temple walls shaking and trembling as the three combatants clashed. Jasiah's flames, strengthened by Darius's wind, danced and flickered with incredible ferocity, but they were no match for the masked man's Cosmic powers.

The man's blast was like a vortex of destruction, pulling everything towards it with an unstoppable force. Darius, however, was not about to let Jasiah take the fall. With a fierce cry, he leapt forward, his wind swirling around him like a protective shield. He raised his hands, and a maelstrom of air erupted from his palms, striking the masked man with incredible force.

The man stumbled backward, his eyes wide with shock as Darius's wind ripped into him like a hurricane. The air was filled with the sound of shattering stone, the temple walls cracking and crumbling as Darius's attack ripped through the masked man's defenses.

Jasiah, taking advantage of the distraction, unleashed another blast of flames, the inferno erupting from his palms with incredible force. The masked man, battered and bruised, stumbled backward, his eyes flashing with pain as the flames engulfed him. But the man refused to fall.

With a snarl of rage, he summoned a blast of Cosmic energy, striking Darius with incredible force. The wind wielder stumbled backward, his eyes flashing with pain as the energy ripped into him. Undeterred, Darius launched himself forward, his wind swirling around him like a vortex of destruction. He struck the masked man with incredible force, their battle raging on with unrelenting intensity.

The blast of Cosmic energy struck Darius with incredible force, his eyes flashing with pain as the power ripped into him. But the wind wielder refused to fall, his determination and rage fueling his movements.

With a snarl of anger, Darius launched himself forward, his wind swirling around him like a vortex of destruction. He struck the masked man with incredible force, their battle raging on with unrelenting intensity. The masked man stumbled backward, his eyes flashing with pain as Darius's wind ripped into him.

The man's anger was growing, his face twisted with rage as he gazed at the two boys. "Tch, annoying little brats!" he spat, his voice venomous. With a sudden gesture, the masked man summoned fifty Skull Wolves, the creatures erupting from the shadows like a horde of demonic beasts. Their eyes glowed with an eerie red light, their jaws snapping with hunger as they surrounded Jasiah and Darius.

The masked man seized the opportunity to escape, his movements swift and silent as he vanished into the shadows. Jasiah's eyes widened in alarm as he gazed at the Skull Wolves, their numbers overwhelming. But Darius was not concerned. He gazed at the creatures with a calculating eye, his wind swirling around him like a vortex of power. With a sudden burst of speed, he launched himself forward, his wind striking the Skull Wolves with incredible force.

The creatures stumbled backward, their eyes flashing with pain as Darius's wind ripped into them.

But they refused to fall, their numbers too great as they continued to press the attack. Jasiah's flames danced and flickered, his movements swift and fluid as he struck at the Skull Wolves. But despite his best efforts, the creatures seemed to be everywhere, their numbers too great as they surrounded him.

Darius, however, was partially toying with the Skull Wolves. He struck them with precision and power, his wind ripping into them with incredible force. But he was holding back, his movements calculated as he assessed the creatures' strength. The Skull Wolves continued to press the attack, their numbers seemingly endless as they surrounded Jasiah. The young fire wielder struck back with determination, his flames dancing and flickering as he unleashed blast after blast of fire. But despite his best efforts, the creatures seemed to be everywhere, their jaws snapping with hunger as they closed in on Jasiah.

    The air was thick with the scent of smoke and sweat, Jasiah's movements growing more desperate as the Skull Wolves closed in. Darius, however, was a different story altogether.

He struck the Skull Wolves with precision and power, his wind ripping into them with incredible force. But he was holding back, his movements calculated as he assessed the creatures' strength. The wind wielder's eyes gleamed with a fierce intensity, his focus solely on the battle at hand.

He didn't seem to care that the Skull Wolves were gaining the upper hand, his expression almost...amused. Jasiah, on the other hand, was starting to feel the strain. His flames, once so fierce and powerful, were now mere sparks, flickering weakly from his hands.

His lack of training was catching up to him, his fire wielding skills rusty from disuse. "No...no...no..." Jasiah muttered, his eyes wide with desperation as he struggled to summon more flames. But it was no use, his body too exhausted to respond. "Damnit!" Jasiah exclaimed, his voice cracking with frustration. He stumbled backward, his eyes scanning the battlefield for an escape route.

But there was none, the Skull Wolves closing in on him like a vice. Darius, however, seemed oblivious to Jasiah's plight, his focus solely on the battle at hand. The wind wielder's wind howled and whipped, striking the Skull Wolves with incredible force. But even Darius's power seemed limited, the creatures' numbers too great as they continued to press the attack.

Just when all hope seemed lost for Jasiah, a medium-sized boulder seemingly came out of nowhere, hurtling towards the Skull Wolves with incredible force. The rock crushed twenty-five of the creatures, their bodies splintering beneath its weight.

Before the remaining Skull Wolves could recover, a blast of water struck seven of them, sending them tumbling to the ground. Jasiah's eyes lit up as he saw where the attack had come from, his face breaking into a wide smile. "You guys!" Jasiah exclaimed happily, his eyes shining with relief.

But before any further reunions could take place, Michael's gaze fell upon Jasiah's appearance, and his eyes widened in shock. "Nah bro, what happened to your hair? You're practically half bald now!" Michael burst out laughing, his voice echoing through the temple.

Neveah shot Michael an unamused look, her eyes flashing with annoyance. Darius, meanwhile, looked confused, his gaze flicking between Michael and Neveah. "Who are these people?" Darius asked, his voice laced with curiosity. "My friends," Jasiah replied, his smile faltering as he gazed at his friends. But before any further introductions could be made, the Skull Wolves began to stir, their bodies reforming as they prepared to attack once more. Jasiah's eyes fell, his exhaustion evident as he realized he couldn't fight anymore. His overuse of flames had left him drained, his body weak and trembling.

Michael and Neveah stepped forward, their eyes determined as they prepared to defend their friend. Michael summoned a blast of water, the liquid rushing forth with a weak but determined force.

Neveah, meanwhile, called upon the earth, the ground trembling as she summoned a small tremor.

But it was clear that neither Michael nor Neveah was a trained Ninja, their Elements weak and unpracticed. Darius, on the other hand, was a different story altogether. His wind howled and whipped, striking the Skull Wolves with incredible force as he prepared to take on the remaining creatures alone...

The small tremor Neveah summoned was barely enough to make the Skull Wolves stumble, their bodies quickly recovering as they continued to press the attack. Michael's water blast was equally ineffective, the liquid splashing harmlessly against the creatures' fur as they advanced.

Darius, on the other hand, was a force to be reckoned with. His wind howled and whipped, striking the Skull Wolves with incredible force as he prepared to take on the remaining creatures alone. The wind wielder's eyes gleamed with a fierce intensity, his movements swift and deadly as he struck at the Skull Wolves.

Despite Darius's best efforts, the Skull Wolves refused to back down. They seemed to be driven by a singular purpose, their hunger for destruction and chaos fueling their movements as they continued to attack.

The battle raged on, the four friends fighting for their lives against the relentless Skull Wolves. The air was thick with tension, the sound of snarling and growling filling the air as the creatures closed in. Jasiah's eyes were wide with fear, his body trembling with exhaustion as he struggled to stay upright. Michael and Neveah fought valiantly, their elements weak but determined as they struck at the Skull Wolves.

But it was clear that they were no match for the creatures. The Skull Wolves were too strong, too fast, and too relentless. They seemed to be drawn to Jasiah, their eyes fixed on the young fire wielder as they closed in for the kill. Darius's wind howled and whipped, striking the Skull Wolves with incredible force. Even the wind wielder's power seemed limited, the creatures' numbers too great as they continued to press the attack. The four friends were surrounded, their backs against the wall as the Skull Wolves prepared to strike the final blow.

The air was thick with tension, the sound of snarling and growling filling the air as the creatures closed in...

As the Skull Wolves closed in, the temple began to crumble, the ancient stones groaning and shifting beneath their feet.

The air was thick with tension, the sound of snarling and growling filling the air as the creatures prepared to strike the final blow. "Guys, we gotta get out of here!" Neveah shouted, sprinting towards the exit of the temple. But as she reached the cavern connected to it, she realized that it too was crumbling, the rocks and debris tumbling down around them.

Michael followed close behind, his eyes scanning the cavern frantically as he searched for an exit. "Jasiah and wind guy, let's go!" he yelled, not waiting for a response as he kept running.

Darius followed, his wind whipping around him as he ran. Jasiah stayed back, his eyes fixed on the scroll the man had dropped after summoning the Skull Wolves. "Jasiah, what the hell are you doing?!" Darius shouted, noticing that Jasiah wasn't running. "I gotta get the scroll!" Jasiah exclaimed, before quickly grabbing the parchment and sprinting out of the temple into the cavern.

The group ran in a zigzag line, dodging falling rocks and debris as they desperately sought an exit. The cavern was dark and foreboding, the air thick with the smell of dust and decay. "I know where an exit is, follow me!" Darius exclaimed, before running to the left. The group looked confused, but followed anyway, their hearts pounding in their chests.

As they ran, the cavern walls seemed to close in around them, the rocks and debris tumbling down in a deadly cascade.

Darius led the way, his wind blowing back the dust and debris as he searched for a way out. But as they turned a corner, Darius's face fell, his eyes widening in shock. The exit of the cavern was closed off by boulders, the rocks piled high and impenetrable. "No...no...no..." Darius muttered, his eyes scanning the area frantically as he searched for another way out. But it was too late, the cavern was collapsing around them, the rocks and debris tumbling down in a deadly avalanche...

The group was trapped, their only hope of escape dwindling with every passing second.

The Skull Wolves were closing in, their snarls and growls growing louder as they sensed their prey was cornered. Trapped, their only hope of escape dwindling with every passing second. The Skull Wolves were closing in, their snarls and growls growing louder as they sensed their prey was cornered.

Neveah seemed to panic, her eyes darting back and forth as she searched for a way out. But then, suddenly, her eyes gleamed a bright green color, and a green flash illuminated the cavern. The group was enveloped in a blinding light, and when the light faded, they found themselves standing in the forest they had been in before falling into the cavern. "Hey... how did we get here?" Jasiah asked, looking around in confusion. "Good question," Michael replied, shrugging his shoulders.

Darius shook his head, a wry smile on his face. "Well, obviously, genius, the girl did," he said, pointing at Neveah. "I did?" Neveah asked, looking equally confused. "People with earth energy can teleport?" Jasiah and Michael said in unison, their eyes wide with surprise. Darius's facepalmed. "Are you two dumb? Yes, they can," he said, exasperated. Michael rolled his eyes.

"Whatever, pretty boy," he said, before turning and seeing the Monastery on the mountain. "Hey! We're almost back! It's time to finally get back from the mission Mr. Kamar sent us on!" Michael exclaimed, sprinting towards the mountain. "From today and so on, I hate CAVES!!" Michael shouted as he ran, his voice echoing through the forest. Darius looked confused. "Who's Mr. Kamar?" he asked. "That's our teacher," Neveah said, walking after Michael and Jasiah. "Oh, that makes sense," Darius said, following behind them.

Jasiah also ran after Michael. "Wait up!!" he said, running after his friend. "Nah, idiot!" Michael yelled out, not slowing down. Darius asked Neveah, "Are they always like this?" Neveah sighed, shaking her head. "You mean stupid and retarded? Yes."Darius raised an eyebrow, but followed after them, even though he had mostly been working alone.
He supposed that having some company wouldn't hurt, especially after that harrowing adventure.
As the group began their ascent up the stairs of the mountain, Michael was practically sprinting, his hunger and exhaustion propelling him forward.
He couldn't wait to get something to eat after what felt like an eternity without a single morsel. "Geez, slow down!" Jasiah exclaimed, struggling to keep up with Michael's breakneck pace. "You can't beat me, I'm gonna be first!" Michael proclaimed, a competitive glint in his eye. Jasiah's eyes narrowed, his face set in determination.

"Wanna bet on that?!" he argued, picking up speed as he chased after Michael. Neveah and Darius followed at a more leisurely pace, watching the two friends with amusement. Darius chuckled to himself , shaking her head at the antics of the new boys. "I've never seen anyone as hungry as Michael," he said, turning to Neveah with a smile.
Neevah raised an eyebrow, his eyes fixed on the two friends as they continued to race up the mountain. " And I've never

seen anyone as competitive as Jasiah," he continued with a dry tone in his voice. As they climbed higher, the air grew thinner and the stairs steeper, but Michael and Jasiah showed no signs of slowing down. They were like two bulls, charging up the mountain with reckless abandon, their hunger and exhaustion fueling their determination.

Finally, after what seemed like an eternity, they reached the top of the mountain, the Monastery's imposing structure looming before them. Michael and Jasiah burst through the doors, panting and gasping for air, their faces flushed with exertion.

Neveah and Darius followed more sedately, their faces calm and composed. As they entered the Monastery, they were greeted by the familiar sight of Mr. Kamar, his wise eyes watching them from across the room.

Mr. Kamar smiled, his eyes twinkling with amusement.

"Ah, I see you three returned," he said, his voice trailing off as he gazed at Darius, who stood taller than the trio. "And you are?" Kamar asked, his curiosity piqued. "The wielder of wind, Darius Breeze, at your service," Darius replied in a calm tone, his eyes meeting Kamar's. "He helped us on the mission!" Jasiah exclaimed, his enthusiasm barely contained. "There was a man in a mask and robe, and he completely wiped the floor with me in the temple! And he used some type of slash on me, but I dodged it, and now..." Jasiah's words were cut off by Michael, who chimed in with a mischievous grin. "And now you're half bald!" Michael teased, chuckling at his friend's expense.

Jasiah's face reddened, and he shot Michael a withering glance. "Shut up!" he growled, his embarrassment evident.

Kamar chuckled, his eyes crinkling at the corners. "Ah, I see you've already gotten into a fight with one of the members of the Kahos Kollectivite," he said, noticing the scroll in Jasiah's hand. "Oh, you got the scroll?" Jasiah nodded, handing the parchment to Kamar. "Oh, yeah!" he said, his pride evident. Kamar's eyes scanned the scroll, his face serious. "Good! Now, there are a total of six more to retrieve," he said, his voice filled with a sense of purpose.

The group fell silent, their minds racing with the implications of Kamar's words. They knew that their mission was far from over, and that the road ahead would be fraught with danger and uncertainty.

They also knew that they were ready, ready to face whatever lay ahead, as long as they stood together. "So, what's the plan, Mr. Kamar?" Neveah asked, her eyes shining with determination. Kamar's smile was enigmatic. "Ah, my young friends, the plan is to retrieve the remaining scrolls, no matter the cost. We will need to be cunning, resourceful, and brave if we are to succeed."

Darius nodded, his eyes gleaming with excitement. "I'm in," he said, his voice was firm. Jasiah and Michael exchanged a look, their faces set in determination. "We're in, too," they said, their voices in unison.

Neveah smiled, her eyes shining with a sense of camaraderie. "Then let's get started," she said, her voice filled with a sense of purpose. The four friends made their way to the kitchen area, where they were greeted by the warm aroma of freshly baked bread and the cheerful chatter of Camillia.

As they entered, Camillia's eyes lit up, and she rushed towards Neveah, enveloping her in a tight hug.

"Oh my gosh! You're alive and okay!!" Camillia exclaimed,

her voice filled with relief. Michael rolled his eyes, a hint of annoyance in his tone. "We're alive too, you know?" he said, sighing. Camillia pulled back,
a sheepish grin on her face. "I know," she said, her eyes sparkling. "And we got a new member?" she asked, her gaze fixating on Darius. Darius waved slightly, a laid-back air about him. "Yo," he said, his voice casual. Camillia's eyes crinkled at the corners as she smiled. "Hmm, you're a pass," she said, her tone enigmatic. Jasiah's face screwed up in confusion, his brow furrowed. "Pass what does that even mean?" he asked, his innocence and naivety evident. Darius's face lost its usual calm, a hint of embarrassment flickering across his features. "Do you know the game smash or pass?" he asked, his tone hesitant.

Jasiah's eyes widened, a look of confusion still etched on his face. "Huh, yeah?" he asked, his voice uncertain. Darius's face flushed, and he cleared his throat. "She means that," he explained, his words awkward. Jasiah's eyes lit up, comprehension dawning on his face. "Ohh!!" he exclaimed, a laugh bursting forth. As the group chuckled, Michael spoke up, his voice laced with a hint of emotion. "Hey, Camilla, where's Haneul? We still have a score to settle." Camillia's face turned serious, her eyes clouding over.
"He's on a mission right now!" she said, her voice firm.
As they sat down to eat, Darius's mind began to wander, his thoughts drifting towards Jasiah's half-bald head. A mischievous grin spread across his face as he turned to Jasiah. "Know what, Jasiah?
Your half-bald head is hideous, so let's fix it," Darius said, his voice laced with amusement. Jasiah's eyes widened in protest, his hands instinctively reaching up to defend his hair. "Wait,

no! My half-dreads are fine," he protested, his voice rising in alarm. But Darius was too quick, and before Jasiah could react, he was lifted off the ground by the back of his red ninja robe.

Camillia appeared beside them, a shaver and other hair-styling tools in her hands. "I'll get the materials," she said, her eyes sparkling with amusement. Jasiah tried to wriggle free, but Camillia was prepared. With a quick flick of her wrist, she summoned her plant elemental, which wrapped its vines around Jasiah, restraining him. "ASSAULT!" Jasiah protested jokingly, his laughter echoing through the kitchen. Darius chuckled, his hands deftly taking out the right side of Jasiah's dreads.

He then shaved the right side of Jasiah's hair, the sound of the razor humming through the air. Michael and Neveah watched with humor, their eyes fixed on the spectacle unfolding before them.

Finally, Darius stepped back, a flourish of his hand signaling the end of his masterpiece.

Jasiah's hair was now styled in a mid-fade, slightly messy and with small little bangs that looked a bit spiky. "Anddddd done!" Darius exclaimed, his grin triumphant. Jasiah's eyes widened as he took in his new look, his face momentarily stunned.

Then, a slow smile spread across his face, and he burst out laughing.

"Damn, Darius, you're a genius!" Jasiah exclaimed, his laughter echoing through the kitchen. As Jasiah laughed, his whole body shook, his eyes sparkling with mirth. Michael and Neveah joined in, their own laughter echoing through the kitchen, creating a symphony of joy and camaraderie.

Camillia smiled, her eyes crinkling at the corners, as she watched the group's antics. The kitchen was filled with the warm scent of freshly baked bread and the sound of clinking utensils, but it was the group's laughter that brought the space to life.

For a moment, they forgot about their mission, their battles, and their worries. They forgot about the weight of their responsibilities and the danger that lurked around every corner. In that moment, they were just a group of friends, enjoying each other's company, and reveling in the simple joy of being together.

The kitchen was transformed into a haven, a sanctuary where they could be themselves, without fear of judgment or rejection. As they laughed, the tension and stress of their journey began to melt away, replaced by a sense of warmth and belonging. They knew that they could face whatever challenges lay ahead, as long as they stood together.

Finally, their laughter began to subside, leaving behind a warm glow of happiness. Jasiah wiped tears from his eyes, his face still flushed with laughter. "Thanks, Darius," Jasiah said, his voice still shaking with mirth. "I think I needed that." Darius grinned, his eyes sparkling with pride.

"Anytime, bro," he said, clapping Jasiah on the back. Michael and Neveah nodded in agreement, their faces still flushed with laughter. Camillia smiled, her eyes shining with a sense of contentment.

As they settled back into their seats, the group knew that they were ready to face whatever lay ahead. They were ready to take on the challenges of their mission, armed with the knowledge that they had each other's backs.

CHAPTER 16
START OF AN RIVALRY

As they finished their meal, Michael's eyes sparkled with mischief as he gazed at Jasiah. "Hey, Jah, now that we know how to use our elemental powers, let's spar! Unless you're too scared, of course," Michael continued, a taunting glint in his eye.
Neveah and Camillia's faces fell, their expressions a picture of exasperation. "Why did I know this was gonna happen?" Neveah sighed, shaking her head. "Well, I'm gonna have to get used to them bickering," Darius said, a dry tone to his voice. "Oh, you don't even know the worst of it," Camilla said, rolling her eyes. But Jasiah just grinned, his eyes flashing with excitement. "Yeah, I'm gonna kick your ass for sure!" he exclaimed, cracking his knuckles in anticipation. Michael chuckled,
a confident smile spreading across his face. "We'll see about that, Jah." The two friends strode down to the dojo, their footsteps echoing through the halls. As they entered the spacious room, they stood on opposite sides, their eyes locked in a fierce stare. The air was electric with tension, the only sound the soft hum of the dojo's energy field.

The walls were lined with mirrors, reflecting the intense gaze of the two opponents.
Jasiah cracked his neck, his fingers flexing into fists. Michael smirked, his eyes glinting with amusement. The battle was about to begin, and the group knew that only one person

would emerge victorious. The question was, who would it be? Camillia, Neveah, and Darius watched from the sidelines, their faces tense with anticipation. They knew that this sparring match would be intense, and that only the strongest would prevail.

The air was electric with tension as Michael and Jasiah faced off, their eyes locked in a fierce stare. They began to circle each other, their footsteps silent on the dojo's mats.

Without warning, they charged at each other, their fists flying in a flurry of punches and kicks. The hand-to-hand combat was intense, with both opponents exchanging blows and counterattacks. Michael's movements were fluid and precise, Jasiah, on the other hand, relied on his raw strength and agility to hold his own.

As they fought, the dojo seemed to shrink, the walls closing in on the two combatants. The sound of their breathing, the thud of their footsteps, and the crack of their punches filled the air. Suddenly,

   Michael jumped back, creating distance between himself and Jasiah. His eyes gleamed with a mischievous spark as he raised his hand, and a stream of water burst forth from his palm.

The water jetted across the room, a crystal-clear arc that threatened to engulf Jasiah.

Jasiah leapt to the side, dodging the water with ease. But he didn't stay defensive for long. With a swift gesture, he summoned a blast of fire from his fingertips.

   The flames roared to life, a fierce inferno that illuminated the dojo. Despite not having a lot of training with their elements, Michael and Jasiah were determined to push themselves to the limit. They may not have been experts, but they were eager to learn and adapt.

The water and fire clashed in mid-air, a spectacular display of elemental power.

The sound of the collision was deafening, a crackling explosion that sent shockwaves through the dojo. The flames danced and spat, as if alive, while the water rippled and churned, its surface torn apart by the fire's fury. The air was filled with the acrid scent of smoke and ozone, a pungent smell that stung the eyes.

The sound of the collision echoed through the dojo, a deafening crackle that seemed to shake the very foundations of the building. The flames and water continued to clash, their elemental fury unrelenting as they battled for dominance.

   Michael and Jasiah stood frozen, their eyes fixed on the spectacle before them. Their faces were set in determined grins, their bodies tensed and ready to respond to the other's next move. The air was thick with tension, the smell of smoke and ozone hanging heavy over the dojo.

The flames danced and spat, as if alive, their tongues of fire licking at the air. The water rippled and churned, its surface torn apart by the fire's fury, sending plumes of steam shooting upwards. The dojo's energy field hummed and crackled, struggling to contain the elemental power unleashed by the two friends. The walls seemed to vibrate with the force of the collision, the mirrors reflecting the intensity of the battle.

Michael's eyes narrowed, his focus fixed on Jasiah. He could see the fire burning in his friend's eyes, a fierce determination that would not be extinguished. Jasiah's face was set in a fierce snarl, his teeth bared in a savage grin.

Jasiah's flames surged forward, a wave of fire that threatened to engulf Michael. But Michael was ready, his own elemental power responding to the challenge. A wall of water erupted from his hands, crashing into the flames and sending them reeling back.

The battle raged on, the two friends exchanging blows and counterattacks in a frenzy of elemental power. The dojo shook and trembled, the air thick with the smell of smoke and ozone. Camillia, Neveah, and Darius watched from the sidelines, their faces tense with anxiety. They knew that the stakes were high, that the loser of this battle would be left weakened and vulnerable.

As the battle raged on, Michael's water energy began to gain the upper hand.

With each exchange of blows, he expertly manipulated his element to counter Jasiah's flames. He summoned wave after wave of cool, clear water, each one precision-targeted to extinguish Jasiah's fiery attacks. Jasiah, fueled by his determination to win, refused to back down. He unleashed a torrent of flames, each one more intense than the last, but Michael was relentless.

He countered each blast with a deluge of water, pouring all his energy into quenching the flames. The dojo's energy field hummed and crackled, struggling to contain the sheer force of the elemental battle. The air was thick with the smell of smoke and ozone, and the sound of crackling flames and rushing water filled the air.

Camillia, Neveah, and Darius watched in awe as Michael's strategy began to pay off. Jasiah's flames, once a raging inferno, began to falter, dwindling to mere embers as Michael's water energy continued to wash over them.

As Camillia, Neveah, and Darius watched, Jasiah's flames continued to dwindle, reduced to mere sparks as Michael's water energy washed over them. But Jasiah was far from defeated. He had a plan, and he was just waiting for the perfect moment to strike. That moment came when Michael, confident in his victory, let his guard down. Jasiah saw his chance and seized it, unleashing a blast of flame that seemed to come out of nowhere.

Michael, caught off guard, grinned as he countered with a wave of water, creating a smoke screen that obscured his vision. But as the smoke cleared, Michael's grin faltered. He looked around, confused, and that was when he realized Jasiah was no longer in front of him. He spun around, his eyes scanning the room, and that was when he saw Jasiah standing behind him, a triumphant grin spreading across his face.

"You're too slow!" Jasiah exclaimed, his eyes gleaming with mischief. Michael's eyes widened as he saw Jasiah's flame-encased fist hurtling towards him. He tried to dodge, but it was too late.

Jasiah's fist connected with a loud thud, sending Michael crashing to the ground. But Jasiah wasn't done yet. He followed up his punch with a swift kick, sending Michael flying across the room. Michael crashed into the wall, the wind knocked out of him, as Jasiah stood over him, his chest heaving with exertion. Michael struggled to his feet, his chest heaving with exertion, his eyes fixed on Jasiah with a fierce determination. He knew he had to turn the tables, and fast, if he wanted to get back in the game. Jasiah, still grinning with triumph, didn't notice the subtle change in Michael's stance. He didn't see the faint glimmer of water energy building up in Michael's hands. That was, until it was too late. With a swift motion, Michael conjured up a lasso of water, its tendrils whipping through the air with deadly precision.

Jasiah, caught off guard, didn't have time to react as Michael's water lasso snared his foot, pulling him off balance. In a flash, Michael yanked the lasso, sending Jasiah flying across the room.

Jasiah crashed into the wall, the impact sending shockwaves through the dojo's energy field. But Jasiah was far from defeated. As he hurtled through the air, he summoned up one final blast of flame, its intense heat illuminating the darkening room. The flame blast erupted just as Jasiah was about to hit the wall, its force propelling him forward like a human fireball. Michael, caught off guard, stumbled backward as Jasiah careened off the wall, his flames burning brighter than ever.

   The dojo was plunged into chaos, the air thick with the smell of smoke and ozone. Camillia, Neveah, and Darius watched in awe as the two friends clashed, their elemental powers locked in a struggle for supremacy. Michael, his eyes flashing with determination, summoned up a massive wave of water, its cresting foam threatening to engulf Jasiah's flames. But Jasiah was ready, his eyes burning with a fierce inner fire.

Michael, his eyes blazing with determination, raised his hands, and a massive wave of water erupted from his fingertips. The wave crashed down on Jasiah, its cresting foam threatening to engulf his flames.

But Jasiah was ready, his eyes burning with a fierce inner fire. With a swift motion, Jasiah summoned up a blast of flame, its intense heat illuminating the darkening room.

The flame clashed with Michael's water, the two elements locked in a struggle for supremacy. The dojo was plunged into a maelstrom of sound and fury, the air thick with the smell of smoke and ozone. The battle raged on, the two friends locked in a dance of death, their elemental powers raging out of control. Camillia, Neveah, and Darius watched in awe, their eyes wide with amazement as the two friends clashed. The water and fire clashed, the two elements locked in a fierce struggle.

The dojo's energy field hummed and crackled, the air thick with the smell of smoke and ozone. The sound of crackling flames and rushing water filled the air, the two friends locked in a battle to the death. But as the clash continued, it became clear that Michael was gaining the upper hand.

His water energy was too strong, too powerful, and Jasiah's flames were beginning to falter. The fire was dwindling, its flames dying out as Michael's water washed over them. Jasiah's eyes widened in shock as he realized he was losing. He summoned up one final blast of flame, its intense heat illuminating the darkening room. But Michael was ready, his eyes fixed on Jasiah with a fierce determination.

With a swift motion, Michael countered Jasiah's flame with a wave of water, its cresting foam engulfing the flames and snuffing them out. The dojo fell silent, the only sound the heavy breathing of the two combatants.

Michael stood tall, his chest heaving with exertion, his eyes fixed on Jasiah with a triumphant gaze. Jasiah, on the other hand, looked defeated, his flames extinguished, his energy spent. The dojo erupted into cheers as Michael was declared the winner of the battle.

Camillia, Neveah, and Darius rushed forward, congratulating Michael on his victory.

Jasiah, on the other hand, grinned, his eyes flashing with admiration for his friend. As the cheers died down, Camillia stepped forward, her eyes shining with a warm, nurturing light. She raised her hands, and a gentle, green glow began to emanate from her fingertips. The glow enveloped both Michael and Jasiah, bathing them in a soothing, healing energy. Michael's eyes fluttered closed, a look of relief washing over his face as Camillia's plant element began to repair the damage done to his body. Jasiah, too, closed his eyes, his chest rising and falling as he absorbed the healing energy.

The group watched in silence as Camillia worked her magic, her plant element weaving a delicate, intricate pattern of healing and restoration.

Slowly but surely, the wounds and bruises on Michael and Jasiah's bodies began to fade, replaced by a warm, healthy glow. Finally, Camillia lowered her hands, a soft smile on her face. "All better," she said, her voice gentle. Michael and Jasiah opened their eyes, looking at each other with a newfound sense of respect and admiration. They nodded to each other, a silent understanding passing between them.

The group began to disperse, each member making their way to their respective dorms. Camillia fell into step beside Darius, guiding him through the winding corridors of the monastery. "I'll show you where your dorm is," she said, her voice friendly. "You're still getting used to the layout, right?" Darius nodded, his eyes wide with gratitude. "Thanks, Camillia. I don't know what I'd do without you guys." Camillia smiled, her eyes shining with warmth. reached Darius's dorm, Camillia bid him goodnight, leaving him to settle in. She made her way back to her own dorm, her mind already turning to the next day's classes.

Meanwhile, Jasiah made his way to his own dorm, his mind still reeling from the battle. He flopped onto his bed, his eyes closing as he let out a deep sigh. For a moment, he just lay there, his body and mind recovering from the exertion of the battle. Then, slowly, he began to let his mind wander, his thoughts drifting into his own private world.

He started to think about the battle, about the strategies he could have used, about the ways he could have improved.

He thought about Michael, about the way his friend had outmaneuvered him. And then, he started to think about the next battle, about the ways he could come out on top. His eyes grew distant, his mind consumed by the thrill of competition, the rush of adrenaline that came with fighting alongside his friends.

As Jasiah's mind wandered, his thoughts grew more intense, his competitive spirit burning brighter with every passing moment. He couldn't help but think about the next battle, about the ways he could improve, about the strategies he could use to outmaneuver Michael. Finally, after what felt like an eternity of mental preparation, Jasiah sat up, his eyes snapping back into focus.

He swung his legs over the side of the bed, his feet thudding onto the floor as he stood up. With a determined stride, Jasiah walked over to his desk, his eyes fixed on the notebook and phone that lay waiting for him. He sat down, his movements economical and precise, as he began to prepare for his next move.

First, he opened his notebook, the blank pages staring back at him like an empty canvas. Jasiah's hand began to move, his pen scratching out notes and diagrams as he started to plan his next attack. But as he wrote, Jasiah's mind began to wander again, his thoughts straying back to the thrill of battle, to the rush of adrenaline that came with competing against his friends.

He needed inspiration, and he knew just where to find it. With a swift motion, Jasiah picked up his phone, his fingers flying across the screen as he searched for "cool fire attacks" on YouTube. The search results flashed up, a list of videos stretching out before him like a tantalizing promise. Jasiah's eyes scanned the list, his heart racing with excitement as he clicked on the first video.

The screen flickered to life, a montage of fiery attacks and blazing special moves flashing before his eyes. Jasiah watched, transfixed, as the videos played out before him. He saw fireballs and flames, blazing punches and kicks that ignited the air. He saw fire wielders, their powers blazing like miniature suns as they took on their opponents. As he watched, Jasiah's mind began to spin, his thoughts racing with ideas and strategies. He saw himself, his flames burning brighter than ever before, as he took on Michael and the others in the next battle.

The videos played on, Jasiah's eyes glued to the screen as he absorbed every detail, every trick and tactic. He was a sponge, soaking up knowledge and inspiration like a dry sponge absorbs water.

As the hours passed, Jasiah's eyes remained fixed on the screen, his mind drinking in every detail, every trick and tactic. He watched videos on fire manipulation, on flame propagation, on the art of wielding fire like a precision tool.

He saw fire dancers, their bodies weaving intricate patterns as they spun and leaped across the screen. He saw fire breathers, their mouths exhaling flames like miniature dragons. He saw fire wielders, their powers burning bright as they summoned blazing infernos from thin air. Jasiah's fingers flew across the keyboard, his searches taking him deeper and deeper into the world of fire energy.

He discovered tutorials on fire shaping, on crafting flames into precise, deadly forms. He found videos on fire augmentation, on amplifying his powers to new heights. As the night wore on, Jasiah's room grew darker, the only light coming from the glow of his phone. His eyes felt dry, his head throbbing with the intensity of his focus. But he couldn't stop, wouldn't stop, until he had absorbed every last detail.

He watched videos on fire projection, on casting flames across vast distances. He saw fire wielders summoning blazing shields, their flames protecting them from harm. He saw fire elementalists, their powers calling forth storms of flame and fury. Jasiah's mind reeled, his thoughts spinning with the sheer scope of what he was learning.

He felt his powers growing, his flames burning brighter and hotter with every passing moment. As the videos played on, Jasiah's fingers began to move, his hands weaving intricate patterns in the air. Flames danced at his fingertips, tiny sparks of fire that flickered and died.

But Jasiah knew that it was just the beginning, that with time and practice, he would master the art of fire energy.

The night wore on, the hours ticking away like seconds. Jasiah's eyes remained fixed on the screen, his mind drinking in every last detail. As the hours ticked away, Jasiah's focus never wavered, his eyes glued to the screen as he absorbed every last detail. His fingers continued to move, his hands weaving intricate patterns in the air as he practiced the techniques he was learning.

The flames at his fingertips grew stronger, the sparks of fire burning brighter and more steadily. Jasiah's mind hummed with excitement, his heart racing with anticipation.

The videos played on, Jasiah's eyes darting back and forth as he scanned the screen for every last detail.

He watched as fire wielders summoned blazing infernos, as they crafted flames into precise, deadly forms. He saw fire elementalists calling forth storms of flame and fury, their powers raging like untamed beasts. He saw fire dancers, their bodies weaving intricate patterns as they spun and leaped across the screen.

Jasiah's mind reeled, his thoughts spinning with the sheer scope of what he was learning. He felt his powers growing, his flames burning hotter and more steadily with every passing moment. And then, suddenly, Jasiah realized it was 1:34 AM. The clock on his phone glowed brightly, the numbers stark and unforgiving. Jasiah's eyes widened in surprise, his mind racing with the realization. He had been watching videos for hours, his focus so intense that he had lost all track of time. Jasiah's body ached, his eyes feeling dry and gritty from the prolonged exposure to the screen.

But even as he felt the fatigue creeping in, Jasiah knew he couldn't stop. He couldn't afford to, not when he was so close to mastering the art of fire energy.

With a deep breath, Jasiah settled back in, his eyes fixed on the screen as he continued to watch and learn. The night wore on, the hours ticking away The hours ticked away, the night wearing on as Jasiah continued to watch and learn.

His eyes felt heavy, his lids drooping as the fatigue crept in. But he refused to give in, his determination to master the art of fire energy driving him forward. As the minutes dragged on, Jasiah's body began to slump, his head nodding forward as his eyes grew heavier.

The screen blurred, the images melting together as his vision grew dim. Finally, after what felt like an eternity, Jasiah's eyes closed, his body surrendering to the exhaustion. He slumped forward, his head crashing onto the desk as he fell into a deep, dreamless sleep.

But as he slept, Jasiah's mind began to wander, his subconscious conjuring up a world of fire and flame. He found himself standing in a charcoaled place, the sky above him a deep, smoky orange. The air was thick with heat, the ground beneath his feet crackling with embers. Jasiah looked around, his eyes taking in the desolate landscape. And then, he saw her.

A girl made of flames, her body crafted from fiery tendrils that danced and swirled around her. She had long hair, Jasiah could see, and some type of armor that glowed like hot coals. But her face was indistinct, her features hidden behind a veil of flames. Jasiah tried to speak, but his voice was muffled, the flames blocking his words. The girl's voice, on the other hand, was soft and angelic, her words dripping with an otherworldly calm. "Do your best, ok?" she said, her hand reaching out to touch Jasiah's cheek. Jasiah's eyes widened, his heart racing with confusion. He tried to speak again, but the flames blocked his words, muffling his voice.

He reached out his hand, his fingers stretching towards the flame girl. But she drifted away, her body dissolving into the fiery landscape. Jasiah's voice was muffled, his words trapped behind the flames as he reached out again and again.

And then, as suddenly as it had begun, the dream was over. Jasiah's eyes snapped open, his body jerking upright as he sat back in his chair. The screen in front of him was dark, the room around him silent. Jasiah's heart was still racing, his mind reeling with the intensity of the dream.

CHAPTER 17
KHAOS KOLLECTIVITE

In a dimly lit chamber, a figure lay in a regeneration chamber, his body a mess of broken bones and torn flesh. His face was half-peeled off, revealing the muscle and bone beneath, and his right side of his chest was crushed, giving him an ugly, disfigured appearance. His;long black hair was disheveled, and his eyes burned with anger. "What do you mean!? You failed to capture the wind wielder Darius!? You failed to get the scroll and let a bunch of kids take it!?" the figure, Maledict, growled from his chamber. The masked man standing before him cowered, his eyes downcast.

"I'm sorry, Maledict," he apologized, his voice trembling. Maledict's response was immediate and fierce. "Sorry, doesn't cut it! How can you fail something so simple?!" he yelled from his chamber, his voice echoing off the walls. The masked man took a step back, his eyes fearful. "I-I didn't expect the kids to be so resourceful," he stuttered. Maledict's gaze narrowed, his eyes burning with fury. "You should have expected the unexpected," he spat. "You should have been prepared. Now, because of your failure, we've lost the scroll and Darius is still on the loose."

The masked man bowed his head, his shoulders slumped in defeat. "I'll do better next time, Maledict," he promised. disdain. "There won't be a next time," he said, his words cutting through the air like a knife. "You're finished. You're no longer part of the Kahos Kollective." The masked man's eyes widened in shock, his face pale with fear. He knew what it meant to be cast out of the Kollective.

He knew that he would be hunted, that his life would be forfeit. "You're...you're banishing me?" the masked man stuttered, his voice trembling with terror.

Maledict's gaze was unyielding, his eyes burning with a fierce intensity. "I'm not banishing you," he said, his voice dripping with malice. "I'm giving you a chance to redeem yourself. But if you fail again, there will be no mercy. Do you understand?" The masked man nodded, his head bobbing up and down like a puppet on a string.

"Y-yes, Maledict," he stammered. "I understand." Maledict's gaze narrowed, his eyes piercing through the masked man's very soul. "Good," he said, his voice dripping with satisfaction. "Then you know what you must do. Find Darius, retrieve the scroll, and bring it back to me. And don't fail again." The masked man nodded once more,

his eyes filled with a desperate determination. He knew that he had to succeed, no matter what the cost. He knew that his life depended on it. The masked man nodded once more, his eyes filled with a desperate determination. He knew that he had to succeed, no matter what the cost.

He knew that his life depended on it.

As he turned to leave, he stopped and looked back at Maledict. "Actually, sir, there's something you should know," he said, his voice hesitant. Maledict's gaze narrowed, his eyes piercing through the masked man's mask. "Oh, is there?" he spoke, his voice dripping with curiosity. The masked man nodded, his throat bobbing up and down.

"Yeah... one of the kids... I fought him, and I saw... he had fire... and during my fight with him... I've seen that look... it looked like... her..." The masked man's voice trailed off, his eyes fixed on Maledict's reaction.

Maledict's face was a mask of surprise, his eyes wide with excitement. "Oh, I see," Maledict exclaimed, his voice rising with enthusiasm. "Perfect! Just perfect! This generation just gets more and more beautiful every day!" The masked man's half-smirk seemed to amuse Maledict, who chuckled to himself. "Capture that boy too, then," Maledict continued, his eyes gleaming with excitement. "But not now. We'll hold off... we only have yet to see his potential... and I want to be the one to kill him once we get all seven scrolls.

I can be healed." Maledict's voice was rising with excitement, his words tumbling out in a rush. The masked man's eyes were fixed on Maledict's face, his expression unreadable. "Yes, sir," the masked man said, his voice flat. Maledict's gaze snapped back to the masked man, his eyes burning with intensity. "And don't fail again," he spoke, his voice dripping with menace. The masked man nodded, his eyes downcast. "I won't, sir," he said, his voice barely above a whisper.

As the masked man nodded and retreated, another member of the Kahos Kollective spoke up, his voice laced with skepticism. He was a tall, imposing figure, with coffee brown skin and piercing emerald eyes that seemed to bore into Maledict's very soul. A messy mullet framed his face, and a horizontal scar above his nose added a touch of ruggedness to his features.

He stood at around 6'3, and his early twenties physique was

accentuated by the plain white long-sleeve tee shirt with a black short sleeve shirt layered over it, complete with double pockets. His jogger jeans were a casual touch,
but his overall demeanor exuded an air of confidence and authority. "What's the point of trusting Nicholas with that mission if he's already failed once?" the man, Abyss, said bluntly to Maledict, his voice dripping with disdain. Maledict's gaze snapped towards Abyss, his eyes flashing with anger.
"Cause unlike you, he doesn't give mercy to people," he replied, his voice cold and calculating. "Don't question me, Abyss." Abyss snorted, rolling his eyes in disgust. "You can't really judge me on that," he said, his voice laced with sarcasm. "You're the one who's stuck in a recovering chamber for how long? Just so you can stay alive, old fuck." Maledict's face twisted with rage, his eyes blazing with fury. "Watch your tone, boy," he spat, his voice venomous. Abyss raised an eyebrow, unfazed by Maledict's outburst. "Or what?" he said, his voice dripping with defiance. "You'll try to kill me? Please, Maledict. You're not even in a position to threaten me right now."

 The tension between the two was palpable, the air thick with unspoken threats and veiled insults. The other members of the Kahos Kollective watched in silence, their faces expressionless as they waited to see how the confrontation would unfold.

 Maledict's anger seemed to dissipate as quickly as it had flared, his face smoothing out into a calculating mask. "No, Abyss," he said, his voice dripping with menace. "I'll let you live... for now. But don't think you're above me, boy. I'll watch you, and I'll wait. And when the time is right, I'll strike." Abyss smirked, unfazed by Maledict's threats. "I'm shaking in my boots, Maledict," he said, his voice dripping with sarcasm. But Abyss didn't stop there. He continued, his voice laced with contempt. "Honestly, you know what I think?" he said, his eyes fixed on Maledict's face. Maledict's eyes flashed with anger, his face twisting into a snarl. "Shut up," he snapped, his voice cutting through the air like a whip. But Abyss just continued, his voice unwavering.

"I think having to send other people to kidnap little kids who happen to have elemental powers for your own thing is kinda weird and pathetic and downright sad," he said bluntly, his words hanging in the air like a challenge.

The room fell silent, the tension between the two men crackling with electricity. Maledict's face was red with rage, his eyes blazing with fury. Abyss, on the other hand, seemed completely unphased, his expression calm and collected. The other members of the Kahos Kollective watched in silence, their faces expressionless as they waited to see how the confrontation would unfold. The air was thick with tension, the atmosphere heavy with unspoken threats and veiled insults. Maledict's chest was heaving with anger, his breathing rapid and shallow.

His eyes were fixed on Abyss, his gaze burning with intensity. "You know, Abyss," he said, his voice dripping with venom. "You're really pushing your luck." Abyss raised an eyebrow, his expression skeptical. "Oh, am I?" he said, his voice laced with sarcasm.

Maledict's eyes narrowed, his face twisted into a snarl. "You think you're so clever, don't you?" he said, his voice dripping with malice. "You think you can just mouth off to me and get away with it?" Abyss shrugged, his expression nonchalant.

"I'm just telling the truth," he said, his voice unwavering. "You're the one who's getting worked up over it."
The tension between the two men was palpable, the air thick with unspoken threats and veiled insults.
unspoken threats and veiled insults. The silence that followed was oppressive, weighing heavily on the shoulders of the other members of the Kahos Kollective.

Abyss wasn't finished yet. He spoke up again, his voice laced with a hint of menace. "And I hope you're well aware, I could just break your little healing chamber, which will kill you instantly," he said, his smirk growing wider. Maledict's face turned white with rage, his eyes blazing with fury. "You wouldn't dare," he spat, his voice trembling with anger. Abyss shrugged, his expression nonchalant. "Oh, I wouldn't?" he said, his voice dripping with sarcasm. "You're the one who's been playing games with people's lives, Maledict. I'm just calling your bluff." The room was silent, the only sound the heavy breathing of the members of the Kahos Kollective.

Maledict's eyes were fixed on Abyss, his gaze burning with intensity. The air was thick with tension, the atmosphere heavy with unspoken threats and veiled insults. "What's stopping me, huh?" Abyss continued, his voice rising in challenge. "You think you're above the law, Maledict? You think you're above death itself?" Maledict's face twisted into a snarl, his eyes flashing with anger. "You're just trying to distract me, Abyss," he said, his voice dripping with venom . "You're just trying to take attention away from your own failures." Abyss laughed, a cold, mirthless sound. "Failures?" he repeated, his voice laced with scorn. "You're the one who's been failing, You're the one who's been playing with fire and getting burned."

Maledict's face turned red with rage, his eyes blazing with fury. He took a step forward, his fists clenched at his sides. "How dare you," he spat, his voice trembling with anger. Abyss turned, shooting Maledict a last, scathing glare.
For a moment, the two men locked eyes, their hatred and contempt for each other palpable. Then, Abyss turned and walked out of the meeting room, leaving Maledict seething with rage. The other members of the Kahos Kollective watched in silence as Abyss departed, their faces expressionless.
The tension in the room was still thick, the atmosphere heavy with unspoken threats and veiled insults. Maledict's chest was heaving with anger, his breathing rapid and shallow.

He turned to the remaining members of the Kahos Kollective, his eyes blazing with fury. "You all saw that," he spat, his voice dripping with venom. "You all saw how Abyss disrespected me." The members of the Kahos Kollective nodded in silence, their faces still expressionless. But Maledict's anger was not assuaged. He turned to the masked man, his eyes flashing with anger. "Nicholas, take care of Abyss," he spat, his voice venomous. "Make sure he knows his place." The masked man nodded, his expression unreadable. "Yes, sir," he said, his voice flat. The masked man nodded, his expression unreadable.

"Yes, sir," he said, his voice flat. Without hesitation, Nicholas charged out of the meeting room, his footsteps echoing down the corridor. "Bastard!!" he shouted, his voice ringing out with anger. Abyss, who had been walking away, suddenly flashed stepped behind Nicholas, his movements swift and silent. Before Nicholas could react, Abyss swiftly broke his hand, the sound of bones snapping echoing through the corridor.

Nicholas cried out in pain, clutching his broken hand to his chest. Abyss stood over him, his eyes blazing with anger. "Don't challenge me, low rank," he said, his voice dripping with disdain. Nicholas glared up at Abyss, his face twisted with rage and pain. But Abyss just turned and walked away, leaving Nicholas to nurse his broken hand. The corridor was silent once more, the only sound the heavy breathing of Nicholas. He glared after Abyss, his anger and resentment simmering just below the surface.

He knew that Abyss had just made a powerful enemy, and he vowed to make him pay for his insolence.

As Nicholas stumbled back to the meeting room, his broken hand throbbing with pain, he couldn't help but wonder what other secrets Abyss was hiding. He knew that Abyss was not what he seemed, and he was determined to uncover the truth. The game of cat and mouse had just begun, and only time would tell who would emerge victorious.

But one thing was certain - the stakes had just been raised, and the consequences of failure would be dire. Nicholas stormed back into the meeting room, his face twisted with rage and pain. Maledict looked up at him, his eyes narrowing with concern. "What happened?" he asked, his voice laced with venom. Nicholas glared at him, his anger and resentment simmering just below the surface.

"Abyss," he spat, his voice venomous. "He broke my hand." The room fell silent once more, the tension between the members of the Kahos Kollective palpable. The game of cat and mouse had just begun, and only But back at the monastery, Jasiah, Michael, Neveah, Camila, and Darius were

unaware of the brewing evil. They were in the kitchen area, chilling and enjoying each other's company. The atmosphere was relaxed, with laughter and chatter filling the air.
Jasiah, however, got up and walked out into the hallway, his mind consumed by thoughts and questions.
Would he be able to find who he really was, besides being the reincarnation of Aria? Would he even be ready when he had to fight his best friend Michael to the death? Would he win? And was he even strong enough?
The doubts and fears swirled in his mind like a vortex, threatening to drown him.

   He knew he had made a good choice choosing to stay at the monastery, even if it meant leaving his mom and his normal life behind. He knew he had the life of a ninja now, and no one would care about the old, timid and weak Jasiah. He would have to become stronger, tougher, and more resilient if he had to save anyone. The weight of his responsibilities settled heavily on his shoulders, but he steeled himself for the challenges ahead. As he walked down the hallway, he felt a sense of determination growing within him.
He would face his fears, and he would overcome them. He would find a way to defeat Michael, and he would save the people he cared about. The darkness that had once threatened to consume him was slowly receding, replaced by a fierce determination to succeed. Jasiah's eyes narrowed, his jaw clenched, and his fists tightened. He was ready to face whatever lay ahead, no matter how daunting it may seem. Was slowly receding, replaced by a fierce determination to succeed. Jasiah's eyes narrowed, his jaw clenched, and his fists tightened.

He was ready to face whatever lay ahead, no matter how daunting it may seem. He continued to think, his mind racing with thoughts of the future, of battles to be fought and won, of challenges to be overcome. But as he stood there, lost in thought, he realized that he didn t have to think about that right now.

He didn't have to worry about the future, or dwell on the past. All he had to do was focus on the present moment. He looked down at his fist, clenched in determination, and a slow smile spread across his face.

He knew that he was ready, that he had the strength and the courage to face whatever lay ahead. And in that moment, he felt a sense of peace, of calm, wash over him. Jasiah's eyes gleamed with determination, his smile growing wider as he gazed at his clenched fist. He knew that he was ready to take on the world, to face whatever challenges came his way.

With that thought, he smiled, a sense of confidence and determination radiating from every pore. And so, Jasiah stood there, his fist clenched, his smile triumphant, ready to face whatever the future may hold. And with that thought, he smiled, a sense of confidence and determination radiating from every pore. And so, Jasiah stood there, his fist clenched, his smile triumphant, ready to face whatever the future may hold. Just then, Michael's voice pierced the air, shattering the tranquil atmosphere. "Hey Jasiah! We're gonna go outside! You coming or you just gonna look at your fist like a weirdo?" Michael said teasingly, a hint of amusement dancing in his eyes. Jasiah's reverie was broken, and he turned to face Michael, a look of confusion crossing his face.

"Huh? Oh yeah!" Jasiah said, his voice laced with enthusiasm, as he realized what Michael was saying. He turned to the group, knowing they were probably gonna have a lot of fun outside.

The others were already making their way towards the door, chatting and laughing, and Jasiah's heart swelled with excitement. He quickly fell into step behind them, his fist still clenched in determination, but a wide grin spreading across his face. As they emerged into the bright sunlight, Jasiah felt a sense of freedom wash over him.

The fresh air and warm breeze invigorated him, and he couldn't help but feel a sense of joy and contentment. He was surrounded by his friends, and they were all here to have fun and enjoy each other's company. Jasiah's eyes sparkled with mischief as he gazed at the group, already planning the various pranks and antics they could get up to. He knew that with Michael, Neveah, Camila, and Darius by his side, they would have an unforgettable time.

Together, they set off into the unknown, ready to face whatever adventures lay ahead, armed with nothing but their wit, courage, and an insatiable appetite for fun.

www.ingramcontent.com/pod-product-compliance
Lightning Source LLC
Chambersburg PA
CBHW070727160426
43192CB00009B/1348